Class Strategies and the Education Market

Modern state education was essentially formed around the needs and interests of the middle class. The middle classes are currently very much at the centre of all politicians' electoral concerns. Nevertheless sociological and educational research has tended to neglect the middle class. *Class Strategies and the Education Market* examines the ways in which the middle classes maintain and improve their social advantages in and through education.

Drawing on an extensive series of interviews with parents and children, this book identifies key moments of decision-making in the construction of the educational trajectories of middle-class children. Stephen J. Ball organizes his analysis around the key concepts of social closure, social capital, values and principles and risk, while bringing a broad range of up-to-date sociological theory to bear upon his subject. From this thorough analysis, valuable and thought-provoking insights into the assiduous care and considerable effort and expenditure, which go into ensuring the educational success of the middle-class child, emerge.

The middle classes are a sociological enigma, presenting the social researcher with considerable analytic and theoretical difficulties. *Class Strategies and the Education Market* provides a set of working tools for class analysis and the examination of class practices. Above all, it offers new ways of thinking about class theory and the relationships between classes in late modern society.

Stephen J. Ball is Karl Mannheim Professor of Sociology of Education and Director of the Education Policy Research Unit at the Institute of Education, University of London.

Class Strategies and the Education Market

The middle classes and social advantage

Stephen J. Ball

 RoutledgeFalmer
Taylor & Francis Group

LONDON AND NEW YORK

First published 2003 by RoutledgeFalmer
11 New Fetter Lane, London EC4P 4EE

Simultaneously published in the USA and Canada
by RoutledgeFalmer
29 West 35th Street, New York, NY 10001

RoutledgeFalmer is an imprint of the Taylor & Francis Group

© 2003 Stephen J. Ball

Typeset in Sabon by GreenGate Publishing Services, Tonbridge, Kent
Printed and bound in Great Britain by The Cromwell Press, Trowbridge,
Wiltshire

British Library Cataloguing in Publication Data
A catalogue record for this book is available from the British Library

Library in Congress Cataloging-in-Publication Data
A catalog record for this book has been requested

ISBN 0-415-27277-7 (pbk)
ISBN 0-415-27276-9 (hbk)

For John Ball 1381/1994

When Adam delved
and Eve span
Who was then
a gentleman?

From The Peasant's Revolt of 1381

Contents

Illustrations

Figures

Tables

Acknowledgements

A lot of people have helped me with this book, in many different ways. Most important among them is Trinidad without whom it would never have got started and would certainly not have been finished – I cannot say enough.

Richard Bowe, Miki David, Jackie Davies, Sharon Gewirtz, Sheila Macrae, Meg Maguire, Diane Reay and Carol Vincent were the main protagonists in fieldwork and interviewing and many extracts from interviews they conducted are quoted in the text. Agnes van Zanten commented on chapters and the work we did together on several comparisons of education in England and France was very useful to me. Carol Vincent had the patience and stamina to read and comment on everything, for which I am very grateful. Harry Brighouse and Alan Cribb undertook my philosophical education and made me think differently, especially about Chapter 6. Meg Maguire gave me the usual hard time, especially over Chapter 8. Val Hey, Hugh Lauder, Philip Noden and Tim Butler also read parts of the book. Jim Scheurich fed me relevant research from the US. Thank you to Caroline Gill for her multi-tasking and Anjali Kothari who made the diagrams for me. I also thank Annie and Rebecca for helping me cope and Geraldine for the house. Whatever weaknesses remain are down to me.

1 Introduction

Between structure and hermeneutics

Of course, personal initiative is the hallmark of the middle classes ...

(Lockwood 1995: 10)

... the middle class has in many ways been the central symbol of twentieth-century life in the west, a reflection of western anxieties and hopes ...

(Owensby 1999: 11)

This introduction is an exercise of meta-writing, an attempt to draw some lines and limits around a piece of work that constantly goes beyond itself and at every turn 'stumbles against what it does not mean' (Foucault 1974: 17). I therefore want to draw these lines in particular by accounting for what this book is not about, what it does not do. In this respect I shall endeavour, perhaps fruitlessly, to clarify the standpoints from which the book is written and guide the reader towards a position from which the book might be read as eclectic but nonetheless coherent. I do this in part because the book has some unconventional aspects to it, although in another sense it is a throw-back, a re-invention of old themes and concerns from within the sociology of education – in particular the multifaceted relationships between families, public institutions and educational inequalities. In this introduction then I will sketch in the general orientations of the project; specific aspects of these orientations are taken up in more detail in later chapters. Each of the substantive chapters focuses upon one or more key themes and works on these in interaction with empirical materials.

This is a book written between rather than against.[1] It defines itself as different from rather than opposed to and I am certainly not 'trying to reduce others to silence' (Foucault 1974: 17). Neither is this an attempt to have the last word, far from it; no closure is sought or claimed and I will be working on rather than closing off these concepts. It is intended to be read as a set of statements to be worked on, to be developed further in relation to an obdurate and brute reality. My project here has a particular concern with 'appraising concepts as possibilities for future thinking' (Colebrook 2000: 5).

> ... the peculiar difficulty of sociology, then, is to produce a precise science of an imprecise, fuzzy, woolly reality. For this it is better that its concepts be polymorphic, supple and adaptable, rather than defined, calibrated and used rigidly.
>
> (Bourdieu and Wacquant 1992: 23)

I am interested in subtleties and nuances here rather than stark and distinct patterns and relationships, indeed this is not a field of analysis that lends itself to that sort of style of interpretation – if you are looking for some kind of clear-cut class story of stark oppressions and determinisms then you are reading the wrong book. To use a sociological cliché, this account is addressed primarily to 'the revelation of complexity within cultural processes' (Watson 1993: 193). In good part, as I have indicated, the task of the book is the assembly of a toolbox of analytic possibilities rather than the display of findings. It is a cautious and stumbling text. It is a pragmatic or synthetic sociology rather than an ideological one. It is about exploring the way 'the social' works. It is about mapping rather than explaining. There is no pristine theoretical exposition to be displayed nor any avant-garde posturing. I am attempting to gather together and elaborate a particular package of concepts, or a 'moral vocabulary' (Parkin 1979: 115) that may be useful for 'the exercise of making things intelligible' (114). In articulating this vocabulary I have sought, as far as possible, to escape from the seductive simplicities and the 'comforts of certainty' (Stronach and MacLure 1997) offered by the binary. Both in class research and in qualitative analysis binaries have a certain obviousness to them. But binaries can obscure as much, if not more, than they reveal; they avoid complexity and divert our attention from what lies between, that which is neither one thing nor the other. This text is littered with the promises and pitfalls of the dual classification and not all of these are eschewed but neither are they indulged in without care. Finally, the division of the text into chapters does not indicate neat divisions nor a linear narrative. Indeed, as you will see, the issues addressed and concepts deployed interweave, elaborate and build upon one another.

   This text is, then, a hybrid. It is part empirical; data are deployed in various ways – sometimes to illustrate, sometimes to demonstrate, sometimes to speculate and I shall endeavour to be clear about which is which. The aim is to achieve a degree of plausibility. The text is also, as already noted, in part conceptual. I am attempting to define, develop and relate together a set of concepts which offers 'perspective' in understanding the complex relationships between social class and social justice in contemporary educational settings with a specific focus on the middle class. I shall focus on the rhythm and murmur of middle-class voices; their changing cadences and concerns, their expression of dilemmas and ambivalences. These are voices of confidence and uncertainty, which are sometimes also confused, voices which are articulate, persuasive and authoritative but also careful, measured and thoughtful. These voices are quoted at length in the text, in part because of what they tell us about class practices but also because they are a medium of practice. The middle class gets things done at home, work and in engagement with 'expert systems' through talk of a particular sort. They represent and perform themselves as moral subjects, as efficacious social actors and as classed agents, through talk.

I shall be working across the surfaces of class and trying to eventualize class. This is one form of what Savage (2000: 41) calls 'a kind of "strategic inductivism"'. My focus is on key moments of anxiety, fear, action and efficacy, on the micropractices of social reproduction, and on the situated enactment of class skills, resources, dispositions, attitudes and expectations. These are moment of ordinariness and exclusivity (Savage 2000). I shall be dealing with tendencies and patterns here, and dominant discourses, but, where I can, I shall avoid trading in a simple essentialism of the middle-class subject. I am certainly not dealing here with a set of mindless inevitabilities – again complexity is favoured over parsimony. Thus, I am interested in the power and usefulness of exceptions and spend some time, at various points, on these. Also this is not an exercise in methodological individualism; my individuals are thoroughly embedded in social relations. I am interested in the ways in which 'class structures are instantiated in people's lives' (Savage 2000: 150). I am seeking to excavate and interrogate the common sense and the naturalness which underpins individual reasoning and practices, what Eder (1993: 9) calls the 'cultural texture' of class 'that is prior to the motivations of actors and their individual class actions'.[2] In all this I am very conscious of Bourdieu's warning that:

> ... the perfectly commendable wish to see things in person, close up, sometimes leads people to search for the explanatory principles of observed realities where they are not to be found (not all of them in any case) namely, the site of observation itself.
>
> (Bourdieu *et al.* 1999: 181)

This is also a further development of my work towards a policy sociology and more specifically the 'policy cycle' (Bowe, Ball and Gold 1992; Ball 1994; Ball 1997b). This account focuses on particular moments in the policy cycle and the practices of policy enacted by groups of parents who are 'called up' by and 'into' policy as 'choosers' and 'consumers' of education. Each of these moments is represented by a different corpus of data, drawn from different research studies (see Appendix I). These moments are major points of transition and differentiation at which times key class resources are brought into play and issues of identity, responsibility and aspiration are up front. When advantage is at stake, I suggest, habitus comes fleetingly into view. In effect we have the possibility of seeing the same children and same parents in action at four different points of transition in the education/care system – arranging pre-school child care, the move from primary to secondary school, compulsory to post-compulsory education, and the choice of higher education. At these points classed capitals and dispositions engage with classed policy regimes and, I shall argue, are differently legitimated and privileged. I shall also consider the relationships between middle-class parents and the state in other respects.

I am working hard here to embed education within broader trends of social change and changes in the class structure – and thus to relate the field of education to general social theory and class analysis. I draw heavily on Bourdieu throughout, and Parkin (1979) and Brown (2000) (see Chapter 2), and Crook (1999) in Chapter 7, and Jordan, Redley and James (1994) are key interlocutors in Chapter 6, as is Savage (2000) in Chapter 8 and elsewhere. In passing, I refer to Giddens' (1994) and Beck's (1992) work on individualism but express a number of concerns about the generality of their theorizing and their failure to recognize the relational nature of identity formation. I suggest that they give inadequate attention to the different ways in which different social groups are confronted by 'systemic contradictions' and the uneven distribution of resources, of different kinds, which enable reflection and choice, despite some passing disclaimers.

I have to say that I am not making, indeed cannot make, any kind of clear and simple argument claiming that the processes and perspectives that are described here are different from before. Nonetheless, at times this may be a logical and valid interpretation based upon the data presented – at least that which represents the perceptions of parents. In this respect, as we shall see, there are both continuities and differences to be addressed. Before-and-after comparisons are not my main concern here. What I am doing primarily is to indicate how things are within the current regime of policy in education. However, I am arguing that various conditions and contexts encourage or hail certain actions and attitudes in a different way from before (see Chapters 2 and 7).

For the middle classes it is the best of times and the worst of times; a time of affluence and risk, opportunity and congestion, celebration and anxiety. As always by definition this is a class-between, a class beset with contradictions and uncertainties. As Ehrenreich (1989: 15) puts it: 'If this is an elite, then, it is an insecure and deeply anxious one'. Roberts (2001: 162) echoes this, suggesting that 'the present day middle class is anxious rather than complacent and comfortable'. And yet, this was ever so. Lewis and Maude (1950: 273) wrote that 'the attitude of the middle classes towards the future is much what the attitude of the individual breadwinner always is: an amalgam of dread and confidence', and the 'middle classes are beset with worries. But this is no new sensation' (288). The combination of dread and confidence is a recurring theme in this book (see also Owensby's, 1999, account of the Brazilian middle class).

In some respects, as noted already, as a recasting of the sociology of education this exercise is a return to the beginnings of work on class inequalities in the 1950s and 1960s, with its emphasis on locating the motor of inequality within the family (Craft 1970; Douglas 1964; Floud, Halsey and Marton 1956). While I would not want to turn back the clock as far as underplaying the role of institutional differentiation and other social factors in producing educational inequalities, there has been a neglect of the actions of families, and particular family members, in recent times (with a few exceptions like Crozier 2000; David 1993; Vincent 2000 and Reay 1998b). We now have the theoretical resources which enable attention to be paid to the differences within and between families without an immediate collapse into social pathology. According to Nash (1990: 446):

> Through Bourdieu's work we have been able to reconstruct a theory of the family and recover the centrality of family resources to educational differentiation within a radical context which allays fears of a retreat into cultural deficit theory.

Why are the middle classes interesting? In part simply because they constitute a major contemporary phenomenon in their own right. They are worthy of attention because they are there. Because there are so many of them: 'The middle class is now Britain's second largest; it is pressing on the heels of the working class and accounts for roughly a third of the population' (Roberts 2001: 141). But further they are of particular importance within the sociology of education within education, because their actions produce or contribute to the perpetuation, inscription and reinvention of social inequalities both old and new. New forms of old inequalities and new forms of inequality. As Savage (2000: 159) argues:

> If there is still a role for class analysis it is to continue to emphasize the brute realities of social inequality and the extent to which these are constantly effaced by a middle class, individualized culture that fails to register the social implications of its routine actions.

With more than a little over-simplification contemporary work on social class takes three main forms: class theory, the attempt to define classes theoretically, and recently to incorporate race and gender within such definitions (Anthias 2001; Crompton 1997); class analysis (or social stratification), the attempt to establish and operationalize systems of class categories, 'who belongs where', which can then be used for various kinds of correlational, comparative or mobility research (Goldthorpe 1980; Goldthorpe 1996; Halsey, Heath and Ridge 1980); and class practices, which incorporates a variety of work ranging from consumption research, work on identity, workplace studies and experiences of oppression, inequality and social reproduction – the last includes recent auto/biographical work on working-class girls 'made bad' (Mahony and Zmroczek 1997). Looking from the outside in on all of this is a more recent critical tradition which explores the demise of class (see Crompton 1998 for a definitive overview and below). However, within all of this, despite the recent upsurge of empirical interest in the middle classes, alongside a long-standing debate around the issues of definition and theorizing (see Scott 2000 for a good account), there is relatively little empirical or conceptual development around middle-class practices apart from the important work done by Savage and Butler and their colleagues and one or two others (e.g. Butler and Savage 1995; Savage, Barlow, Dickens and Fielding 1992; Savage 2000; Sulkunen 1992; Wynne 1998; Walkerdine, Lucey and Melody 2001 and Power, Edwards, Whitty and Wigfall 2002). This text engages neither with class analysis (boxes) nor class theory (abstraction). The focus is upon class practices. Specifically, this study contributes to a body of recent work which is attempting to return to an emphasis on the lived realities, the situated realizations, of class and class reproduction (Butler and Robson 2002a; Butler and Robson 2002b; Jordan, Redley and James 1994; Maguire 2001; Reay 1998b, etc.). I also locate myself theoretically and take up issues laid out within what Brown (2000) calls Positional Conflict Theory (see Chapter 2). As such my discursive terrain is hemmed in on all sides by analytic niceties and categorization systems, theoretical fideism, and postmodern scepticism – the idea that class is no longer that important.

Concepts of class, class analysis and class society are, as Pakulski and Waters (1996: 2) validly claim, 'notoriously vague and tenuously stretched' and as they go on to say: 'The debate about classes combines issues of semantics and substance' (2). Indeed the conceptual and methodological quagmires in which class is embedded often means that 'one hardly knows what one is talking about' (Foucault 1996: 447). So let me try to be clear. I shall be using and troubling these concepts at the same time. Holding some ambivalence towards the usefulness of class, set against a very strong sense of the presence of class within the politics and practices of contemporary education. In writing this classness into being I will inevitably give emphasis to its facticity. My topic becomes a resource.

I take it that class 'is something that happens (and it can be shown to have happened) in a human relationship' (Thompson 1980: 8–9). Class here is an identity and a lifestyle, and a set of perspectives on the social world and relationships in it, marked by varying degrees of reflexivity. Identities, lifestyles, perspectives and relationships are 'constituted in the course of collective history' and 'acquired in the course of individual history', which 'function in their practical state' (Bourdieu 1986a: 467). Class, in this sense, is productive and reactive. It is an identity based upon modes of being and becoming or escape and forms of distinction that are realized and reproduced in specific social locations. Certain locations are sought out, others are avoided. We think and are thought by class. It is about being something and not being something else. It is relational. Class is also a trajectory, a path through space and time, a 'history of transactions' (Walzer 1984). We are not always the same, or always able to be the same. Our current sense of who we are may be deeply invested in once having been someone different or wanting to be someone else in the future. Similar class positions are held and experienced differently, and have different histories. Class positions and perspectives are produced from and invested with the traces of earlier choices, improvizations and opportunities as well as being inflected by chance. Transactions are cumulative; 'aspects of action and interaction are constantly being negotiated, reformulated, modified and so on as a result of experience' (Devine 1997: 9). Each new choice or point of decision is confronted with assets or capital (economic, social and cultural) to be exchanged or invested; for an individual or a family volumes of capital may be 'increasing, decreasing or stationary' (Bourdieu 1986a: 120). Advantages in the form of capitals can be stored and accumulated for future use (Lee 1993). In other words, I take class to be dynamic and emergent, as Savage (2000: 69) puts it 'people now have to achieve their class positions'. As such, reproduction is never guaranteed and mobility, up or down, is always possible (see Chapter 4). Such mobility is both contingently and strategically dependent. Here class and class inequalities are treated and 'understood dynamically' (Savage 2000: 69) as 'a longitudinal process rather than a cross sectional one', but nonetheless the analysis here primarily addresses the issue of the relative stability of class relations – stable and static are not the same: 'real world classes are constantly being constructed around us, people are constantly doing class' (Connell 1983: 148). This is about how class is achieved and maintained, and enacted rather than something that just is! Class is realized and struggled over in the daily lives of families and institutions, in consumption decisions, as much as in the processes of production, and particularly at moments of crisis and contradiction as parents think about the well-being and happiness and futures of their offspring. Class is about knowing how to act at these defining moments. Class is of course a massively over-represented subject, this is a further contribution to that over-representation. But it is important to be clear that class is only one possible position from which parents act – some of the others are very evident in what follows.

The action here takes place within the field of educational choices and its particular grid of power, and the social agents at work in this field are located according to the type, composition and volume of their multiple capitals. Embedded in this field, I shall suggest, are a set of social–symbolic and material oppositions which structure it. Oppositions which are manifested in struggles of access, closure and advantage, a particular kind of class struggle; which is not necessarily constituted by overt antagonisms. The:

> character of educational provision is itself a battleground within the middle classes as well as between middle and working classes, in which those already endowed with cultural capital are engaged in conflicts with those who have not.
>
> (Savage, Barlow, Dickens and Fielding 1992: 152–53)

Closure is a very decisive feature within this field of social action, a very particular form of a 'space of relations', or more precisely, relations within a set of sub-spaces. However, here, only one set of social locations within this space are addressed. This enterprise is about 'education as an *aspect* of class' (Rikowski 2001: 1). Education as a field of distinctions and identities is crucial in high modern society in changing and reproducing the borderlines of class and distributing unevenly and unequally forms of social and cultural capital.

As noted already, Bourdieu's concepts and his thinking about class and education are a key resource in this exercise. I share Annette Lareau's view that Bourdieu's various accounts of the interplay of structure and agency and his conceptual paraphernalia offer a way of tracing the reproduction of social inequality into the 'strategies and actions that individuals follow in their daily lives' (Lareau and McNamara Horvat 1999: 38) and thus a way of seeing the structuring process at work, and exploring the work of 'social structure in the head'. Lareau also makes the point that Bourdieu 'has not always been sufficiently aware of variations in the ways in which institutional actors legitimate or rebuff efforts by individuals to activate their resources. Nor has he given sufficient attention to the moments of reproduction and exclusion, although both these points are implied in Bourdieu's work' (38). Thus, this is an effort to ground and eventualize Bourdieu in some specifics of capital activation.

Again, I should make it clear that the question as to whether there is more inequality than within previous policy regimes is not a primary concern here. I am more concerned with the kinds of inequalities currently embedded in education and how they work. Nonetheless the 'logic of the market', as I interpret it, would suggest more inequality and the great bulk of the research, although not all, does seem to indicate that there is relatively greater inequality in market systems than in the systems that immediately preceded them (see Chapter 3). That is to say the weight of evidence, of diverse kinds, from various sources and locations, does seem to tip the balance towards the conclusion that inequality is more prevalent in 'post-welfare' education systems.

As should be already evident, the interpretational calculus of my account rests upon an approximation of Bourdieu's basic analytical framework. That is, the relationship between structure (system properties), dispositions and recognisable social practices, with the addition on my part of an explicit role for the state. The particular rendering of this is encapsulated in Figure 1.1. My approach here is thoroughly embedded in Bourdieu's (1986b: 243) 'general science of the economy of practices', applied to and developed within this specific field.

While not centre-stage in this tragedy of class relations the 'somber reality of the state' (Parkin 1979: 119) is crucial to a proper understanding of the particular class practices with which we are concerned (see Chapter 3). Here, following Parkin, I offer a 'conceptualization of the state as the political

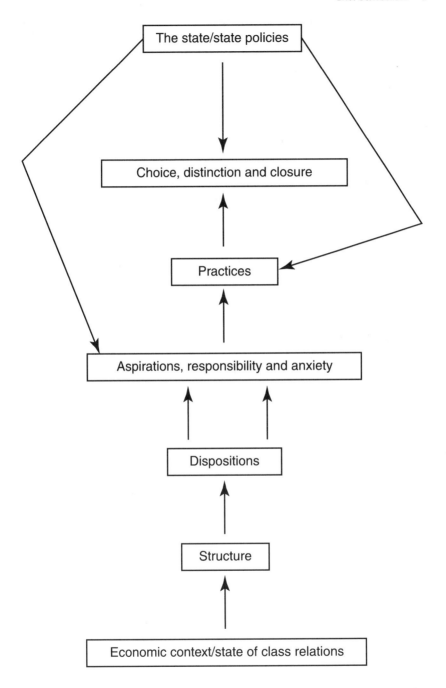

Figure 1.1 Structure, class and state: an analytic framework for education policy and practices

locale or the distillation of class antagonisms' (140), as a 'dependent variable', or a 'condensate', as Poulantzas (1973) would have it. This gives rise, I
would suggest, to the embedding of particular versions of 'class thinking'
within the policy making of the state, and thus gives a particular emphasis to
the ways in which the state acts upon class relations and class struggles (see
Ball 1993).

Class perspectives then have to be understood as they are articulated
from within changing political discourses and policy regimes, in particular
within the discursive framework of 'the market society' and 'the aesthetic of
consumption' (Bauman 1998). The difference from 'before' as Bauman
(1998: 24) puts it 'is one of emphasis, but that shift of emphasis does make
an enormous difference to virtually every aspect of society, cultural and
individual life'. Put simply, in a 'market society' markets and market relations are the basic frameworks for understanding social order (Slater and
Tonkiss 2001: 1).

It is probably evident already that throughout this endeavour the conceptualization of class is essentially Weberian.[3] That is, my representation
of class is located in the market rather than within the social organization of
production. In Weberian terms I conceive of educational decisions and
choices as forms of 'market exchange' in which assets are traded. For Weber
(1961: 82) 'the kind of chance in the market is the decisive moment which
presents a common condition for the individual's fate'. Importantly, the
Weberian market-based model of class and class conflict allows us to examine the multidimensionsal nature of struggles within the marketplace and
commonalities of fate. Weber was also very aware of the dynamic nature of
capitalist societies and therefore of class groups and concomitantly the
dynamic nature of monopolization as 'a fundamental process in the economy' (Collins 1986: 127). Here we are concerned with the monopolization
of particular educational sites and trajectories. This and his assets-based
class categorization provides the basis for a consideration of variations and
divisions within the middle class. Such a conceptualization also provides a
direct link to Bourdieu's analytic framework for class. That is:

> The primary differences, those which distinguish the major classes of
> conditions of existence, derive from the overall volume of capital,
> understood as the set of actually usable resources and powers – eco-
> nomic capital, cultural capital and also social capital.
>
> (1986a: 114)

In part the preference for this model of class rests, as Parkin (1979: 112)
puts it, 'on the claim that it draws attention to a set of problems and issues
that are otherwise obscured'. The class relations, and struggles, explored
here are best understood as competition and exclusion, although they may
also be thought of as forms of symbolic violence.[4] It is difficult to represent
them meaningfully as forms of direct exploitation or oppression, although

they are caught up within the reproduction of more general relations of exploitation. Relationships of domination remain as 'a latent social relationship' (Eder 1993: 167) within the middle classes.

As should already be apparent my discussion of class here does not rest primarily upon any 'independently defined structure of positions' (Parkin 1979: 113) but rather collective modes of social action and social practices are taken as the defining features of class. However, it is clearly necessary that I draw some boundaries around my conception of the middle class (see Appendix I), and specify some bases for identifying intra-class differences. Even so, the general strategies or modes of action of the middle class as a whole remain in the foreground of my concerns rather than an attempt to systematically identify fractional variations (see Chapter 6).

All of this suggests the need to live with a degree of fuzziness in the categorization of class here. The various categorizations referred to in the text are useful in different ways but focus upon slightly different aspects of class position and class perspective in each case. They illustrate the multidimensionality of class, and in some respects the gaps between objective position and the lived realities of class. They also draw attention to the complex trajectories of families we might want to call middle class. While the families represented in the text are similar in many respects, they are different in others. Their relation to a class identity in terms of values, and in some cases attendant practices, vary from entrenched to ambivalent. The role of liberalism, and the degree of competitive individualism evident within these middle-class families produce significant variations in themselves (see Chapter 6).

I am not then, in a traditional sense, interested in 'sterile attempts to map out class structures' (Savage 2000: 158). I am not what Rikowski (2001) calls a 'box person', preoccupied with 'definitions' of class. But I am interested in the ways in which the middle class represent their class location to themselves, their awareness of a class identity. I shall argue that in their euphemistic talk and in their social practices they do evince a form of such awareness of class (see Chapters 4 and 5). Class is inexplicit but pervasive in their educational strategies – 'encoded in people's sense of self-worth and their attitudes to an awareness of others – in how they carry themselves as individuals' (Savage 2000: 107), or in their lifestyles (Berking 1996: 199) 'that today appear to fill in the blank space left by the modernization process in the exchange between individual and society'. For Berking lifestyles are socially distinctive variants of cultural practices; 'Life styles include the subjective and group-related constructions of actors who in this way fashion their reality' and 'invest it with meaning' (199). However, while I am dealing here with the subjective states of actors I am certainly not intending to lose touch with the material bases of class difference at least as regards the distribution of financial and property assets.

Nonetheless, it would certainly make some sense to see the recognitions and rejections embedded in education markets, the comfort and discomfort expressed by the respondents in the field of education in terms of such group-related constructions (see Chapter 5). Especially if we accept Berking's argument that: 'Lifestyles present themselves as relatively homogeneous entities of collective intentions of representation and rules of observation' (199). Theoretically this links very straightforwardly with Bourdieu's point that: 'The division into classes performed by sociology leads to the common root of the classifiable practices which agents produce and of the classificatory judgements they make of other agents' practices and their own' (1986a: 169). And empirically, with Savage, Barlow, Dickens and Fielding's (1992) analysis of divisions among middle-class consumption patterns.

A colleague once described my work as unfair to the middle classes. This is not the point. I am not interested in condemning or redeeming the people referred to or who appear in this text, either individually or collectively. I am not intent upon labelling and judging them. Rather, my concern is with understanding them, or some small aspect of their lives and in doing so to unpack some of the mechanisms that animate the education marketplace – the workings of the 'hidden hand' if you like, and thus the operation of class perspectives and dispositions, their emotions, values and perceptions of risk, and the role of middle-class capitals. I am concerned with some of the ways in which their social world is uttered and constructed 'in accordance with principles of vision and division' (Bourdieu 1992: 232). Also I want to attempt generally to represent their dilemmas, fears and anxieties. In this respect I shall try not to trade too much in and upon the simplicities of 'qualitative cut-outs'. I hope that some of these families might seem familiar and at least at times sympathetic.

However, all of this begs questions about the 'I' which recurs through the text. How do I relate to these middle-class families? Who is the 'I' in text? It is not a single unified 'I' that is for sure. There is the 'I' who was a working class 11-year-old, uncomfortable and 'out of place' in a middle-class grammar school, faced for the first time, mental arithmetic aside, with the bitter tears of school failure. The 'I' undergraduate, first in his family to go to university, reading about himself in the works of Jackson and Marsden (1962) and Lacey (1970), and finding a vocation. The 'I' research student studying working-class children in a comprehensive school. The 'I' professor, without children of his own, safe on the moral high ground, 'othering' the middle class as an analytic stance. All of these Is are imbricated in the text and implicated in my interpretive work.

Topics and themes

The main chapters in the book are organized around a set of topics or concepts each of which provide a focus for discussion. They are: social class, strategy, policy, social closure, social capital, risk and values and principles. However, cutting across these are a number of analytic themes which recur and interweave, in different forms, throughout the book. These are: boundaries, ambivalences, responsibility, fear and uncertainty, individualism and reflexivity. These themes in particular, and the analytic orientation of the book generally, work against any simplistic binarizing across class divisions. While, on the one hand the text does articulate a class binary of working-class/middle-class differences, on the other, there are various asides to and forays into the messiness of class fractions. For the most part my analysis avoids dislocated grand narratives like individualization, risk society, consumerism, post-modernity. The focus here is on the proximate world of everyday life. That is, the situatedness of class, within an economic and social structure, and its realization in practices, in specific locations and at particular, critical moments.

2   Class and strategy

Classes may have changed but they still count ...

(Crompton 1998: 226)

This book is about 'selection and differentiation ... [in education] ... produced by the action of families' (Gewirtz, Ball and Bowe 1995: 56) and the ways in which families' 'choices tend not merely to reflect but to augment and amplify social-class differentiation' (Hatcher 1998: 20). The book takes up lines of analysis which have been central to my work in the sociology of education for almost 30 years. These began in my undergraduate work with my tutor Denis Marsden (see Jackson and Marsden 1962) and were then taken up in my PhD (Ball 1981), supervized by Colin Lacey (Lacey 1970). More recently these lines have been pursued through a series of studies of education markets and choice (Gewirtz, Ball and Bowe 1995; Reay 2000; Vincent 2000; Ball, Maguire and Macrae 2000). More specifically the book takes up and builds upon ideas and analyses touched upon in a series of papers published during the 1990s (Ball 1993; Ball, Bowe and Gewirtz 1995, 1996; Ball 1997a; Reay and Ball 1998; Ball and Vincent 1998). The agenda to be pursued here was in fact outlined schematically in the first of these papers: 'Education markets, choice and social class: The market as a class strategy in the UK and the USA'. I do not think quickly! I argued, somewhat grossly, in that paper that: 'The market works as a class strategy by creating a mechanism which can be exploited by the middle classes as a strategy of reproduction in their search for relative advantage, social advancement and mobility' (Ball 1993: 17). This book takes that proposition seriously and takes it further.[1]

The substance of the book is a set of interpretative forays into the field of post-welfare education. This involves a secondary re-working of data from four choice projects.[2] In this chapter I will lay out the theoretical and conceptual background to that re-working. Four things are involved. First, I will acknowledge some of the most important influences that bear upon my thinking and outline the terrain within which the theoretical 'viewpoints' taken up within the substantive analytical work are set. Second, I will make a very brief excursion into the dangerous and controversial arena of class analysis. I will defend the relevance of a continuing concern with class inequalities and comment upon the complexities of the middle classes. Third, a discussion of contexts of choice. I will argue that strategies of social advantage, while always in evidence, have assumed even greater importance to the middle classes in the last 10 to 15 years. Fourth, I will address more specifically the concepts of strategy and choice, which are central to the whole exercise.

Influences and viewpoints

As indicated already this project represents a set of on-going concerns and a return to my sociological roots, to the examination of social class differentiation and the explanation of class successes and failures (see Ball 1981). It is unashamedly a modernist exercise and seems to me to be an exercise of particular importance within the era of New Labour (and its counterparts) and global education reform. The text can be read as part of a recent rediscovery of social class in educational research but is also set over and against various arguments which suggest that 'class is dead' (Pakulski and Waters 1996) (see below). Theoretically speaking, as indicated in Chapter 1, the viewpoint adopted might broadly be described as something like 'Weber meets Bourdieu!'. This concatenation is certainly reflected in the main influences which play upon the analysis and interpretational framework.

On the one hand, there are a group of Weberian 'social exclusion theory' (SET) scholars (Brown, Collins, Hirsh, Jordan, Parkin and Savage and Butler) who argue for an understanding of educational qualifications as 'a screening device' (Hirsch 1977: 6) and education as an arena of competition and social exclusion. They draw our attention to the way in which 'the positional competition for a livelihood is structured to reproduce existing class, gender and ethnic relations' (Brown 2000: 635). As Weber put it '... educational certificates support their holders' claims ... above all ... to monopolise social and economically advantageous positions' (1945: 241–2, quoted in Brown 2000). The theoretical and ontological grounds of this kind of conceptualization (the relationships between agency and reproduction) are sometimes a little opaque but I am certainly assuming that we have to take seriously Weber's insistence on theoretical adequacy *both* at the level of meaning *and* at the level of causality (see further below, the discussion of choice and strategy). Thus, while I want to construct an argument which attempts to capture changes in positional competition in general terms, I also intend to ground these changes in the social action of individuals and families; 'since human agency is an irreducible element of social events, a tenable explanation must *contain* claims about the intentions and beliefs of actors and how they are translated into action' (Hatcher 1998: 12, my emphasis). As Hatcher goes on to say: 'Specifying micro-mechanisms is often necessary for establishing macro-level explanations' (12).

Embedded inside most of this SET work lies, unacknowledged for the most part (Giddens 1971: 241), some kind of assumption about rational action and strategic behaviour (see below) – that is, people behaving according to their interests and attempting to maximize the utility of their decisions. Decisions are arrived at via the rational calculation of risks, benefits and the possibilities of success and failure within a framework of ends or goals and an awareness of competition. In our field of concern education is viewed as an investment good. While SET theorists typically use a language of social practices – tactics, closure, mobilization, competition, definition, preference and planning – there are relatively few examples of empirical engagement with the 'dense fabric of micro-practices' (Hatcher 1998) which infuse choice and decision-making. Jordan, Redley and James (1994) is an exception (see Chapter 6).

On the other hand, standing over and against the work of the rationalist/exclusion theorists, there are what Hatcher (1998) calls 'culturalist' explanations of choice. In particular, Bourdieu and various Bourdieurian scholars (Hatcher, Nash and Reay, and Gewirtz, Ball and Bowe draw heavily on Bourdieu) who argue that decisions can be understood as the operation of 'practical sense', a principle of 'strategies devoid of strategic design' (Bourdieu 1990: 108); that is, the mental structures and dispositions from which choices derive are generated within the habitus. Habitus is a 'conditioned and conditional freedom' and generates 'things to do or not to do, things to say or not to say, in relation to a probable 'upcoming' future' (Bourdieu 1990: 53). In this way structure is embodied, working in and through people's dispositions and activities, rather than on them (see Reay 1998c). This is a world of common sense and self-evidence, that is 'intelligible, foreseeable and hence taken for granted' and 'what is and is not "for us"' (Bourdieu 1990: 64). This 'does not even require active consent, merely the non-occurrence of a refusal' (Connell 1989: 297). It is at this point that the 'practical principles of division' (Bourdieu 1986a: 471) and in particular 'the distances that need to be kept' (472) begin to come into play. This is what Bourdieu calls 'the objectivity of "second order" – symbolic templates for practical activities' (Bourdieu and Wacquant 1992: 7). There is more than a passing resemblance here to the way in which SET theorists describe exclusionary tactics as being embedded in social relations.

Habitus thus produces and reproduces regularities but, also, as it is constantly subjected to experiences it generates diversity. Despite its apparent determinism Bourdieu is adamant that habitus represents an escape from the structure/agency binary and encompasses the possibilities of improvization and invention. 'This degree of indeterminacy, of openness, of uncertainty, means that one cannot depend on it entirely in critical, dangerous situations' (Bourdieu 1990: 78) – which may well describe the situations at hand (see below; contexts of competition). The crucial point about habitus is that it is 'durable but not eternal' (Bourdieu and Wacquant 1992: 133). Despite its having entered the common parlance of educational analysis the concept of habitus remains somewhat elusive and decidedly difficult. Also, 'Bourdieu's theory, however', warns Nash (1990), 'although a socialization theory, is not designed to explain individual actions' (441). It is often loosely or improperly used. Indeed it seems sometimes that the more Bourdieu talks and writes about it, the more elastic the concept appears. Nonetheless, as Hatcher (1998: 19) suggests, habitus provides a 'way of thinking which powerfully illuminates the processes by which social reproduction can take place routinely and unplanned'.

Here then we have two very different ontological positions: one which sees social actors as essentially strategic and consciously hyper-rational, constantly weighing up choices in relation to outcomes; the other conjuring up an actor who is spoken by a practical and natural logic of necessity, following a pre-adapted disposition with little in the way of deliberate or conscious planning. As the reader may guess I wish to pick my way between these positions, balancing SET's rationalism against Bourdieu's open determinism. I also embed these natural logics firmly within the specifics of social class, working at the level of individual or familial action. I return to this below in the discussion of choice and strategy.

Class analysis

Pakulski and Waters (1996), announcing 'the death of class', see the 'new times'/high/post-modernity as having changed the basis on which inequality is constituted. They argue that 'advanced societies are riven by unacceptable divisions of inequality, conflict and domination that are often marked by coercive or exploitative practices. However, they can no longer be sheeted home to class and any insistence in sociology that class should be our primary focus will divert attention away from these conditions' (viii). This analysis, as should be very evident already, rests upon the antithesis of Pakulski and Waters' position. That is, while there is certainly overwhelming evidence of global economic changes which have both made class more permeable in some settings and reordered class structures, class remains a key factor in the explanation of inequality and conflict. As Marshall (1997: 5, original emphasis) suggests, 'we may have mistaken changes in the *shape* of the class structure for changes in social fluidity or the degree of *openness*'. Class relations in education may differ in some ways from those prevalent in the past but they have by no means disappeared. Thus, I would agree with Savage and Butler (1995: 347) that 'exploring continuity and change simultaneously' is necessary to reconcile the arguments of those who emphasize long-standing patterns of inequality *and* those who point to their transformation as a result of fundamental social and economic change. This does not mean that class is the only basis of educational inequalities. But as a *bottom line* to this I want to refer to the conclusion of Crompton's (1998: 226) recent review of debates over class and stratification: 'There have been shifts in the morphology of inequality'; nonetheless, she concludes, life chances and social and material reward continue to be determined by class structures: 'a combination of market position and rights and powers over productive resources' (226) (see also Adonis and Pollard 1997 and Beynon

1999). Crompton goes on to emphasize that '… increasingly societal frag-
mentation may render these facts more opaque' (227). Even so, I take it
then that social classes are 'stable social collectivities' (Savage, Barlow,
Dickens and Fielding 1992: 5) with a degree of distinctiveness 'in terms of
their life chances, their lifestyles and patterns of association, and their
sociopolitical orientations and modes of action' (Goldthorpe 1983: 467).
Some aspects of this distinctiveness are explored in Chapters 4 to 7.

Within all this the perview of this study is limited in a number of ways.
My focus is upon the processes of, rather than patterns of, class inequality;
that is, upon the achievement or reproduction of class advantage and the
'different means of mobilising power for purposes of staking claims to
resources and opportunities' (Parkin 1979: 5). Robson and Butler (2001:
10) argue that middle-class groups 'skilfully, assiduously and strategically
use the sphere of education to their advantage in processes of class formation and maintenance'. I want to ask: What are the skills, attitudes,
perspectives and aspirations at work here? And can this assiduousness be
identified and examined? Furthermore, the scope of the analysis is limited
to the middle class(es), while recognizing the significance of the plural. The
distinctiveness of the middle class is subject to internal divisions and differentiations founded, in Savage, Barlow, Dickens and Fielding's (1992) terms,
on different kinds of usable resources and powers or *assets* – property, organization and cultural (see also Power, Whitty, Edwards and Wigfall 1998).
In particular, Savage, Barlow, Dickens and Fielding (1992) identify a whole
series of significant differences in social mobility, security, lifestyle and
career between professional and managerial workers. Where feasible I will
explore this differentiation at the level of the social action and choices of
individual families. Savage, Barlow, Dickens and Fielding also note that,
'most work on educational inequality rarely distinguishes between different
middle-class groups' (151). Power, Whitty, Edwards and Wigfall (1998) and
Power, Edwards, Whitty and Wigfall (2002) are an exception to the rule.

The changing context of class competition

Weber argued that class struggles over assets and market position are historically contingent or as Parkin (1979: 114) puts it 'any form of organized
closure will arise on the basis of certain economic and social factors, which
can be intelligibly described in the particular case'. This is important.
Drawing on Phil Brown's work I suggest a number of ways in which the context of class competition in education has changed and intensified in the past
twenty years and the class perspectives and strategies of the middle classes
have changed with them. I want to organize and articulate these context
changes, employing a framework I have used previously in a slightly different way (Ball 1990: 8–11). The framework focuses attention on the changing
economic, ideological and political parameters of competition and the inter-
relationships between these. The three dimensions or levels are derived from

the work of Althusser (1969) and his analysis of the complexity of the total social system. Together these dimensions constitute a *dispositif*, 'a cluster of power relations sustaining, and being sustained by certain types of knowledge' (Foucault 1980: 196) – 'a tangle, a multilinear ensemble' (Deleuze 1992: 159). See Table 2.1.

I will discuss each dimension in turn and sketch in some of the inter-relationships. I suggest that each dimension is classed. In a series of papers Brown (1990, 1997, 2000) has undertaken a broad theorization of the relationship between labour market change and global economic changes. In the simplest sense his argument is that economic restructuring and the globalization of economic relations have had profound effects on local and national labour markets and thus the job security of workers. One particular, and very material, aspect of all this is the very dramatic interruption to the trajectory of economic growth and patterns of employment which provided the basis for the massive post-war expansion in the middle classes and the creation of the so-called 'new middle class'. Several factors are at work here, including:

- the stripping out of middle-management positions in the downsizing and re-engineering of large corporations to produce flatter/flexible hierarchies;
- the breakdown of career security by contracting out and the introduction of fixed-term and performance-related employment leading to serial or portfolio career structures;
- the overproduction of professional graduates in fields like law and architecture;
- the closure of financial services branches and their replacement by call centre and e-commerce systems;
- the commercialization of the private and public professions (see Ball 1994; Hanlon 1998; Gewirtz 2002);
- in the UK, the expansion of higher education participation from 13% to 34%.

These factors, and others, contribute to what Savage (2000: 139) calls the 'individualising of the middle-class career', which rests in particular on the rapid increase in forms of self-employment and the creation through organizational restructuring of a core and a peripheral workforce. There is, as Savage (2000: 140) explains, a 'de-coupling of the career from its anchorage in bureaucratic hierarchy'. As these changes work both in and back upon the

Table 2.1 Three levels of analysis as a unified system

Economic	Restructuring	New labour markets
Ideological	Cultural/discursive change	Individualism
Political	Policy change/public sector reform	Choice and competition

education system they contribute to the development of a new, or reinvented, 'regime of risk identification' (Crook 1999, see Chapter 7) within which the relationship of individuals to the state and to the labour market is one of 'prudentialism' (O'Malley 1996). That is, a regime of risk identification which rests primarily upon individual responsibility – or a 'duty to the self', 'putting the family first' – although, as O'Malley suggests, this new regime might also encourage collective, community responsibility for services. In all this the imagined futures of the middle classes and those of their offspring are now under threat from the unmanaged congestion in the old and new professions and in management positions. The expansion of higher education participation threatens, as Bourdieu (1988: 163) puts it, 'a generalized downclassing' which is, he argues, 'particularly intolerable for the more privileged'. A hiatus is created 'between the statutory expectations – inherent in the positions and diplomas which in the previous state of the system really did offer corresponding opportunities – and the opportunities actually provided' (163) at the moments we are considering. Reay (2000: 578), from her study of mothers of primary schoolchildren, found that 'involvement in children's schooling generated intense class anxiety, in particular, for some middle-class mothers who expressed fears that credential inflation and increased marketization within education was making it more difficult than in the past for children from middle-class backgrounds to attain appropriate jobs'. The response of the middle classes to the increase in insecurity and risk involved in their established strategies of reproduction has been an intensification of positional competition. Those middle-class parents who can exert their market power to gain a competitive advantage for their children are increasingly likely to do so, to maximize their chances of gaining access to elite institutions. Hatcher (1998: 29) makes the same point. Market power is exercised through the 'strategies of social distinction' of a particular class with the result that education is being 'transformed back into an oligarchic good' (Jordan, Redley and James 1994: 212).

The relationships and inter-relationships of these labour market shifts with cultural and discursive changes are not difficult to conjure up. In a reworking of Parkin (1979), Brown (2000) argues that this economic restructuring is accompanied by changes in the 'rules of exclusion' and the movement from *meritocratic* to *market* rules.

> Meritocratic rules of exclusion are based on the ideology of individual achievement in an 'open' and 'equal' contest ... However, meritocratic rules do not assume equality of outcome, only that inequalities are distributed more fairly ... The increasing importance of *market* rules reflects the political ascendancy of neo-liberalism since the late 1970s in Britain and the United States ... The Right were able to claim a moral legitimacy for the market system in education dressed in the language of 'choice', 'freedom', 'competition' and 'standards'.

(639)

The implication is that these rules operate ideologically and discursively at both a family and political level within the new politics of uncertainty, in particular via the virtues of competitive individualism. The fears, concerns, perspectives and strategies of social subjects are re-interpolated within a discourse of responsibility and a 'vocabulary and ethics of enterprise' – 'competitiveness, strength, vigour, boldness, outwardness and the urge to succeed' (Rose 1992) – a new 'style of conduct' in Weber's (1915/48) terms. Lane (1991: 318), citing Deutsch, suggests that 'as a psychological orientation competitiveness embraces cognitive, motivational and moral aspects'. There is within this the potential of a move away from what Nagel (1991) calls 'the duality of standpoints' which he sees as the basis for practical ethics and moral stability – that is the nexus of equality and partiality – towards the ethics of the 'personal standpoint' – that is the personal interests and desires of individuals. The egalitarian concerns of the 'impersonal standpoint' are deprecated and obscured. This feeds what Plant (1992: 87) calls a 'culture of self interest' or what Kenway (1990: 155) calls the 'cult of selfishness'; a practical logic of individualism and competition. Personal motives are given systematic preference over impersonal values and a new moral environment is constituted (see Chapter 6). Within the market rules of exclusion both consumers and producers are encouraged by the rewards and disciplines of market forces, and are legitimated by the values of the personal standpoint in their quest for positional advantage over others. 'The more social resources were distributed on a competitive basis, the more "competitiveness" was rewarded' (Marginson 1997: 169). The cultural, economic, political and social assets of families are mobilized 'to stay ahead of the race' (Brown 2000: 637). One effect of this, I suggest, has been a loss of support among the new middle class for efforts to democratize education and social policy and the progressive experimentation in educational methods and pedagogies (see Chapter 4). However, I will go on to make the point that while the market rules and the discourse of positional competition are dominant and well sedimented among the middle class, they are not absolute or unchallenged (see below). Not every middle-class parent thinks or chooses this way. As we shall see there are varying degrees of reflexivity towards and resistance to these rules and the contexts of choice in general.

Following Hirsch (1977), Brown (2000: 638) reminds us that we need to retain here a distinction between resources *in* the marketplace and influence *over* markets – that is 'the mobilization of social groups seeking to change the rules of the game'. The changing rules of the game brings us to the dimension of policy. It is at the level of policy that the discursive and ideological terms of the new rules of exclusion are translated into practice. Policies then become sources of discursive articulation and legitimation for new styles of conduct and (in the case of market rules) arenas of opportunity for those families holding relevant and transposable assets and resources. This produces the framework for what (Brown 1990: 65) calls *parentocracy*

– 'where a child's education is increasingly dependent upon the *wealth* and *wishes* of parents, rather than the *ability* and *efforts* of pupils'. The relationships between class and policy are addressed in Chapter 3. The key feature of a parentocracy or market rules is the deregulation of school recruitment and the deployment of choice; the resulting competition between institutions and the granting of institutional autonomy to schools enhance the opportunities for the use of family resources at various key points and moments of decision-making (see Chapter 3). As Hatcher (1998: 22) points out, 'choices are not one-off events but a recursive process'. Furthermore, familial resources may be mobilized to change the rules of the game at the institution as well as in making and getting choices.

A final word about these contexts. It should be evident that at each level and between the levels there are problems and complexities of cause and effect – so it is possible to talk about the effects of economic restructuring on positional competition and the consequences of competition in terms of individualism. Then again, the increased intensity of uncertainty and risk experienced by the middle classes can be seen as having effects on policy, in as much that 'the state ... performs its functional task in regulating the system by responding to the particular way in which different classes mobilize around system contradictions' (Saunders 1981: 193). In another way policies have legitimating effects in terms of competitive behaviour and the ethics of the personal standpoint. The particular form of governmentality thus produced also does ontological work, in giving rise to particular 'practices through which we act upon ourselves and one another' (Rose 1992: 161) which underpin 'the new regime of the autonomous, choosing self' (162). I do not see it as my task here to attempt to separate out or privilege particular relations of cause and effect within these contexts. The point is that the contexts together, as a social totality, make certain behaviours and strategies obvious, likely, necessary and appropriate – but not inevitable. Furthermore, there is a paradox at the centre of these changes. That is, as the values and practices of competitive individualism are ever more widely disseminated, in particular by the insertion of choice and competition into public services, then the dream of order that is deeply embedded in the class imagination of the middle class comes under threat. Plant (1992: 89), among others, argues that 'without some sense of civic virtue, or orientation to values that are not of a self-regarding kind, market behaviour will require growing regulation in the interests of the market itself'.[3] Arguably, in the UK we are seeing the expansion both of public sector markets and an increase in their regulation.[4] It may be that 'disorganised capitalism' (Lash and Urry 1987) is beginning to dissolve the conditions of consensus and social cohesion upon which it depends in order to continue. This in itself increases risk and decreases the reliability and trust which are immanent in 'the contexts of day-to-day social interaction' (Giddens 1991: 36).

Choices and strategies

My final concern in this chapter is to consider more carefully the key concepts of choice and strategy. Together these form the basis for my examination of the practices and practical logics of middle-class families in their 'tightly formed relationship' (Savage, Barlow, Dickens and Fielding 1992: 46) to the education system. The issues involved in delineating the two concepts are very much the same. I shall draw again on Hatcher's discussion of rational choice and Crow's (1989) discussion of the use of the concept of strategy. There are three key points to be made. First, it is important not to allow the notions of choice and strategy to be subsumed within a view of social action dominated entirely by rational calculation. As Crow (8) puts it: 'There is a very real danger when analysing household strategies of reading more calculation into the process whereby action is determined than is in reality present'. Educational choices and strategies may well be invested with 'a mixture of rationalities' (Pahl and Wallace 1985: 380) and an element of the 'fortuitous and haphazard' (Morris 1987: 136). Choices are sometimes made, strategies undertaken for varieties of reasons, not merely to achieve advantage. Foucault also warns against importing an 'excess of rationality' into our analyses. Peripheral vision is important here (Bateson 1994: 11). In particular it is vital to recognize the role of non-rational aspects of choice and strategy (see Chapter 6); '... agents do not simply weigh courses of action in terms of their efficacy in achieving a desired goal, they evaluate the desired goals themselves in relation to a framework of personal values that is not reducible to personal utility' (Hatcher 1998: 17). In other words, utility is not the only criterion for decision-making. An exclusive emphasis upon rational calculation, however important it may be, can lead to 'the diminishment of our moral understanding of human agency' (Morgan 1989: 29) and 'the exclusion of the richness and complexity of social action' (Hatcher 1998: 16). Relatedly, there is a problem of categorization here. How do we recognize rationality when we see it? What is the standard for rationality? And, further, there are ethical issues involved here; 'when sociologists impute objectives which actors to whom they are imputed would not necessarily recognise and may object to?' (Crow 1989: 20). Second, again in relation to both choice and strategy, there are difficulties in terms of the balance between agency and autonomy and structure and constraint. This was rehearsed in part earlier in the discussion of habitus. A singular and myopic focus upon strategic conduct is not helpful. I have signalled already the importance of a new *dispositif* for an understanding of contemporary middle-class choices and strategies, and thus conceptually we may want to give 'primacy to practical and discursive consciousness' but 'within defined context boundaries' (Giddens 1984: 22). Nonetheless, the impetus and opportunity to act varies. Boundaries are practical and material – as we shall see at some points of middle-class educational decision-making non-educational constraints are predominant – but choices and strategies are also made up within particular discursive repertoires and vocabularies of motives as argued above. Responses are discursive and dispositional but may occasionally be creative or unorthodox. Constraints also work in other ways. The opportunity to act is also related to capacity. As Morgan (1989: 27) puts it: 'Without resources there can be no strategies'. Capacities vary in relation to the assets and other relevant resources available to families. Capacities also change over time as resources are accumulated and as strategies are refined or learned. As Bourdieu suggests, the relevance of education as a means of social reproduction may be evaluated differently at different points in time and thus the relevant resources for achieving reproduction may be different. Third, there is a question of level. I mean two things by this. One is interpretational. Empirically my focus here is upon the individual family as a relatively independent decision-making unit, pursuing its own goals, values and interests; although in Chapter 3 some of the interventions described involve collective actions. Nonetheless, as SET theorists do, I want to relate individual or family actions to collective effects – exclusion, closure, class advantage. Strategies and choices achieve change and 'the analysis of household strategies is a crucial element in the understanding of social reproduction and social change' (Morgan 1989: 26). The other point is that at the level of the family itself there are differences to be taken into account. Most obviously, gender roles in decision-making. As previous research suggests mothers are usually the key figures in educational decision-making (David, West and Ribbens 1994; Gewirtz, Ball and Bowe 1995; Ball, Maguire and Macrae 2000). But this is not so in all families; patterns vary and families are not always harmonious. The sexual division of labour within families is not always 'resolved without conflict between the sexes' (Yeandle 1984: 171). Decision-making can be fraught. It is certainly often highly emotionally charged and a source of stress and anxiety, as we shall see. The role of the child or young person also varies (see Reay and Ball 1998) and is sometimes difficult to ascertain or understand clearly (see Chapter 6). Finally, the constitution of the family and the household varies. Some variations may have implications for strategic capacity.

As indicated above this book draws upon a related set of research studies conducted over a ten-year period which were primarily concerned with educational markets and choice.[5] The details of these studies, a great deal of direct data, and findings and issues arising thus far are available elsewhere (specifically see Gewirtz, Ball and Bowe 1995; Ball, Maguire and Macrae 2000; Vincent and Ball 2001; Ball, Davies, Reay and David 2002). Here I present and explore a particular set of issues that are embedded in, and arise from, these studies. In doing so I will present and discuss some of data from those studies and subject this to a further analysis (Chapters 4–7). In Chapter 3 I review the findings of a number of other published studies from various settings and countries which address the relationships between education markets and social class; and in particular I will examine the evidence available related to the class use of market opportunities.

3 Class and policy

To try to advance merit and retract class advantages as a basis of selection in a system that remains highly selective is likely to rankle too many entrenched interests. Those who lose privileges could be expected to fight to retain them ...
(Raftery and Hout 1993: 60).

The middle class is a social class that has become a historical actor ...
(Eder 1993: 164).

The purpose of this chapter is to explore the relationships between social class and education policy. I intend to argue a case for two related propositions; first, that currently, in developed societies around the world, education policies are primarily aimed at satisfying the concerns and interests of the middle class. In effect, policy thinking is classed in particular ways and particular policies present the middle class with strategic advantages in education. Second, I will argue that the middle class is active in various ways in influencing and effecting education policies in their own interests. This takes place at various levels from national to local, and institutional. I shall explore and exemplify the workings of middle-class interest at each level. Embedded in these propositions are a number of different conceptualizations of policy – I see these as complementary rather than as competing. They overlay one another and reinforce patterns of social advantage. They are: (a) a pluralist view which focuses on the direct actions of parents in contesting or effecting policy directly by expressing and advancing their preferences; (b) a view of policy as non-decision-making, 'in which decisions are prevented from being taken on *potential* issues over which there is an observable *conflict* of (subjective) *interests*' (Lukes 1974: 20). One prime example here is the English DfES' steadfast exclusion of issues of poverty and social class from debates concerning educational achievement and 'failing schools' and the substitution of School Effectiveness/School Improvement policies which give primary emphasis to institutional factors to explain performance differences (see Thrupp and Ball 2002). I suggest that this can be seen as representing and legitimating a more general re-working of the meaning of and priorities related to educational need which facilitate the movement of resources from those with social disadvantage to the able and gifted; in effect, reasserting an historic continuity in English educational thinking and practice; (c) a view of policy as a condensate of class interests and class struggle, that is as invested by class thinking, such that conflict is latent and 'consists in a contradiction between the interests of those exercising power and the *real interests* of those they exclude' (Lukes 1974: 24–25). In other words, current policies in play provide the middle class with the means to exercise power in various educational settings, although such power relations are always 'complex and dislocated' (Poulantzas 1973: 113). This is analytically more difficult terrain but I will attempt to demonstrate that, in particular, parental choice policies, which have a near hegemonic grip on education policy thinking around the globe, are a prime example of this third dimensional view of policy.[1] Of course, these three views of policy mirror Lukes' (1974) three dimensions of power.

Lukes' language of 'interests' is particularly apposite here, although the notion of 'real interests' is fraught with difficulties (see Chapter 6). Nonetheless, as I hope to illustrate, it is possible to identify concrete moments at which the 'interests' invested in policies are made apparent as class groups, here the middle class, act to project or define their interests within or against policy. This interpretative position with regard to class and policy is central to Parkin's 'closure model' (see Chapter 4).

> State powers can … be harnessed in support of many forms of exclusionary closure, not only those that promote and sustain class exploitation. The closure model conceptualises the state as an agency that buttresses and consolidates the rules and institutions of exclusion … Indeed, a class, race, sex or ethnic group only accomplishes domination to the extent that its exclusionary prerogatives are backed up by the persuasive instruments of the state.
>
> (Parkin 1974: 138)

This is then a two-sided thesis. I shall argue that the particular policies of choice and competition give particular advantages to the middle class, while not appearing to do so, in the way that selection policies did in a previous policy era (not that selection has gone away), and that the middle class are adept at taking up and making the most of the opportunities of advantage that policies present to them. The former is part of what Brown (2000) calls 'rigging' and the latter 'ranking'. In effect, the discourse of choice legitimates forms of exclusion and social differentiation and plays its part in class reproduction and the reproduction of fault lines of ability (see Chapter 4). It also serves to exclude or marginalize other principles of association and modes of resource allocation with more general consequences for social conflict and social inequality. As US philosopher Walzer (1984: 221) puts it, when policies like vouchers and ability grouping in schools operate, especially from the early years of schooling, 'it is not the associations of citizens that are being anticipated, but the class system in roughly its present form'.

Following Parkin (1974) then, and Brown's (2000) updating of his analytical framework, I am here attempting to indicate the various ways in which market rules of exclusion offer possibilities for strategic action which many middle-class families are very willing and very able to take up. However, while one set of exclusionary rules, with its attendant ideological system, may be predominant, this overlays rather than totally displaces other sets of rules and other ideological systems. We can see this in particular in the case of Wilson High (below). What I will call policy regimes – ensembles of inter-related policies which can be reduced to specific principles of integration – rarely operate in unadulterated form. Policy is almost always, to some extent, messy, incoherent and *ad hoc*, as the state responds to different sorts of problems and contradictions and interests and, as noted already, new policies are sedimented into a history of previous policies which may be superseded but are not necessarily expunged. Furthermore, while, as I suggest below, there is a recognizable global orthodoxy to education policy in the twenty-first century, policies also have a national specificity. New policies enter different political histories and are inflected by them as much as they inflect those histories, the mobility of policies is 'neither uniform nor predictable' (Levin 1998: 131). In the main examples of policy struggle presented below – from France, the USA and England – the national political histories produce different mixes or repertoires of rules and ideologies, or 'abstractions', as Oakes and Lipton (2001) call them. In each case appropriate 'abstractions' can be deployed to support or critique policy without the encumbrance of appearing to speak for one's own self-interest.

In focusing 'on how positional competition is experienced by individuals and social groups' (Brown 2000: 637), in this case the middle class, what we will see is in fact a mix of strategies, a mix which varies both in relation to the rules and the 'widely held abstractions' (Oakes and Lipton 2001: 11) in play, and in relation to the assertion of these strategies at different points, and at different moments, in the education system. Strategies both within and between, both individual and collective. The rules are not absolutely limiting and they do not exclude other tactics; middle-class families are opportunistic; they will use their capitals differently as the need arises (see Chapter 4). Tactically, the cultural skills of the middle class enable them to take up the possibilities of different rules and 'abstractions' – those of *choice*, *ascription* and *meritocracy/social good* (see Chapter 4), or market, membership and meritocracy, as Brown (2000) calls them. Or putting it in yet another way, they will use exit, voice or loyalty according to which seems best suited to support and further the interests of their children within any particular set of contingencies.

I want to point to another history in all this, the history of contingencies. Adeptness and strategy vary in importance over time in relation to changes in socio-economic conditions. This is explored further below, but the point is that education policy itself, I suggest, can be interpreted as being responsive to changes in the size and constitution of the middle class and to specific contradictions which emerge as a result within the education system and between the education system and the labour market (see Chapter 2). In saying this I realize that I am skirting around the issue of how class gets into policy. So let us take a short diversion here and I will sketch out, and no more than that, some ways of thinking about this. As elsewhere simple recourse to a single theory explanation seems unhelpful and inadequate but deployment of a set of theoretical affinities might get us somewhere. If this seems uninteresting then skip to the next section.

Class in policy

So, I will switch to a different theoretical language for a moment. In Poulantzas' terms, and through his particular theoretical lens, the state, and thence its policies, is a condensation of class struggles, or in Parkin's (1979) terms it is the 'political locale or the distillation of class antagonisms' (140).[2] The state thus responds, not simply to the interests of the dominant class, but to the political balance of class forces at any particular point in time – at any 'conjuncture'. In this way the state functions to manage and regulate system contradictions. Thus, it is at the political level that one may map the indices of change. The state responds to political struggles around contradictions by interventions of various sorts, and classes articulate and pursue their interests through these struggles. 'Political struggles are thus an inherent aspect of class practices that is, classes do not first constitute themselves as economic categories ... ' (Saunders 1981: 191). 'Class interests are situated in the field of practices' (Poulantzas 1973: 109).[3] As I am trying to establish throughout this text classes, and here specifically the middle class, are to a great extent constituted through their practices, although perhaps not in the grander political sense that Poulantzas meant.[4] 'The state thus performs its functional task in regulating the system by responding to the particular way in which different classes mobilize around system contradictions' (192). While at the same time fragmenting classes through an ideology of individualism within which 'members of these classes come to conceive of themselves and to live their lives as atomized individual subjects rather than as class agents' (193). The response of the state brings into play different 'rules of closure' through different 'policy regimes'. These are articulated in terms of public and national interest, 'the unity of isolated relations' (Poulantzas 1973: 134), which stand in place of 'class interest'. This unity also becomes firmly embedded in the assumptive worlds of policy and policy-makers. Parents are homogenized and differences in interests are obscured within 'everyone wins' policies.

Poulantzas (1973: 109) goes on to argue that class interests 'are in no way a "psychological" notion'. However, and this will come as no surprise to the reader by now, along with Saunders, Pickvance, Sayer and others, I would want to add that such a form of analysis of the state remains incomplete without some accommodation to the problem of meaning. That is: 'In order to explain how class practices mediate structural contradictions, it seems necessary to understand how the members of different classes come to interpret their objective situations' (Saunders 1981: 202). Moments of contradiction then provoke struggles which lead to responses by the state. I suggest that the usurpation of comprehensive education over tripartitism[5] in the UK in the early 1960s can be seen in these terms, as the expanding middle classes found their opportunities for grammar school education increasingly competitive and unsatisfactory, and very uneven between locations. 'Scarcity of places was the crucial factor' (Halsey, Heath and Ridge 1980: 217) in bringing about reform. Further, it is tempting to see the Labour Party's deliberate unwillingness to define and prescribe the meaning of comprehensive education at this time (Ball 1981), as thence allowing for the possibility of the re-inscription of middle-class advantages within the new, and temporary as it turned out, but much more open (relatively porous), set of rules of exclusion which replaced tripartitism – in most parts of the UK. The middle class were quickly able to assert their monopoly of privileged trajectories, particularly access to higher education, within the comprehensive system. This was anticipated by Halsey, Heath and Ridge (1980: 217) when they note that 'inequality survived the 1944 Education Act and may find accommodation in a comprehensive system ...'.

As I argue in Chapter 2, as the economic, political and cultural 'conditions of possibility' shifted again in the 1980s and 1990s, new contradictions emerged, with 'both an increased demand for technical, managerial and professional workers and a more intensive struggle for competitive advantage in education and the labour markets' (Brown 2000: 637), the processes of democratization which were at work within parts of comprehensive education became increasingly intolerable, a new set of rules were set in place – competition and choice. It should be clear then that in developing a critique of the market rules of exclusion here I am not then defending some previous period or golden age of education in which class closure was absent, rather I am referring to different regimes of closure which are more or less porous or *open*, in terms of rules, and more or less *diverse* in terms of abstractions, but which in different ways allowed the middle class to achieve their social reproduction. At the points at which that achievement comes under threat struggles for or against change ensue in different arenas (see Ball 1990).

In some ways, Glassman takes this argument a stage further in suggesting that we are now witnessing around the world, 'with different funding alternatives' (Glassman 2000: 11) the emergence of a new '*extended*' welfare state. This new welfare state, 'set in different ideological garb from nation to nation' (43) is a response to 'the shared needs' (43) of the new middle class, arising in particular from the 'decline of the extended family' (6) – that is, another set of more general system contradictions. Specifically, these shared needs are related to problems involved in the management of risk (see Chapter 7). There are several processes embedded in this emergence.

Responses to new kinds of social problems, the search for new methods of welfare funding and welfare delivery, and the attempt to ensure and retain the commitment of the middle class to the state provision of welfare services. The politics of choice is a key element of this retention. Within all this, the interests of the state and those of the middle class come together in the relationships between individual positional advantage and the state's fostering of international economic competitiveness. However, the argument for the new, extended welfare state is not as straightforward as it may at first seem, in as much that the old welfare state was also used to considerable effect and advantage by the middle class: 'contrary to common belief, fewer individuals in households with low rather than with high incomes received social services in kind of substantial value' (Townsend 1979: 222 and Le Grand 1982: 128–129). Again my point is that different policy regimes offer different kinds of, and possibilities for, advantage to the middle class and are related to different kinds of contingencies.

Choice policies, I argue, in the current socio-economic context, are an effective response to the interest anxieties of the middle class. To support this I will deploy evidence from different national locations to illustrate a clearcut pattern of class advantage. While some of this evidence is contested and while there are very few examples of countervailing evidence, my point here is that there is an irresistible bulk of findings which reiterate very similar outcomes of advantage and inequality from choice policies of various kinds. I am not so much interested in the fine detail here as the bigger picture – who benefits? I will not spend too much time either on reviewing this material or on the global policy trends which support and facilitate the dissemination of choice politics, in part because I have written on these issues elsewhere (see Ball 1998a; Ball 2001b; Ball 2001c), and in part because I want to spend more time on the strategic action of middle-class families in relation to education policy.

For neatness, the discussion here is organized by levels – that is global, national, local and institutional. This is a presentational and analytic convenience and therefore the levels should not be taken as mutually exclusive or descriptively equivalent across settings.

Global

Education reform is a global movement. We are seeing in education and social policy generally, working at different speeds with different degrees of intensity in different locations, the establishment of new generic modes of organization, governance and delivery of state education, and indeed public sector services more generally; that is, a 'policy epidemic' (Levin 1998: 131). There is the emergence of a new orthodoxy made up of 'Remarkably similar claims and solutions' (Dehli 2000: 75). Typically, this orthodoxy comes as a package; that is, very schematically: competition, choice, devolution, managerialism and performativity (Ball 2000). At different times in different locations, different aspects of the package may be emphasized and others played down. The processes of enactment of reform have to be viewed over time and in terms of the changing relationships of various elements. More specifically, the implementation of the package is part of a general alignment, within developed countries, with the policy positions espoused by organizations like the OECD, the World Trade Organization (WTO) and the World Bank and thus the further opening up of these economies, in all sectors, to global capitalist institutions. The World Bank and International Monetary Fund in particular are firmly committed to the Americanization of the world economy along these lines. Their staff is primarily American and their headquarters are in the US with most of their funding coming from the US Treasury. 'Building free capital markets into the basic architecture of the world economy had long been, in the words of the US Treasury's (then) Deputy Secretary Lawrence Summers "our most crucial international priority"' (Wade 2001: 125). Closer to home, so to speak, Rikowski (2001) maintains that education is a core element of the WTO agenda and he outlines the WTO strategy for opening education up to corporate capital.

However, the reform package is not just a matter of introducing new structures, opportunities and incentives. When taken together, these policy moves bring about new forms of social relationships, cultures and values. Client choice is one of the primary constituents of the global reform package, or more specifically in education, parental choice. In OECD-speak, this involves 'the replacement of highly centralised, hierarchical organisational structures by decentralised management environments where decisions on resources allocation and service delivery are made closer to the point of delivery, and which provide scope for feedback from clients and other interest groups' (OECD 1995: 8).

Parental choice seems to be, at face value, like mothers and apple pie, one of those things that must be good and is difficult to criticize. It is certainly attractive to politicians – it wins votes and brings about a shift in the locus of responsibility for educational performance! It is presented by its advocates as a 'magic bullet' which will transform and revitalize moribund bureaucratic education systems. Powers and Cookson (1999: 104–5) suggest that 'school choice is best understood as a social movement ... led by politicians, policy advocates, and public personalities ...'. At the practical level it is very much an urban policy, an example of metropolitan concerns driving national policy outcomes. Once given it is very difficult to take away (Adler 1997). Put simply, in the language of economics, the case for parental choice policies rests on two premises: that they deliver improved productive and allocative efficiency, that is, raised standards of achievement and greater social equity in access to schools. In other words, the argument is that the hidden hand of the market, the individual choices of independent consumers, is a better mechanism for driving up performance and evening out inequalities than state planning and regulation. However, the weight of evidence from around the globe indicates that choice fails to deliver on either count. German economist Manfred Weiss (2000: 14) in a recent review of research reaches the conclusion that:

> The insights provided by international educational research into the way quasi-markets in schooling function and the effects they have suggest that the functionalisation of competition and decentralisation has not achieved any convincing success in attaining efficiency goals anywhere ... The findings produced so far rather imply that quasi-markets tend to increase existing disparities in school performance and in inequalities of opportunity.

In another recent paper Carnoy (2000: 19) arrives at a similar conclusion: 'When the information is assembled in the US and abroad, the evidence suggests "marketizing" education increases school choice for a certain fraction of parents but most likely does little or nothing to improve overall student achievement'. Powers and Cookson's (1999: 109) overview comes to the same conclusion about the social effects of choice.

> Perhaps the most consistent effect of market-driven choice programs ... is that [they] tend to have the effect of increasing stratification to one degree or another within school districts. This stratifying effect of choice has even been found in programs that specifically target low-income families.

Writing ten years earlier, US political scientist Maddaus (1990: 289), in another review of research, came to the same conclusion: 'although conservatives and liberals alike have advocated parental choice of public schools as a means of promoting excellence while ensuring equity, this review of research findings suggests problems with both objectives'. However, taking a much more hesitant position and writing more specifically about voucher schemes Goldhaber (2000: 21) argues that 'we do not know enough about how different voucher designs would impact educational and social outcomes in various contexts to form a conclusion pro and con'.[6] Fuller and Elmore (1996) also have doubts and argue that it is difficult to be clear whether stratification is a general effect of choice or the outcome of the design of specific programmes. This point seems academic; it is choice in practice that is the issue. More boldly, Moe (1995) dismisses worries about stratification, arguing that the 'skimming effect' in choice programmes is less than that which occurs in existing allocation systems within which middle-class parents exercise choice by moving house.

Nonetheless, looking globally at the research on equity and choice there seems to be a decisive and inescapable pattern across systems and societies that are very different from one another. Lauder *et al.* (1999) in a New Zealand study of choice sum this up with their conclusion that on the demand side, in market systems of education: 'Students from high SES backgrounds have the greatest opportunity to avoid working-class schools, and most take it' (101). And that, on the supply side: 'schools will also use whatever means at their disposal to insulate themselves from the 'rigours' of the market' (134). In other words, there are both supply and demand side behaviours. The authors conclude that the social mix of intake is the most significant factor in understanding differences in school performance but that the market works to 'exacerbate the polarisation of school intakes that already existed on the basis of residential segregation' (135). To reiterate, these effects are produced from both ends of the market relation. Certain middle-class parents are seeking out certain sorts of schools – high status schools, irrespective of the quality of instruction – and all schools are seeking to maximize their intake of students who are easy to teach and likely to perform well (see Woods, Bagley and Glatter 1998) in order to attract other such choices or achieve performance requirements.

Of the three English studies that have examined the social distribution of school intakes since the introduction of school choice, giving some indication of the effects of the strategies noted above, two of the three, Gibson and Asthana, and Noden, conclude that polarization has increased. Gorard (1997) demurs and reports an uneven national pattern (as one might expect) and overall a 'modest decrease in segregation' up to 1997, but the interpretations of this analysis seem to shift from paper to paper (e.g. see Gorard 1999 and Gibson and Asthana 2000). Overall Gorard, Fitz and Taylor (2001: 22) conclude that 'the school system in England and Wales is certainly fairer than it was in 1989, but the most recent trend, long after the maturation on the school choice process, is once again towards unfairness'. These authors also point to the difficulties involved in the interpretation of evidence and suggest six sorts of explanations for their findings. Different measures and indicators are deployed in this debate, which adds to the overall lack of clarity. Noden's (2000: 382–3) analysis concludes that: 'Using (his own version of) the index of isolation and the Gorard index of dissimilarity to analyse data for the whole of England during the period 1994–99, we have seen that there has been a net increase in segregation … the "established market" in England has seen average levels of segregation increasing consistently'. However, Noden also points out that the pattern is irregular, with different profiles over time in different Local Education Authorities and like other commentators he questions the efficacy of the free school meals indicator which is used in these analyses as a surrogate for social class. He points out that 'as many previous research studies have suggested, it is at the local level that the educational quasi-market and competition between schools must be understood' (383).[7] Gibson and Asthana's work is focused on lived, local markets. This is an important caveat to any general conclusions about choice and most examples quoted below are based upon local rather than general, national studies of choice and competition. It is only within these local, lived markets that choice is meaningful, either for actors or analysts.

Let us look as some other evidence. Echols and Wilms's (1997: 4–5) work in the Scottish education system again reports finding a segregation effect: 'the research provides strong evidence that parental choice is one of the contributing factors to the increase in between-school segregation in Scotland ... Greater segregation is likely to result in greater inequalities in achievement ... although some students benefit marginally from parental choice, the cost for others and for the system as a whole are high. Schools serving pupils in disadvantaged areas have lost many pupils to schools with high socio-economic status, despite effective teaching practices'. What is important here for middle-class parents is quality but also context. Wilms's findings introduce a further issue into the consideration of choice – the possibility that beneficial effects for some will have negative consequences for others. Fossey's (1994) research in Massachusetts identified a similar effect. The possibility of choice in that state, taken up almost exclusively by middle-class families, resulted in the movement of middle-class students out of low SES districts and into high SES districts, taking their attached funding with them. This is one indication of the way in which the choices of some affect the opportunities of others. Fossey (332) comments that:

> ... depending on the severity of the penalties for districts that lose students, open enrolment plans may be more than ineffective; they may actually hinder districts that lose students from improving their educational programs. By taking money away from districts that lose students – often districts with fewer resources and lower socio-economic levels than receiving towns – such programs could make it more difficult for districts that are already handicapped to obtain higher levels of performance.

Those schools and school districts which need funds most are losing funds and those which least need additional funds are gaining more. Fowler-Finn (1994: 60), a Massachusetts School Superintendent makes the same point and adds that 'politicians have ignored the fact that the reasons for leaving a school are not necessarily connected to the quality of education'. Jimerson (1998) reports the same effects in Minnesota. Several other studies in the USA have also drawn attention to the deleterious effects of choice and competition, both where choice produces movement between public and private school systems or where there are forms of school specialization in the public system. Hershkoff and Cohen (1992) demonstrate how in Choctaw County, Alabama, state subsidies for private school choices have diminished financial support for public schools, produced racial and economic segregation and stigmatized the public school system and its students. 'Parental choice has led to the creation of a dual system that has had a devastating impact on the public schools and the children left behind in them' (3). Here, choice is a 'sorting mechanism' that separates children along racial and class lines. In very different settings (magnet school programmes in New

York, Chicago, Boston and Philadelphia), Moore and Davenport (1990) reported a very similar pattern of sorting based on race and class. In part the sorting effect is again a reflection of the 'inclination to choice' among high income groups (see below). However, in these programmes the discretion of the selecting schools and the complexities of the admissions procedures also contributed significantly to the segregation effects.

> Given the discretion exercised in recruitment, screening, and selection, there was an overwhelming bias toward establishing procedures and standards at each step in the admissions process that screened out 'problem' students and admitted the 'best' students, with best being defined as students with good academic records, good attendance, good behaviour, a mastery of English, and no special learning problems
> (201).

Again, the point is that within competitive systems of schooling, the values of competition encourage and legitimate strategic action on both sides, and on both sides these values work in the interests of middle-class families. Chenoweth (1987) found similar processes at work in San Francisco's magnet programme (see also Blank 1990). Goldring and Shapira (1993) reporting on four elementary 'schools of choice' in Tel Aviv, Israel, also note the unrepresentatively high SES composition of the schools of choice. Wells and Associates' (1998) study of 17 charter schools in California found many of these located in low-income areas while attracting more highly educated parents from among the low-income groups. This is another theme which stands out in research findings in very different national settings, that is, the over-representation of atypical members of low-income groups among those taking up the opportunities of choice schemes; 'choosers tend to come from smaller and more highly educated families than non-choosers' (Powers and Cookson 1999: 109–110). For example, both the Milwaukee choice programme (Witte, Thorn, Pritchard and Claiborn 1994) and the UK Assisted Places Scheme (Edwards, Fitz and Whitty 1989) attracted large numbers of these atypical families. Beales and Wahl (1995) confirm the Milwaukee findings and Heise, Colburn and Lamberti (1995) found the same thing in Indianapolis. Indeed this trend within research findings can be traced back to Jackson and Marsden's (1962) classic study of the families of 88 working-class students in Huddersfield who gained places in the local grammar school, who were different in several respects from their immediate peers.

Moore and Davenport (1990: 221) go on to conclude from their study that 'Public school choice is a reform strategy whose advocates have thus far failed to prove that it can bring about the widespread school improvement that is essential in the nation's big cities. School choice has proven risks and unproven benefits for students at risk, and has typically represented a new and more subtle form of discriminatory sorting …'. And Hershkoff and Cohen (1992: 25) warn that 'any educational improvement that a market approach might bring comes at a price: the creation of an underclass of dis-favoured and underfunded schools' (see also Gewirtz, Ball and Bowe 1995). Van Zanten's work in a commune just outside Paris also shows the use of choice as a means of escape for middle-class students into the more presti-gious Paris school system or private schools, leaving behind an increasing working-class state school system in the commune itself. The result she sug-gests is a widening of 'the gap between "advantaged" schools – those relatively protected from the effects of mass schooling and non-selection – and "disadvantaged" ones, in which workers' and foreigners' children, those with the greatest scholastic difficulties are situated' (Broccolichi and van Zanten 2000: 58). Carnoy's extensive work in Chile (Carnoy 2000 and McEwan and Carnoy 2000) paints a similar picture. 'For-profit schools, which sprang up like mushrooms in Chilean cities when vouchers were made available, are no better at producing high achievement scores for a child of a given socio-economic background than are public schools' and 'there is some evidence that privatisation increased stratification in the 1980s, as private schools cream-skimmed better (higher social class, more able) students from public schools and tended to locate in high income municipalities' (Carnoy 2000: 18). This is reinforced by Espinola (1992) who found that higher-income groups, urban and rural, chose the private sector and lower-income households stayed in the municipal system. Arnove, Torres, Franz and Morse (1997), Munin (1998) and Tedesco (1994) also report negative social effects for students from poor backgrounds arising from the Chilean reforms (see Narodowski and Nores 2002, for a review of studies of Chile).

Muth (1993: 3), from an analysis of the local debates around choice in the US, dramatically argues, in terms which echo the social closure perspective, that 'choice became a byword for competition for scarce resources and reseg-regation' and that 'when the smoke of rhetoric clears, that those who most strongly favour market-choice options, vouchers, or other choice strategies which decrease public control also favour segregation by race or class' (13). Moore and Davenport (1990: 216) starkly conclude their study of magnet choice programmes in four US cities, that these programmes create the possi-bility for a 'new form of segregation based on a combination of race, income level, and previous success in school'. Henig's (1994) analysis of the school magnet programme in Montgomery County, Maryland provides a further example of these patterns. Choice, he concludes, appears to exacerbate rather than ameliorate racial segregation. White families were most likely to request transfers into schools with low proportions of minorities, located in higher-income neighbourhoods (see Chapter 4). Minority families were most likely to opt for schools with high proportions of minorities in low-income neighbourhoods, irrespective of the character of the schools themselves (Ball, Reay and David 2002). Parental choice surveys indicated that parents employed racially influenced criteria which drew heavily on informal word-of-mouth 'information' rather than 'sharply defined clues about which schools are likely to benefit their children'. Parker and Margonis (1996: 2) conclude their review of race issues in US school choice research by stating that 'market driven choice plans serve to ossify and reinforce already established social divisions based on wealth and race' and they see such plans as part of 'the politics of urban racial containment' and as related to 'the political galvanization of white self interest around the issue of race' (10). Back in the UK, Ball, Macrae and Maguire (1998) found 'racial choosing' to be an important dynamic in post-compulsory educational choice and some further education colleges were concerned that their 'ethnic mix', particularly working-class African-Caribbean boys, would act as a deterrent to other white middle-class choosers. Again, we see the two sides of the market at work.

What I have been seeking to do here is to establish a prima-facie case for the proposition that, internationally, school choice policies are taken advantage of and primarily work in the interests of middle-class families. Fairly conclusively the research quoted demonstrates that when choice is available it is taken up most enthusiastically by middle-class families, those who are unable or unwilling to afford the cost of existing private schooling (see Chapter 6), and these families use choice to find settings in which there are large numbers of other families like themselves. Furthermore, such movements both in terms of symbolic effects and especially when associated with funding redistributions have negative consequences for the working-class students left behind. Also, in multi-racial settings, race is a further compounding factor in the choice process and there may well be an increase in racial segregation as a result. Another point to note here is that in a number of studies active working-class choosers appear to be atypical of their community as a whole. All of this raises questions about the advocacy of choice, which is addressed in the next section. The association between choice and class makes it enormously difficult to establish any independent performance improvement effects that are associated with systems of choice and competition (see Naradowski and Nores 2002, for instance).

National

Again, here I need to be selective and specific. I shall concentrate on recent English national politics and point to some contrasts with France, drawing on van Zanten's work. But I am interested here not so much in specificity for its own sake as in developing some generic tools of analysis. I am trying to develop an argument which links choice politics and education markets to the interests of the middle class. I am also suggesting that this is an international phenomenon which cuts across national political traditions but which is nonetheless realized in somewhat different ways in different locations (Ball 1998). Brown (2000: 645–6) makes the point that the reproduction of class advantage through education is itself of increasing international significance. Educational elites compete with one another in the increasingly congested international labour market. Thus, once choice is seen to be effective for achieving social closure in one setting:

> ... not only will market rules be endorsed by social elites who already play by these rules, but the social elites from other countries such as Germany, France and Sweden, may also press for the same rules if they are to maintain a level playing field beyond their national boundaries.

The politics of choice were central to the popularist appeal of the UK Conservative governments of 1979–97. They were part of a more generic privileging of the role of the market form as an instrument of social change. Thus, it is important to recognize that political support for and the political effects of the market do not simply rest on simple economism. The market form carries with it a political vision which articulates a very individualistic conception of democracy and citizenship. This is captured very powerfully in Margaret Thatcher's oft quoted dictum: 'There is no such thing as society. There are individual men and women and families' (*Woman's Own*, 31 October 1987). Morrell (1989: 17) suggests that this remark 'is an expression of the Hayekian view in epigrammatic form'. Morrell goes on to note that 'Hayek is particularly concerned to argue against the involvement of the Government in the life of the citizen'. The new market citizenry is animated and articulated by Hayekian conceptions of liberty, 'freedom from' rather than 'freedom to', and the right to choice. Consumer democracy is thus both the means and end in neo-liberal social and economic change. In effect these policies bring about an alignment of the social with the economic. It is assumed that active choice will ensure a more responsive, efficient public sector and release the natural enterprizing and competitive tendencies of citizens, destroying the so-called dependency culture and dependence on the welfare state in the process and replacing the latter with the virtues of self-help and self-responsibility (see Deem, Brehony and Heath 1995, Chapter 3). This is constitutive of a new moral economy. The role of some of these qualities of neo-liberal social life and their relationship to the values and norms of the middle class is taken up in Chapters 4, 5 and 6.

As many commentators have noted, one of the remarkable facts of the post-1997 New Labour governments in the UK is their reluctance to make any clear break with this Conservative agenda (Power and Whitty 1999; Jones 1999; McCaig 2001). And yet this is also unremarkable for, to a considerable extent, the Labour election successes of 1997 and 2001 were founded on policies, including education policies, which were 'carefully geared to "middle England" voter aspirations' (Tomlinson 2001: 65) and 'Labour's need to reposition itself as a party of the centre in order to retain both the confidence of capital and the support of middle class erstwhile Conservative voters' (Hatcher 1998: 488). This gearing has involved over time a continual reworking of Labour Party policies with respect to choice, and to private schools, grammar schools, other forms of school selection and forms of internal school differentiation, each of which contribute, as Tomlinson (2001: 134) puts it, to offering the middle class various means of 'avoidance of the poor and socially excluded'. Stephen Pollard, Research

Director of the Fabian Society, was one of many Labour intellectuals who argued for a clear commitment to forms of selection inside comprehensive schools as a way both of appealing to 'Middle-class *Guardian*-reading liberals' (Pollard 1995: 3) and raising educational standards. Thus, in first-dimensional, pluralist terms, it is possible to point to choice as part of the promissory politics of parties aiming to attract the votes of the middle class and the concomitant use of increasingly sophisticated techniques for the measurement of sentiment and class opinion in the formation and abandonment of policies.

Michael Barber, then Head of the UK School Standards and Effectiveness Unit (part of the Prime Minister's Office), also made clear in a speech to the Samuel Richardson Foundation (Washington July 2000) the concern of the UK Labour government to convince an 'impatient electorate' and 'aspirant parents of all classes … that we can deliver a service which meets the needs and aspirations of their children'. The orientation to the interests of the middle class is also evident in Prime Minister Blair's speech to Labour's Progress Group (2000) in which he first used his reference to 'bog standard comprehensive schools'. In this, he re-invokes the Conservative derision of comprehensive education, and what he calls the comprehensive 'one-size-fits-all mentality' and reiterates the notion of crisis in schooling. He goes on to articulate instead a form of meritocratic IQism (Gillborn and Youdell 2000) which exactly mirrors the concerns of many of the middle-class parents represented in this text (see Chapter 4) and reiterates a concomitant and historically repetitive political neglect of those other students, the unspoken minority, who constitute the long tail of under-achievement in UK schools. He argued that: 'Comprehensives should be as dedicated as any private school or old grammar school to high achievement for the most able'. The comparative references do considerable work in this comment. I return to this point below.

Labour's steady back-tracking on its opposition to grammar schools and its half-hearted commitment to ending other forms of selection (Webster and Parsons 1999) and advocacy of 'specialist schools' are further indicators of the shift to a meritocratic policy position attractive to middle-class voters. All of this develops Blair's earlier attack on what he calls the 'ideology' of unstreamed teaching in comprehensive schools (Blair 1996: 175; Labour Party 1997: 7) and his commitment to the need for 'setting' by ability in schools (Blair 1995) and a general tactic of distancing New Labour from the 'collective social agents' (Jones 1999: 244), like 'progressive' teachers of old socialism. The educational politics of the UK, or more precisely of England, are now firmly established in a mode which legitimates, indeed celebrates the virtues of choice and differentiation. Within all this the anticipatory and responsive (polls and focus groups) or promissory elements mirror the market behaviour of schools described below.

I want to draw a contrast here between the educational politics of the UK as outlined above, with its public, official and policy endorsement and legitimation of choice and differentiation, and French educational politics which at face value represents a very different legitimatory regime, very different abstractions. The political vocabulary of French education policy eschews notions of choice and differentiation and competition, and conversely represents via the 'republican model' (van Zanten 1997) a vision of a unified, centralized and inclusive system. However, van Zanten's work in various Parisian locations makes it clear that the influence and impact of the interests of middle-class parents produces significant informal, indeed sometimes illegitimate, modifications to official policy (van Zanten and Veleda 2001). On the one hand, there are the attempts by schools and municipalities to keep middle-class parents either in a particular school or in the local schools or in the state sector, for instance, at municipal level the manipulation of school catchment boundaries to give middle-class neighbourhoods access to preferred schools. On the other, more direct pressure from particular parents or groups of parents has led to specific responses in schools, such as the creation of what are called 'ability groups' – separate classes for more able students – or specialist foreign language classes which have the same ability 'creaming' effect; 70 per cent of French secondary schools now operate such illicit differentiation. These sub-policy moves by schools and municipalities, occurring either as direct responses to middle-class pressures or anticipatory responses to middle-class preferences in an effort to retain such parents in socially heterogeneous schools, exactly parallel the UK and US examples but, even more clearly than the US, in a non-market educational system. It would appear that middle-class families are able to use their skills and resources to effect influence and change, to the very same ends, in very different political settings (see also Birenbaum-Carmeli, 1999 below).[8]

Local

Despite the examples of the effectiveness of the middle-class strategies adumbrated here, it is clear that the responsive mechanisms of the market, despite the arguments of market advocates, do not always deliver for or solely work in the interests of the middle class. In the simplest sense, the education market 'does not clear' (Hirsch 1994), and market mechanisms are not available to all middle-class parents equally. In the UK the number of appeals against school placement, where parents do not get the choice of school they want, has risen year on year since 1989; by 1999/2000 appeals had risen to 96 per 1000 new admissions to secondary schools. The number found in favour of parents remained steady throughout this period at around 31–32 per cent. However, where choice or 'exit' (Hirschmann 1970) is not an option then 'voice' in some form is an alternative, and different skills and capitals can be called up. Chapter 4 provides some discussion of individual interventions into schools by middle-class parents. Here I want to concentrate more upon collective mobilization or collective efforts in pursuit of collectively identified self-interest. This involves the use of either positive advocacy in favour of setting, for example, or much more commonly, negative opposition, to de-tracking or mixed ability, or progressive pedagogies or certain curricula materials. That is, in general terms opposition to 'equity-focused reform' (Oakes and Lipton 2001). Again the point made above, that there are two sides to this in market systems of education, choice and responsiveness or proactive recruitment tactics, is important.

Dehli (2000: 2005) in discussing the shift over time in the educational politics of Toronto schools from a 'progressive' to a 'neo-liberal' version of choice, describes the contemporary debates as follows:

> ... a small number of parents are frequently quoted in the media as representatives of parents-in-general. They champion economic efficiency, a return to basics in the curriculum, stronger school discipline, and standards and accountability, presumably on behalf of all parents, as though they form a coherent constituency with identical interests.

These new advocates and their organizations are largely white and middle-class, although they are heard as though they speak for what every parent wants (see below). Here we see again 'the unity of isolated relations' (Poulantzas 1973: 134) obscuring 'class interest'. Their organizations are formed into a coalition – the Coalition for Education Reform – and coalition representatives have been elected as trustees on some of Toronto's local school boards. Among other things, these organizations argue that 'child-centred pedagogy ... is incapable of providing students with the skills and knowledges that are supposedly needed in the new global economy ... [and] that discipline is too lax ...' (2005). While choice has not been a central part of the Coalition's agenda, Dehli argues that they 'have eagerly taken up other themes from neo-liberal ideologies of education' (2007). And the advocacy groups, mostly minority and much more class-diverse, which were working hard to change education in the 1970s and 1980s, with rather different concerns, have been displaced from media attention and marginalized by the new activists. Indeed, Dehli suggests, in the persistent talk of school failure, set against the real needs of ordinary children, despite claiming to speak for all parents, the new activists have racialized policy debate. The referent of the ordinary child is white and middle-class, and minority ethnic children are those who have different needs and difficulties, 'unrelated to the mainstream' (2006) (see also Chapter 4 for the consequences of this logic). Dehli goes on to ask the question: 'While it is not a new phenomenon for middle-class parents, and particularly middle-class mothers, to be involved in local home and school and parent teachers associations, why are they coming together in noisy, angry and political activism now?' (2006). That question goes to the heart of what this book is about. Dehli (2008) answers by saying that: 'Today, more privileged groups of parents, whose access to good jobs and comfortable lifestyles were closely linked to education, feel threatened'.

Let us look at some other examples, local and institutional, of middle-class parents getting angry and getting organized. Oakes and Lipton's (2001) account of Wilson High School in the US offers another example of the classed relationships between the local and institutional. Wilson is one of a large number of US schools where attempts at detracking have been stoutly resisted by 'local elites who immediately see equity reforms as a direct threat to their status, to cultural norms, and to political and economic positions' (7). The parents opposed to reform at Wilson saw detracking as creating classrooms which would involve 'distractions, lack of challenge, or a less comfortable classroom or school environment' (5) for their children. One parent at a Parent Teacher Association (PTA) meeting called to discuss the reform, a meeting at which only white parents spoke, objected to one teacher's reference to parents not in attendance.

> I don't understand when you talk about the parents who aren't here ... Because, yes we are the ones who come to the meetings, and we are pushing our children, but we also know that in these classes, many kids at Wilson do not want to learn, they don't give a darn about what's going on. They are littering the school ... All I am saying is give the kids that care a chance. Put the five who care in one class with the other five who care from another class, with the five who care from a third class. Put them together and let them learn. We're all afraid to say that there are these kids here that don't care, and they're holding the rest of us back.
>
> (quoted by Oakes and Lipton 2001: 3)

Here is a set of themes explored in more detail, in English settings, in Chapter 4. This parent clearly sees the detracking reform as a threat to the well-being and ability to learn of 'our' children and children like ours. The threats come from others who are not like 'our children', as in the case of Toronto. As in Toronto those who are seen as not caring are positioned that way by dominant voices. The solution is to maintain or establish separation. The important point here is the oppositional capabilities and tactics of the local elite parents. Immediately after the PTA meeting an electronic mail listserve 'Wilsonfriends' was set up to provide a focus for oppositional views against detracking. In particular, as Oakes and Lipton (2001: 3) point out, the opposed parents were very adept at mobilizing arguments based on 'a larger social good' to make their case 'in terms of "high standards", "safety" or "meeting individual needs" (for example, the needs of a "gifted" child or the needs of a low performer)' (Oakes and Lipton 2001: 7) – all legitimate abstractions. As one contributor to the message board put it: 'The message [of Wilson's reforms] is: educating capable students is less important than making sure those less capable aren't left behind'. Again what is signalled here is a struggle over scarce resources and over priorities embedded in policy. Furthermore, the struggles at Wilson High, as in the other examples quoted below, are both relational and exploitative, in the sense of 'creating [or seeking to maintain] subordinate social formations' (Parkin 1979: 46). These are the kind of activist, middle-class parents that Jeannie Oakes calls 'Volvo vigilantes' (Kohn 1998: 573).

In a similar vein, McGrath and Kuriloff (1999) describe the ways in which upper middle-class parents in the Minsi Trails school district use social networks and the involvements with their children's schools to keep pressure up to maintain and extend tracking (see Chapter 5). 'Much of the discussion about tracking involved parents trying to separate their less academically successful children from other low achievers' (McGrath and Kuriloff 1999: 618). Other parents, who did not share these concerns, like those of minority ethnic students, were unable to participate in parents' groups or were subtly marginalized. Also, parents with direct access to school knowledge and social contacts pressured administrators for special resources. In response, the school district officials put their energies into holding the line on the existing pattern of tracking.

> Someone told me some schools are heterogeneously placed [untracked] in some districts. I say, okay. But wait till I'm retired. Because they're going to tear the doors of this place.
> (Administrator, field notes, September 26 1995, quoted in McGrath and Kuriloff 1999: 620)

The 'they' are the upper middle-class parents. A number of other studies in the US have revealed the opposition of affluent white parents to detracking programmes and, in the ways that School Districts respond, have distinct parallels with the French case above. Stuart Wells and Serna (1997: 728) describe the findings from their study as follows:

> Within each of our ten schools, when educators penetrated the ideology that legitimates the track structure (and the advantages that high-track students have within it), elite parents felt that their privileges were threatened. We found that local elites employed four practices to undermine and co-opt meaningful detracking efforts in such a way that they and their children would continue to benefit disproportionately from educational policies. These four overlapping and intertwined practices were threatening flight, co-opting the institutional elites, soliciting buy-in from the 'not-quite-elite', and accepting detracking bribes.

In an earlier paper based on the same study, Stuart Wells and Oakes (1996: 138) argue that what they call 'efficacious parents of high-achieving or identified gifted students will demand greater differentiation between what their children learn and what is offered to other students'. All of this is mirrored in Lipman's (1998) study of schools and school restructuring in Riverton, USA. In particular, in her case study of Gates High School, Lipman identifies the work done by Riverton's upper middle-class interests to 'limit and define restructuring through their opposition to the heterogeneously grouped Study and Research Methods class and their ability to reinstate their children's separation from low-achieving African American students' (170). Gates was 'a microcosm of the interplay of competing interests' (142) in the school district. As Lipman goes on to say: 'The web of race and class in these power relations was difficult to untangle' (170) but 'Elite white parents did not seem to object to high-achieving, mainly middle-class African-Americans in honors classes' (171). Essentially, at Gates, certain issues and areas of debate about restructuring were off the agenda – silences and omissions existed. As at Fletcher School mentioned below, and more generally across all of the examples cited, 'equality and educational excellence were framed as competing and separate interests' (170) within the school, the school district and the community. Tracking, or setting as it is called in the UK, is a recurring issue in this and the next chapter. As research on ability grouping over time has shown, there are consistent relationships between social class and set allocation and between set allocation and educational opportunities and resource advantages (Hallam 2002). Setting is not merely a neutral way of organizing teaching but has consequences for both access to longer-term success roles and routes, the distribution of esteem, and of resources (Ball 1981). In the various examples, above and below, we also see setting as a mechanism of social closure.

Birenbaum-Carmeli (1999) offers another case study of the local activism of middle-class parents in the Givat Narki area of Tel Aviv. Here a group of middle-class parents, who felt that their children were unfairly excluded from a curriculum innovation programme, lobbied to set up their own school. By using access to the local media and other social capital these parents managed to get permission from the local authority to set up a school which also separated their children off from their working-class counterparts. 'By employing terms of civil participation and social integration these parents legitimised the prioritisation of their own children's interests, while oppressing less powerful parents, teachers and principals' (Birenbaum-Carmeli 1999: 63). Again, as in the previous examples, these parents were able to deploy abstractions or principles, what Birenbaum-Carmeli (1999: 86) calls 'rhetorics of social responsibility', articulated as in the general social good, to 'promote their own particularistic interests'. This and the other examples point up a contradiction at the heart of attempts to empower and give parents a voice in relation to school in as much that 'this may turn out to be another resource that benefits the powerful' (Birenbaum-Carmeli 1999: 88). Thus, McGrath and Kuriloff (1999: 604) argue that 'increased emphasis on parent involvement and schools' accountability to parents actually may subvert ... egalitarian aims'. This contradiction remains unaddressed by many who advocate the empowerment of parents but homogenize 'the parent' and neglect class differences. Crozier (2000) is a clear exception to this and she contrasts the 'consumerist' interventions or 'struggles' of middle-class parents (39) with the 'deference' (44) embedded in working-class parents' interventions. Not surprisingly the outcomes of these different types of intervention are different. Middle-class parents 'seem to have the upper hand' but 'this was not the case for working-class parents' (39). Crozier (2000) and Vincent (2000) also both make the concomitant point that 'good' parenting is not 'a class-neutral concept' (Vincent 2000: 24: see also Gewirtz 2001). Middle-class parents may be seen as meddlesome by teachers but are also more likely to fit teachers' conceptions of the 'good parent'. More generally, all of the examples quoted would give support to Taylor's (1996) dystopic critique of new social movement theory and his portrayal of middle-class suburban social movements as characterized by a mix of fear, anxiety and aspiration and driven by the 'search for personal economic safety and neighbourhood security' (321).

Overall, Kohn (1998) identifies three areas of concern which have produced responses of collective action from middle-class parents in the US: types of instruction, and particularly the mathematics curriculum; placement, that is, tracking and other forms of grouping and access to special programmes, for example for the gifted and talented; and selecting and sorting, that is, the distribution of awards, grades, rolls and ranks. All of these can be seen in the institutional examples presented next. Kohn also makes the important point that: 'All affluent parents, of course, do not necessarily line up on the same side in every dispute' (Kohn 1998: 570). I come back to this in Chapter 6. For example, there are differences between middle-class parents who favour innovative curricula and those who defend traditional approaches (see Chapter 4). Also, and I come back to this in Chapter 4, struggle, interventions and the voices of middle-class parents do not inevitably produce the desired response or outcome. Vincent (2000: 32) makes this point very starkly, referring to research conducted in two English secondary schools with colleagues Martin and Ranson.

> We found evidence of attempts by (mainly middle-class) parents to challenge the schools on issues such as uniform, mixed-ability teaching, and standards of maths teaching. There were, however, no instances of parents succeeding in their challenge in a way that provoked significant policy changes ...

Institutional

As indicated in the discussion of national educational politics, the work of class influence is not one way and not necessarily overt. Class interests can become embedded in policy-making or are responsively produced within the politics of promissory democracy. The same is true at an institutional level, particularly within settings of parental choice and institutional competition. Where schools compete to recruit students on the basis of reputation and examination performance, then certain types of students become more sought after, that is they are more highly valued in the education marketplace than others. More often than not, those most sought and most highly valued are middle-class. This is in itself another aspect of the classed nature of policy. The logic of the market is that schools will develop policies which are attractive to and serve the interests of middle-class families. Thus, it is not always necessary for the middle class to be proactive in order for their concerns to be attended to. Reay (1998c) describes events in an English comprehensive school, Fletcher, in which a science department committed to mixed-ability teaching, with a successful examination record, is required by the head teacher to reintroduce setting (tracking) as part of a concerted effort by the school to attract and recruit more middle-class parents. Mixed ability, the head teacher argues, is regarded by middle-class parents as not serving their children's best interests. Internal debates at Fletcher Comprehensive were circumscribed by the 'strong authority of the principal' and as noted above a separation of issues of equity from those of excellence. One of the senior teachers explained his view that:

> With the Governors I was aware there was a hidden agenda ... I think, in that a number of the parent governors, I think, felt that they would prefer to have their particular child in what they thought would be top sets. That wasn't necessarily the case, but I know they felt that if we had some sort of streaming or banding their child would be in the top group.
>
> (551)

I return to the issue of setting/tracking below. The head teacher's insistence on setting at Fletcher is one example of the response to what Woods, Bagley and Glatter (1998: 161) call 'scanning', which is 'an integral and continuing aspect of assessing a school's position in its local competitive arena, with a wide range of formal and informal contacts and sources of information feeding into this ...'. Thus, the surveys and interviews conducted by schools and LEAs (see Woods, Bagley and Glatter 1998: 72–73) are intended to make schools more responsive to their clients, or at least some of their clients. And these techniques are essentially the same as those used by political parties to gauge voter preferences.

Another example of the class consequences of the market form and choice, which gives further support to my thesis of classed policy is the way in which, both in presentation and practice, many schools have reoriented their general offering to attract a different kind of clientele. As one aspect of this, since the introduction of the market form there has been a systematic playing down and deconstruction of support for special educational needs (SEN) and a concomitant playing up and redistribution of funds and effort towards gifted and talented programmes of various kinds. In previous research on education markets, in which I was involved (Bowe, Ball and Gold 1992 and Gewirtz, Ball and Bowe 1995), we found that a number of our case study schools were dismantling and de-emphasizing their SEN provision in response to the exigencies of competition. In the former study we noted that: 'schools are aware that there may be longer-term costs involved in giving too high a profile to SEN work; market image, national testing performance and staying-on rates in the sixth form may conspire to produce new kinds of exclusion or marginalisation of SEN students' (Bowe, Ball and Gold 1992: 137). In the latter we quoted three examples from our case study schools of the introduction of schemes for more able students, which seemed to be conceived almost entirely for commercial purposes.

> I have introduced an able pupil's policy because parents with able children are often those who are most anxious about sending their children to a comprehensive school. Now, all the research, I believe, bears out that able children will do as well in a comprehensive as they would elsewhere, but people need convincing of that and if we have a policy that we can explain and offer to parents of what we do to enable them, to ensure they are stretched and they are taught extremely well, [we] will reassure them. And that policy will be new for September.
>
> (Head teacher, Parsons, 20.5.91)

> It's seen as a good marketing tool. I mean when Fiona was acting head last term and she had a bit of extra cash … it was quite a controversial decision within the school and within the staff, that she put the money into an able pupils' project, which as far as I was concerned, I mean she gave a bit of extra staffing to me, and as far as I was concerned that was complete marketing, because as a humanities teacher there's not very much more that we can do for our students than we actually do in the lessons apart from laying on enrichment, but I think just to be able to say, we do things for able pupils will appeal to perhaps those parents … who think their daughters should be in private schools, but perhaps they're not able enough to get there or the parents can't afford the place or whatever.
>
> (Head of Department, Pankhurst, 18.3.92)

> There was a definite push towards having children of a higher ability doing, rewarding those kids, not ignoring them, making them feel worth something within the school, and making sure that parents understood that.
>
> (Deputy Head, Trumpton, 9.6.93)

Bagley, Woods and Woods (2001) report the same change in orientation in their study of three competitive arenas in the English midlands. 'Parents in all three case study areas frequently came away from open evenings with the impression that a particular school was more interested in attracting the academically able' (302). One parent reported that: 'the head teacher scared the life out of me because the only people he is interested in is the top 15 per cent'. Another said, of another school: 'I didn't get a good reception at the school ... I asked what chance she would have to catch up at [school name] and the head teacher just wasn't interested ... and she walked away from me'. Lucey and Reay (2002) report in their study of inner city London schools that by 'September 1999 11 of the 22 secondary schools in the sample had established programmes for those pupils identified as especially bright' (330) and all four children, from their sample of forty-five, who were in these programmes, were from professional middle-class families. This reorientation of schools away from equity-related priorities is mirrored and supported and encouraged by government schemes which are aimed at offering special programmes for the gifted and talented; £60 million were allocated for these schemes in the year 2000/1. In this case it is not so much the scope as the symbolic effect of such commitments that is important. The *Excellence in Cities* programme launched in 1999 (DFEE) announced that:

> ... secondary schools will be expected to develop a distinct teaching and learning programme for their most able five to ten per cent of pupils ... we are already piloting masterclasses, summer schools for gifted pupils and other initiatives ... and partnerships with independent schools, to develop opportunities for gifted and talented children during school holidays ... and university summer schools.
>
> (22)

This represents one part of the process which Bagley, Woods and Woods (2001: 305) call 'privileging the academic'. These 'trends in schooling' (305) produce a 'pronounced misalignment between the policy emphases and market strategies of schools and the consumer interests of, in particular parents of children with SEN' (306).

This re-orientation is also evident in general political discourse in England. In May 2002 the Secretary of State for Education publically called for more 'positive attitudes to excellence'. According to *The Financial Times* (17 May 2002):

> Her speech signalled Labour's determination to break with past policies on the left, which had seen effort concentrated on raising poor standards and which had equated excellence with elitism ... She defended the creation of the comprehensive system in the 1960s as a necessary way of stopping selection at 11. But she said comprehensives now needed to treat each individual pupil according to their talents.

Halpin, Power and Fitz's (1997) work on grant-maintained schools in the UK indicated a re-invented and invigorated traditionalism in these schools; one that was based on a perception that this would appeal to middle-class parents (see Chapter 4 for the other side of this commercial equation). As well as moves intended to signal academic rigour (e.g. plentiful homework, emphasis on exam performance), greater differentiation of the children (through for example, setting and streaming), there have also been signs of growing deployment of signifiers of traditionalism (strict uniform policies in particular) (see also Woods, Bagley and Glatter, 1998 and Gewirtz, Ball and Bowe 1995 for similar developments in the maintained sector). In contrast, the growth in numbers of specialist schools in the UK provide the opportunity for a different kind of modern school image which may appeal to a different fraction of parents (see Chapter 4). Woods, Bagley and Glatter (1998) also identify what they call *social targeting* by some of the schools in their study. Gillborn and Youdell (2000: 65) found the same thing in their case study of Clough grant-maintained school. Woods, Bagley and Glatter (1998: 159) describe social targeting as:

> ... that is, giving priority to promoting the school to middle-class and more able pupils (often done through geographical targeting, focusing on feeder schools located where there are concentrations of middle-class and more able pupils). Such strategies also include: attention to the 'traditional trappings' of the school ... attention to the school's achievement of A to C grades at GCSE [see also Gillborn and Youdell (2000) on the 'A–C economy']; specialisation in a 'strong' curriculum area (such as technology); downplaying at the level of rhetoric at least of the caring , pastoral side of schooling; and generally sending signals indicating what sort of parents are made most welcome.

I am suggesting that, taken together, these small changes, financial and organizational, promotional and symbolic, bring about a reorientation of the education system as a whole to the needs, concerns and interests of middle-class parents. They work to embed class thinking into the policies of schools.

I want to go back now to the issue of parental interventions and examine some further examples of class interest and class struggle in educational settings. In another pre-choice example of the success strategies of middle-class families, Chestnut Heights Elementary School, Sieber (1982: 30) offers an account of their 'long-standing political struggles against the school's staff and other parents'. Chestnut Heights was an area of inner-city gentrification, and the majority of the 'brownstoners' – the middle class in-comers – enrolled their children in local private schools. Only 20 per cent, 'for reasons of cost and political convictions' (35) sent their children to the local elementary school, P.S.4 (see Chapter 6); although many of those with children in private school 'agreed that improvement of the public school was a key element in making the neighbourhood attractive for further middle-class settlement and in enhancing the general quality of community life' (35) – a group was formed. All of this again would fit with Taylor's (1996) analysis of middle-class social movements. Initially, group efforts were focused 'on gaining regular access to the school, gathering information on school practices and personnel, and establishing their presence' (Sieber 1982: 35). Also: 'The brownstoners made a conscious attempt to engender class defer-ence on the part of the school staff' (36), who, significantly, saw themselves as 'a different kind of middle class ...' (36). The newcomers also found them-selves in conflict with the Puerto Rican mothers who were active in the PTA and worked as para-professionals in the school, and whom the brownstoners saw as inappropriately qualified for 'effective, disinterested parent leader-ship' (36). The Puerto Ricans were routed in the PTA elections and increasingly found themselves 'unwelcome at meetings' (37). There are echoes here of both Toronto and Wilson High (above). Again we see parental voice and involvement with schools as a form of struggle between competing class interests. The children of the brownstoners were exclusively concentrated in the top track class in grade 1, even those who 'do not really belong in a1-class', and their parents pressed the school for an open organiza-tional format in this class (a Bernsteinian 'invisible pedagogy' (Bernstein 1990) with 'Liberal allotments of time ... given over, for example, to the cre-ative arts; poetry-writing, painting, sculpting, crafts of all kinds, writing and producing dramas, etc.' (39–40). Furthermore, 'behavioural standards in the upper track classes were more relaxed' (40); the parents expected their chil-dren to be 'self-regulating' (Bernstein 1990: 84). Alongside this the a1-class students dominated student offices and prizes and their classroom was regu-larly shown-off to visitors. 'The teachers saw the children as "special", "bright" and "gifted" ...' (41); although they also regarded them as 'spoiled' and 'arrogant' and their parents as morally and personally unstable (42) (cf Reay 2000) and as a result some avoided the a1-class assignment. For their part, 'The parents were quick to criticize and to make invasive complaints' (43) about the teachers. Again the main themes identified above recur.

In various respects the brownstone parents seem archetypes of Bernstein's new middle class, or professional agents of symbolic control; although the occupational backgrounds of the brownstoners can only be inferred from Sieber's account. At face value they exhibit a strong prefer-ence for an invisible pedagogy (see Chapter 4), with its class-related 'spatial, temporal and control grids' (Bernstein 1990: 84), but this preference is combined with a strategy of exclusion, a monopolization of the schools' traditional success roles and close surveillance of teachers' work. We might also point to the timing of this account – the early 1970s, and the level – elementary. Thus, the context is different from the more recent data but the concerns remain the same – differentiation, closure and advantage. Different kinds of policy opportunities are taken up and different abstrac-tions deployed. The struggle between classes among parents and teachers is more overt here, with the purposes, opportunities and success trajectories of the school at stake. Power is exercised by one class fraction, over and against others, in their own interests.

Another example of intervention, with an almost exactly opposite peda-gogic agenda, comes from Australia and another Riverton, a Queensland primary school. Hatton (1985) describes the activities of the Parents and Citizens Committee (P & C) – 'a very powerful body' (260) made up of upper-middle-class parents. Successive principals at Riverton were unable to handle the P & C which was active and effective in blocking a number of progressive innovations attempted in the school. For example: 'The P & C began to lobby politicians and the Education Department against the provision of open plan classrooms in Riverton. The basis of the P & C protest was disapproval of 'open educational practices' (262). The preference here is for a 'visible pedagogy'. Members of the P & C were also vocal in public meetings. The upshot was the physical division of school space into separate classrooms and the continuation of one teacher–one class teaching at Riverton. (For a similar ethnographic account of middle-class parental resistance to progressive educational practices, see Miles and Gold 1981). More generally Hatton reports that 'children of high status parents, through the intervention of their parents, achieve the best conditions, for example stable, competent staff'. Writing with striking prescience Hatton (1985) concludes that:

> As articulations approximate the market relationship the scope of situated autonomy [for teachers] reduces, and when tensions develop between teachers' pedagogic judgements and decisions and parents' beliefs about what is legitimate and appropriate, interventions are likely to follow.
>
> (270)

These examples are complex and their effects, as noted above, are exclusionary and exploitative. That is, they are relational. In these cases the success of middle-class interventions means that, as Hatton (1985: 269) argues: 'Children of low status parents, on the other hand, suffer adversely as a consequence ...'.

I have tried to establish a case in this chapter for the argument that education policy, at various levels, is strongly classed. In effect education policy is a focus of class struggle. Struggle for opportunity, advantage and closure, and over the distribution of scarce resources. The examples deployed here have illustrated the classing of policy in a variety of ways, as outlined initially; through overt struggles and interventions; through the privileging of certain abstractions and the exclusion of others, especially the privileging of opportunity over equity and the emphasis given to giftedness in policy; through the mechanism of the market itself and the way in which the regulation of the market values some qualities and some kinds of students and devalues others; and through the responsive and anticipatory politics of class now deeply embedded in education policy-making in the UK, and perhaps elsewhere. I have drawn my examples mainly from England, the USA and France and could have given further emphasis to the difference in the particular politics and different class structures of these locations, but instead have tried to highlight the similarities in the anxieties and concerns and efforts of the middle class in each location. I have also drawn my examples from different points in time. This indicates the enduring nature of anxieties, concerns and efforts but perhaps could be taken as weakening my argument that the current point in time is one in which the middle class is particularly anxious and particularly active. I think not. I am not arguing that middle-class strategies of social advantage are a new phenomenon, rather that different policy regimes and their attendant abstractions provide different opportunities for and constraints upon intervention and influence. I do suggest that the current social and economic conditions have raised the stakes in competition for educational success and that market rules and concomitant moves to empower parents have given a specific legitimacy to diverse forms of intervention and participation for which middle-class parents possess relevant skills and resources (see Chapter 5), while treating the parents both as 'as atomized individual subjects rather than as class agents' (Poulantzas 1973: 193) and as a 'unity'. Within previous policy regimes privilege based on ability or equity based on categorical identities provided, and in some cases still provide, legitimation for disunifying families and treating them differently. Even within these different policy regimes we can still see how the state works 'as an agency that buttresses and consolidates the rules and institutions of exclusion' (Parkin 1974: 138). Through this chapter I have noted the recurrence of certain key themes involved in middle-class interventions into schools – they are concerns about modes of instruction, student grouping and the distribution of rewards and success roles. These are picked up again in the next two chapters.

4 Social class as social closure
A strategic approach

Social closure is the means: 'by which social collectivities seek to maximise rewards by restructuring access to resources and opportunities to a limited circle of eligibles'.

(Parkin 1979: 44)

Parents take a much livelier interest in the schoolmates than in the school books of their children.

(Walzer 1984: 215)

This chapter begins by explaining, then elaborating and then deploying, a set of concepts, alluded to previously, drawn from the work of Parkin (1979). Later the discussion is extended to incorporate Bourdieu's work on 'discrimination' and 'social structure in the head' and use is also made of Bernstein's work on social class and pedagogies. This chapter is a companion piece to Chapter 3 in that it takes up again the issue of social closure. In this case the emphasis is not upon the deliberative control of the rules of the game that provide the framework for policies of choice in education, but rather on the use of these rules to achieve and maintain social closure in practice. That is to say, the focus here is upon those 'definite social exertions' (Parkin 1979: 63) that middle-class families must make on their own part 'or face the very real prospect of generational decline' (Parkin 1979: 63). Taking up the framework outlined in Chapter 2, I am suggesting that now more than previously middle-class families 'must approach the task [of achieving closure] more in the manner of a challenge than as a foregone conclusion' (Parkin 1979: 63). In effect status and advantage can 'only be preserved as a result of the adaptation by the bourgeois family to the demands of institutions designed to serve a different purpose, it does not come about as a natural consequence of closure rules themselves' (Parkin 1979: 62). In effect families must work on, in and with public and private institutions to achieve their particular ends and interests. This is not an issue that Parkin himself attends to in any detail, even in his discussion of education and credentialism, but he provides a vocabulary from which to start. In some respects there is a parallel here with the point made elsewhere (Chapter 1) with regard to Bourdieu's work on capitals, that is the need to attend to the 'activation' as well as the possession of these capitals. Here we need to attend to the exertions of families with respect to the rules of closure that are in play. Put another way, while Chapter 3 focused upon the collective mobilization of power, within the state and in public institutions, in the 'distributive struggle' (Parkin 1979: 46) over educational advantage, this chapter focuses upon individual exclusionary strategies. By this I mean the efforts of individual families to monopolize particular educational sites and establish and maintain social cleavages based upon these monopolies. As Allatt (1993: 156) notes: 'while there is a rich literature on the transfer of privilege, there is little on the intricacies and details of the mechanisms through which this is achieved'.

However, the argument developed in this chapter does not rest upon an abandonment of the collectivist basis of closure or a total separation between individualism and collectivism. While I will deploy a particular adaptation of Parkin's diachronic analysis of modes of closure, this is, I believe, consistent with the spirit and thrust of his analysis. What I intend to demonstrate is the ways in which 'the use of ostensibly individualist criteria', that is the use of choice in a market system of education, work 'to produce a pattern of social closure that quietly discriminates via the collectivist criterion of class or racial membership' (Parkin 1979: 65). Two propositions are thus put forward. First, the discourse of liberal individualism which legitimates and describes the market form in fact obscures the work that the market does as a mechanism for collective class advantage and social closure. Second, a close analysis of the exertions of choice, of class practices, provides access to those 'everyday activities in the "we"' (Lash 1994: 161) which are invested in the class identification of the middle classes; that is, a subjective awareness of cultural and more indirectly economic interests held in common. The primacy of choice and the market form indicates, at least for the moment, the triumph of liberalism in social policy, as the market form is installed as the one best way for the delivery of public services and choice is installed ideologically as 'the great equaliser' (Chubb and Moe 1990). Choice provides a novel resolution of what Parkin (1979: 47) calls the 'permanent tension' within the middle class which results from the need for political legitimacy, 'by preserving openness of access' as against 'the desire to reproduce itself socially by resort to closure' (Parkin 1979: 47). This is achieved by calling up unevenly distributed inclinations to and capabilities of choice in the context of a rhetoric of equality through individual choice. As Parkin asserts 'Liberalism finds nothing reprehensible in exclusionary closure *per se*, provided that it is grounded in a genuine and uncompromising individualism ...' (Parkin 1979: 66).[1] Choice serves the purpose wonderfully well. The collectivist basis of social protection is cloaked by the celebration of individual responsibility embedded in choice policies.

This then is the conceptual terrain of the first part of the chapter. I want to look at the purposive exertions and adaptations of middle-class families in asserting social closure, including what Parkin calls 'dual closure', in other words, the use of exclusionary strategies 'employed by one segment' of a class 'against another' (Parkin 1979: 89). In Chapter 6 I return to the 'permanent tension' noted above, again at the level of individual families, to examine the tussles between legitimacy and closure embedded within parents' values and principles, particularly with regard to choice of a private school. Some of these tussles are also evident below.

I want to underline the point made elsewhere in the text that the middle-class parents represented in the data quoted below are localized social phenomena. Their enactment of class is specific. Their view of schools and colleges, state and private, and their decision-making is embedded in their relationship to the opportunity structures of localities. These variations are important but here I am concentrating upon the strategies used in relation to opportunity and (in the following chapter) the use and possession of particular forms and volumes of capital, which are, I suggest, common across locations. Thus, the percentage of parents choosing private or selective schooling, as well as the urgency of closure, varies from place to place in relation to local class structures. It is the press to closure and its achievement with which I am primarily concerned.

Ambivalences and responsibilities

The transcripts are literally littered with references to private schools. The private sector is an ever-present possibility, a temptation, an escape route, an obvious recourse for many of these parents; that is for those who could afford the fees. Parents do position themselves differently in relation to the private sector but it is a major point of reference in school choice processes. Furthermore, part of the exercise of responsibility for parents is that they consider all alternatives, all possibilities, even if this produces a value-conflict. Not to engage in such considerations is viewed as an abrogation of responsibility. Indeed, the heavy weight of such responsibility throws up a wide range of dilemmas between general principles and values and the interests of the child within decisions about education. For example, the short-term happiness of the child can sit awkwardly against the longer-term demands of stretching and the achievement of good qualifications; although Allatt (1993: 146) makes the important point that middle-class parents' notions of happiness also take into account that 'happiness in adulthood was highly dependent upon economic security and, in consequence, the importance of educational success'. I will return to this. Again though, as part of this there is the question of the respect to be given to the child's own judgement and preferences set over and against those of the parents in choosing a school (see Reay and Ball 1998). Responsibility relates to choice also through knowing what is best for *your* child. For these parents making choices which do not take into account the particularity of their child is a failure to take their responsibilities seriously. In some cases this means overriding the child's own wishes. However, there is a confusion in many of the narratives between parental motivations based upon their child's best interests in terms of their particularity (a form of personal orientation perhaps in Bernstein's, 1990, terms) and motivations involving seeking maximal positional advantage for their child (a form of positional orientation perhaps). What 'best interests' are differs in each case. The moral status of these positions, in traditional philosophical terms, would be very different. In practice their separation is very difficult. Even when the child's best interests, of either type, are to the fore, choice is not necessarily obvious. But the particularity of a child could rule out certain possibilities. Some parents chose not to send their child to a private school because they felt that they would not cope or would not be comfortable in such a 'pressured academic environment' (Lacey 1974). Generally, Devine (1997: 4) describes such decision-making as 'complex and precarious'. As Allatt (1993: 149) points out responsibility is about agency. It is about having, or taking, or trying to take, control; 'independence, responsibility, self-motivation and individualism' are blended together into a heady mix that fosters a sense of autonomy but which can also induce anxiety. The flipside of taking responsibility seriously is guilt, the sense that you may have let your child down (see Chapter 6). Such dualities are central to the middle-class psyche. Again, however, it would be wrong to assume that this autonomy is unbounded. The transcripts provide plenty of examples of the frustration of independence or freedom of action and of instances where the limits of capability or knowledge constrain action (see Chapter 7). But it is easy to see in all of this the attractions to these families of educational reforms which empower parents in relation to schools. The interviews both with parents and the older children, can be read as narratives of individualism and responsibility. These narratives were extremely sophisticated and multi-faceted but were by no means guileless descriptions. These accounts show us individualism-in-action as ordinary behaviour, but Jordan, Redley and James (1994: 4) make the point that these ways of accounting for decisions are also ways of rendering 'morally adequate versions of their life choices'. In other words, they describe and legitimate certain sorts of behaviour at the same time. They are a form of identity work.

Among those parents who do choose the private sector there are those, as we shall see, for whom this is not some straightforward rational or marginal decision between alternatives or the weighing up of what is for the best. Rationality is very difficult to arbitrate here. They choose private schools precisely and simply because they are not state schools, because they are different and separate from state sector schools (see also Chapter 7). State schools are the unacceptable 'other', wrong for their child, by definition unable to deliver or ensure their aspirations. They offer no guarantees.

It's a chapter of private education isn't it? I think we discounted the state system whether we were right or not, as not being good enough and presumably our decision was exactly the same as my parents for me and that was to send them to the best education you can get for them.

(Dr Scott)

I never considered in a million years sending them to a state primary school

(Mrs Scott, quoted in Devine 1997: 26)

I resent the fact that we were forced into the private sector. Money wouldn't be easy, we are not sure that our income will actually allow us to keep both of the children in private schools throughout secondary school, and we will be missing out on holidays which would have been very nice for the children ... holidays abroad. We are making sacrifices in order to go to a private school ... the state schools should be good enough, that we didn't have to send them to private schools ... we thought about perhaps moving house to a different area, putting them in the local school for a year but then moving, because I don't want my children to get a second-rate education.

(Mrs Moseley)

There are important differences in all this between those parents who regard choice of private schooling as inevitable, as ordinary and obvious behaviour (Dr and Mrs Scott), and those for whom the issue is a choice between private schools and particular state schools (Mrs Moseley, above and Trisha, below) and indeed those only considering the state sector. The first kind of choosing may be spatially dislocated, in a system rather than a situation, the second and third have a spatial specificity, and are part of a geography of fear and uncertainties, of dangerous places and people. (I return to the location of choice in Chapter 7.) Trisha is confronted by a local, poorly performing, culturally diverse comprehensive as a possible school for her son, and is thinking about private schooling as an alternative. Her daughter already attends a girls' comprehensive. There are recurring themes here; the issue of social mix; the possibility of voice and intervention; the desire to see the child extended; the ambivalence of values.

I think there's a whole band of people like myself who wouldn't naturally send their children privately ... and wouldn't if there was an establishment that was a little bit better than what we've got, I think they would readily support it ... I think Durham school has got a wonderfully committed staff, but it, and you know, it probably doesn't sound very politically correct to say this, but at the end of the day what you're, I mean my child is proficient in English ... and I'm particularly passionate about literature and the English language and I want that fully developed.

I'm not saying that can't happen, but then I think a school like Durham that embraces so many cultures has so much to give, but I also want my child's English extended, and whilst you know, he is mixing with children who haven't that level, I mean OK in other areas yes, wonderful, but you know, I want that side of things developed ... I think that's an issue that has to be addressed because it's one that sounds, very you know, and we had, the primary [school] PTA organised for the head of Durham to come along, and I said the same point there, risking my neck ... but I knew it was in a lot of parents' minds and I felt awful saying it, and I said, you know, this isn't and I'm not the pushy white middle-class parent, well, I suppose I am, but you know, that's an issue that has to be looked at.

(Trisha, white mother, 'Little Polities' project, quoted in Ball and Vincent 2001)

There is a clear element of calculation here, literally in Mrs Moseley's case, but as we shall see, this kind of thinking has a strong emotional/cultural dimension to it and is also inflected, for some, by the play of values and principles. However, for most middle-class parents generally, and many within the studies reported here, private school was either unobtainable, that is unaffordable, or unacceptable (see Chapter 6). On the other hand, the state system, and especially comprehensive education, was an unknown quantity for many, seen as beset by risks of failure and a challenge to parents' sense of responsibility for their children. Such risks would have to be weighed and managed carefully. Choice is not a simple one-off moment of action, it is part of the construction of a complex trajectory of achievement and advantage.

... like everything you experience in your life, isn't it? You tend to want the devil you know rather than the one you don't. You tend to panic ... I mean I think I'm probably ... we are the first generation of middle-class people who haven't ... who are sending their children to state schools. Everyone I know either went to a grammar school or a private school ... so it's something ... comprehensive to me is a complete unknown quantity, so therefore it's alarming, only based on ignorance really. And also you do have to be able to handle those ... varying degrees, you are not in an environment where everybody wants to work.

(Mrs Grafton)

I think Riverway is a fairly middle-class area, but as I said before, you're always going to have the exceptions to the rules ... and that was probably our main concern ... that there are an element there which ... I understand they have a drug problem, that sort of thing, but I think that's going to happen in any school, and hopefully Laura's sensible enough not to get involved with that, but it is something that we did bear in mind and we talked about that.

(Mrs Leonard)

Throughout, a fundamental problem with the state sector generally, and comprehensive schools in particular, is their heterogeneity, or more accurately the possibility of the wrong kind of heterogeneity. There is always the potential of an 'unnatural union' (Bourdieu 1986a: 474). As a consequence, for those parents whose children would be remaining in the state sector, or rather for the majority of these, the maximization of rewards was pursued through different and more subtle forms of social closure (see below). Within both scenarios, in choice of or avoidance of comprehensive schooling, 'classifying practices' assume their importance, expressive order and 'the distances that need to be kept' (Bourdieu 1986a: 472) are made apparent. Practical intuition and a matrix of commonplaces – prejudices if you like, or what Bourdieu calls 'social mythology' (469), organize and inform parents' responses to the social meanings of schools, that is to say, distinctions are made with little sense of 'a distinct knowledge' (466). In other words, these parents appreciate and differentiate and make attributive judgements, again as part of ordinary behaviour. Within this social field of education perception, expectation and choice all relate to and play their part in reproducing social structures. Logic and taste are interwoven in school choice. Schools are assessed by middle-class parents both in terms of their instrumental and expressive orders (Bernstein 1966). That is, both in terms of staffing, pedagogy, organization and leadership; underpinning the acquisition of specific skills and bodies of knowledge – the instrumental; and the complex of behaviour and activities to do with conduct, character and manner, particularly as these are embodied in the students attending the school, as dispositions of the mind and body, including dress, demeanour and voice (see below) – the expressive; although this latter is not exclusively a middle-class concern. To a great extent the parents see the expressive order as produced by the social demography of the school intake rather than as created by the practices or efforts of the school staff: 'that's what you were looking for, the package, which tended to be other people that were going there' (Mr Christie). The students also stand for their parents, who are also part of the 'package'. That is, these parents are looking for other 'parents with similar ambitions' (Mrs Cornwell), or 'the likelihood of finding kindred spirits I think', who have certain 'social and cultural skills' (Mrs Symons). Other parents can also be surveilled and classified by attending open evenings, for example. It is not only the school and its staff that are subject to scrutiny at such events. Again there are expressive and instrumental aspects to such assessments. Mr Christie spoke of the '21 of 24 mothers with a degree' in his daughter's primary school class, and Mrs Symons, of wanting her son to go to a school with 'children from caring homes', or in another interview, 'people likely to have the same ideas … same sort of value system, school to promote the values you are promoting at home' (Mrs Gosling). Or as Mrs Doyle put it, displaying a particular social orientation which gives her 'a sense of her place'; 'it felt local' and there were 'familiar faces'. These familiar settings are ones in which family and school habitus complement each another (see Power, Whitty, Edwards and Wigfall 1998 for other aspects of this complementarity).

The commitment to finding settings in which there are other people like us also arose in the higher education choice interviews. Mrs Atwood wanted her daughter to go to a Cambridge college rather than a campus university:

> where there was, say, a very large student intake, she wouldn't necessarily find a group of people of her calibre, or her interests, in such a large student intake, because people tend to gravitate to the same places, and only a proportion of people, in a very large campus would be of interest to her, and the same calibre ...

For some this sense of mutuality is very clearly a sense of class identification. 'Merrybush is magical, we couldn't believe it when we got there. I mean it is an awfully middle-class school' (Mrs Crichton). (See also mother 2 in Vincent 2001: 356). In the private sector this sense of social structure is made practical and secure by academic selection and cost; 'you're actually buying who else goes to it', as one parent, Mr Christie, put it. For some parents their sense of a place and of place is reinforced by a sense of history and continuity, by a very direct recognition; 'it was just what my old grammar school was like'. A father expressed this very vividly in relation to the private school chosen for his son: 'Alleyns was like a pair of comfy old slippers in some ways' (Mr Crichton). Parents sometimes expressed their recognition and responses as visceral feelings, suggesting deeply inscribed 'schemes of perception and appreciation ... which function [partly sjb] below the level of consciousness and discourse' (Bourdieu 1986a: 466).

> ... you get a gut feeling about a school when you walk into it and I think that's how it was ... we just felt very comfortable there ... partly on our own account because we felt a lot of the parents would have very similar ... well ... have similar ambitions for their children I suppose, and partly we just felt that Sarah would feel very comfortable with the children there. The children seemed very mature and calm ...
>
> (Mrs Cornwell)

However, the recognition of others 'like us' can also be very practical and 'real'.

> I've got three speech therapist colleagues whose children go there, and I think that says something as well ... we must have some sort of value system that is not dissimilar.
>
> (Mrs Gosling)

The other side of all this is what Bagley, Woods and Glatter (2000) call 'negative choice', that is, rejection of schools by parents which they suggest 'may often be more powerful than positive choice in favour of a school' (2). Indeed in Bagley, Woods and Glatter's study, one third of parents they interviewed cited the students attending as a major reason for rejecting a school as unsuitable for their child. The manner and appearance of these students were the main aspects of perception which led to rejection. They were 'different' (7), and such difference rests upon a 'network of oppositions' (Bourdieu 1986a), as below. The parents' discourse of choice activates 'pairs of antagonistic adjectives' (Bourdieu 1986a: 468) which are used to classify and qualify. One mother explained, situating her daughter at an objective distance from the students of Leaside:

> It's a terrible thing to say but we just didn't want her going to Leaside. The appearance of some of the children was appalling. They were so scruffy it was just dreadful. They were smoking, the language was choice. So I said right, you're not going there. She's going to be with children of her own type of background. I don't want her going to a school where children, for whatever reason, think she's a snob.
>
> (quoted in Bagley, Woods and Glatter 2000: 7)

There is a dual element then to these small acts of closure. On the one hand, there is the recognition of others 'like us', a 'class-attributive judgement' (Bourdieu 1986a: 473). On the other is a sense of alienation, of difference, from 'others' not 'like us' – 'aliens among their own species' (Charlesworth 2000: 9). In other words, a sense of social structure. 'Parsons definitely has not ... not such a good socio-economic catchment area ... and yes ... hand on my heart ... honestly ... I think that probably would have an influence as well' (Mrs Gosling). This is what Bourdieu (1986a: 472) calls 'the practical "science" of positions in social space'. The students at Leaside were 'a complex of undesirable traits' (Brantlinger, Majd-Jabbari and Guskin 1996: 581) that this mother did not recognize in herself or her daughter. The Riverway and Northwark parents held similar views about some of the schools they had seen. Mrs Cornwell felt that her daughter 'would be too different from the majority of girls there'. These rejected schools held no sense of recognition. They seemed alien, 'other'. As Parkin (1974: 69) suggests these 'others' are taken to be a *de facto* collectivity 'one defined in terms of an all-encompassing negative status'. We were 'worried the people who went there ... threatening ... what pupils it attracts ... It was a bit of a dustbin school' (Mr Moseley) and 'Goddard doesn't feel part of this community ... it was quiet there, surprising' (Mrs Gosling) and 'The children were noisy, I mean rude ... it didn't seem a particularly nice school' (Mrs Forsythe). This is the 'aesthetic of distance' (Savage 2000: 107). Mr Parker sought reassurance, 'we asked lots of people' that the school she was considering for his son was not 'as it were a sort of sink school, you know only children who didn't seem to have very much hope'. A related and further aspect of the social makeup of a school is, for some parents, related to the distribution of and their child's access to scare resources – the teachers' time and attention and specialist services and support systems. Mrs Henry explained that the main reason she did not choose the local state primary school for her daughter, sending her to a private preparatory school instead, was that:

> loads of children there had special needs and they have lots of children who are refugees who really didn't speak English, and I just thought, its not appropriate for a bright little girl who, you know, is going to need quite a lot of stimulation.

Here the needs of 'my' child is set over and against, in competition with, the needs of others. And specifically others with different sorts of needs which may orient school priorities in a particular way. Within their talk of rejection, such parents also deployed fears based upon social pathologies of those children who were different from their own. Mrs Crichton found Goddard school unacceptable because its instrumental order seemed 'more about welfare than about education, because that is what the children in the catchment areas are perceived to need'. Another parent selected her son's school because it had 'not quite as many problem children ... that sort of idea, slightly further out of London, less an inner city school' (Mrs Rankin). In the former settings the parents experience a grating of habituses, a sense of being uncomfortable, of being in the wrong place. The students at such schools were 'seen as distracting – even contaminating – an impediment or threat' (Brantlinger, Majd-Jabbari and Guskin 1996: 584). These rejections and pathologizations make up what Brantlinger, Majd-Jabbari and Guskin (1996) call 'expurgation strategies' and in the parents' talk are set over and against the 'symbolisation of unity' (Thompson 1990) (above) which locates them and their children within middle-class boundaries. Here: 'Class identity and unity are ideologically constructed through exclusions and the creation of borders' (Brantlinger, Majd-Jabbari and Guskin 1996: 574). However, Pajackowska and Young (1992: 204) would see this as an 'illusory identity' which is 'highly dependent on its others to shore up its sense of security, to reflect back the disowned parts of itself ...'. There are strong emotional undercurrents to this kind of disidentification. Both the essential collectivity, and the 'silent' antagonisms of class' were most poignantly and subtly stated by Mrs Henry, who explained that:

> the state school down the road would have been lovely, except that *nobody* sends their children there. [my emphasis]

Here the working class are invisible, they do not count, they are nobody; those who are somebody, other middle-class children, are somewhere else, somewhere else is where your child should be.

Again here we can see the importance of place in constructing identity, and marking oneself off from others. 'The milieux through which people come to understanding are cultural historical contexts where things count or "show up"' (Charlesworth 2000: 16). The sense of social mix within schools, which is, in inverse, a representation of exclusivity or closure, is located within an experiential awareness of local demography (see Thrupp 1999). Mix, as we shall see, is always relative and this relativity is crucial, either as a potential benefit or as a possible risk. As Mrs Mankell explains it, Riverway offers the right kind of mix 'a nice balance', a 'good mix'. Here the dangers of massification of 'levelling', which threaten 'a fall into the homogenous, the undifferentiated' (Bourdieu 1986a: 469), can be avoided. In other settings, in other schools, the mix is wrong, dangerous, as we can glimpse here.

> ... these kind of London suburbs are quite unique ... and ... they are moneyed ... I hate these terms ... jargon, isn't it ... they're moneyed areas ... people have good standard of lives ... whatever middle class means ... doesn't actually mean they're all middle-class ... but it has a nice balance, I suppose, of children from caring homes. It doesn't have a great ethnic mix. But it certainly has a balance of ... it has a balance between children from less caring and more caring homes ... I wouldn't say it was predominantly middle-class really ... it hasn't got a very good ethnic mix, like a few Asian children, only a couple ... well that's true of the borough, this is not a borough with a high proportion of Asian or West Indian families particularly, but what we do have is a vast mixture from all over the shop.
>
> (Mrs Mankell)

As indicated earlier by Trisha, mix is clearly related to a concern with 'stretching' (see below) and the satisfactions of achievement (Allatt 1993: 152) and both are articulated by parents in relation to their child's 'individual and social needs' (Jordan, Redley and James 1994: 12). '... if you know that you've got a reasonably bright child, you want to know that they're in a school which has got a reasonable number of kids who are academically capable. I mean it's no good if they're the only one, or one of few, then they're not going to extend themselves'[2] (Mrs Archer) – I shall return to this later. Despite the centrality of individualism and autonomy in all of this, the judgements and perceptions which parents use and inhabit are collective, they are embedded in and 'carried by the communal practices of one's immediate group'; they are part of a 'shared intelligibility' (Charlesworth 2000: 16). These parents, as explored in some detail elsewhere (Ball and Vincent 1998), construct their judgements through a complex of different forms of information, but the views of others, who are like them, are particularly highly valued, although not exclusively relied upon (see Chapter 7). This is a world of 'talking and listening' – 'a world full of resonances, of fear and anxiety and of pleasure' (Charlesworth 2000: 21). School reputations are made and circulated through this 'grapevine knowledge' (see also

Chapter 5). In a sense, the circle closes. The search for a place of safety is a search for others like us, informed and reinforced by decisions made by and advice given by those others like us, whom we can trust. A community of aspirations is being sought, people who see and value the future in the same way, a partially closed community, a 'community of fate' (Pakulski and Waters 1996: 90). Central to the process of choosing a school is what Broccolichi and van Zanten (2000: 56), in a very similar analysis of Parisian schools, call 'the search for guarantees' and underpinning such guarantees is 'the quality of a school's pupils' which 'is perceived by parents to indicate the quality of the school'.

> ... you talk to other people who've got children there who come from Riverway, how are they coping and ... you obviously do, you spend a lot of time talking outside the school gates ... to people you know in the same situation, that's how you discover things really.
>
> (Mrs Grafton)

> ... we spoke to teachers in the schools, spoke to other parents, and spoke to my friends who are scattered across the borough and where their children went and what they thought about it.
>
> (Mrs Gosling)

The middle class, the chattering classes, are adept at these forms of talk. They use talk in a variety of domestic and social contexts, to get things done and to establish and maintain collective identity. This kind of talk and the skills of questioning in particular, and other social competencies are part of their cultural capital.[3] They are used to presenting themselves and evaluating others through talk. 'We started asking people's advice, because that's the way you normally go about things' (Mrs Moseley). 'I tried to ask them [teachers] the sort of questions that might be a bit awkward' (Mrs West). One parent used the approach of asking teachers how many students had gone on to places in medical schools, which was for him a good indicator of school performance. A certain set of social competencies and social confidence (see Chapter 5) come to be applied, and a mix of trust and scepticism is involved – the collective and the individual aspects of the class are apparent once again. The middle-class world is realized in unreflexive practices but is also organized around 'self-transparent, conscious projects' (Charlesworth 2000: 22)[4]. These people are attached to their community with a certain degree of reflexivity. They are very much one of a group embedded in the 'shared meanings, practices and obligations' of a 'taste community' (Lash 1994: 161) and individual, self-interested strategists.[5] Again here I want to avoid the simple binary of communal/individual, or in Lash's terms reflexive and non-reflexive community. These inhibit understanding. The middle class are both part of 'everyday activities in the "we"' (Lash 1994: 157), part of a world of meanings and practices into which 'they are thrown' *and* part of a world which one 'throws oneself into' – relations from which they are able to distance themselves, see themselves over and against. They think *about* as well as *from*, and have a sense at times of the arbitrariness of classifications and structures.

> We were also to a certain extent plugged into a local grapevine as well, but a lot of people's children went to Pilkinton. So over the years, long before one started to get really serious about secondaries, you would hear what people were saying ... the good stuff and the horror stories, and then as the time began to approach, and I would say certainly when the children were in what is now the Year 5, at the beginning of that ... a lot of it starts to get really serious thinking about this ... and ... basically I suppose ... I mean I talk and listen to ... anybody who is talking about the local secondaries. There are some parents whose judgement I would trust more than others. I would never depend on just what one or two people say, even people whose opinion I generally respect ...
>
> (Mrs Symons)

These judgements are embedded within a history, in a locality and in a form of community – they draw upon, arise from, and rest on the strength of 'weak ties' (Chapter 5). In this regard, we need to think about the limits of individualism and of autonomy. The parents' commitment to providing for their children what Allatt (1993: 153) calls a 'landscape of possibilities' has to be set against the deeply inscribed grammars of aspiration which circumscribe choice. For some families certain possibilities are unthinkable. The 'transgenerational family scripts' (Cohen and Hey 2000: 5) of some middle-class families 'exert a prospective and regulative influence on actual life chances and choices' (Cohen and Hey 2000: 5).[6] They are pursuing what Du Bois-Reymond (1998) calls a 'normal biography'; although on occasion these can be resisted (see Chapter 6). Normal biographies are linear, anticipated and predictable, unreflexive transitions, often gender- and class-specific, rooted in well-established life-worlds. They are often driven by an absence of decisions. These decisions are rational and they are not. This is the work of 'class wisdom' (Lauder *et al.* 1999); 'intentionality without intention' (Bourdieu 1990: 108). All of this was particularly clear in interviews with middle-class young people preparing to go to university. These young people talked of going to university as 'automatic', 'taken for granted', 'always assumed' – it was what people like you do (see also Pugsley 1998). 'That was the family plan, that was the expectation of everyone', as Tom from Cosmopolitan Boys' School put it. The decision to go to university is a non-decision. To not go is virtually inconceivable as it is part of a normal biography.

Again though, choice and class practices cannot simply be reduced to self-interest. At least the narratives displayed more than a simple pursuit of interest. In Brantlinger, Majd-Jabbari and Guskin's study expurgation and self-interest were set over and against the articulation by parents of a 'liberal educational discourse'. However, they seemed to be 'unaware of the dichotomy' (1996: 588). Similar divisions and tensions between a liberal ideology and a sense of responsibility for their child were apparent in the studies deployed here, although expressions of awareness of these tensions were not uncommon (see Chapter 6). There were moments when what Jordan, Redley and James (1994: 8) call 'the individualist repertoire' or 'putting the family first', a particular kind of 'morally adequate' version of their life choices, at least in terms of their presentations of self in the interview situation, came into conflict with their liberal, impersonal repertoire. At these moments various kinds of repair work or tactical evasions were deployed. Such awareness of tensions may also have played its part in rendering some of the accounts of closure into a subtle lexicon of allusions, asides or unfinished sentences. Gorard (1997) makes the point that school 'ethos', which is another way to render parents' perceptions, is an 'elusive choice factor'. Again subjective and objective assessments 'affect and sense' blend to make certain places impossible, risky or suspicious.

> Northwark Park has the same sort of problem ... though I like the architecture, but that's never had the right image, from what we're actually ...
>
> (Mr Symons)

> ... and the ones ... from Heathfield were going on there and he'd have got to mix with that lot, so a lot of it was on sort of hearsay really ... but you sort of have these things in the background, and you wonder about it. I mean the results on paper didn't look that good ...
>
> (Mrs Doyle)

> If you had say caring parents, they would make sure you didn't go to Northwark Park school ...
>
> (Mr Marsh)

> ... certainly in an urban area I think you're going to get, certainly around here it would be completely different cultures as well, and languages spoken, so it was that kind of thing really that makes you think. I think if we were in the country I wouldn't bat an eyelid about sending them to the local school.
>
> (Mrs Kerr)

In some instances these moral balancing acts, between interest and ideology, became part of the process of choice (again see Chapter 6). Some of the complexity of all of this is embedded in the following extract.

> It was important ... that I wanted a comprehensive school, it was very important that he would have a few children of a similar background as well ... I mean we live in a reasonably big house, we go to France for our

holidays, and at first my eldest son wouldn't admit to going to France, wouldn't admit that actually we owned half a house in France, because he felt that that wasn't right. But I want them to ... not to have to hide how we live ... so it was important that they had other friends that they could mix with that have a similar sort of background.

(Mr Rankin)

Here a commitment to comprehensive education is set over and against a particular recognition of class and lifestyle differences, which may inhibit social mixing and 'being yourself'. Here the openness of comprehensive education is immediately closed down. One sort of mixing is then rendered impossible, divisions and differences are reasserted. A pervasive sense of boundaries and boundary markers and their significance is presented here. A class phenomenology is at work, grounded in perceptual systems which 'require the same ability to mark out boundaries and directions in a given world, to establish lines of force, to keep perspectives in view ...' (Merleau-Ponty 1962: 112).[7] Mr Marsh finds himself confronted with similar ambivalences which represent a mix of social and academic concerns and ambitions for his son, but which lead him to move the child from a state primary to a private secondary school. One set of fuzzy boundaries, which offers mixing with 'different kids' but which also carries the risks of being 'influenced' by 'certain children', are replaced by more decisive, although not exclusive, divisions. Again Mr Marsh wants his son 'surrounded by all sorts of people' but not those who 'find it just cool not to work' – a 'good' mix here seems to be those who are different but the same.

> I think Albert has had a wonderful time at Merrybush because it's been so mixed, and I'm very ... I regret a lot that he'll only start to mix with different kids. Having said that ... I think ... that Merrybush and cer-tain children ... find it just not cool to work, and he's been influenced that way ... so I don't regret it completely, but I ... just want him to be surrounded by all sorts of people, which I ...
>
> (Mr Marsh)

Perhaps here Mr Marsh is displaying the skills involved in 'playing with objective distance by emphasising it' as well as 'symbolically denying it' (Bourdieu 1986a: 472). But, to add further complexity, sometimes mixes can be too narrow! ' ... that worries me slightly in a private school, that he's going to mix with a far narrower range of kids'.

Setting and streaming

As noted above, boundaries and demarcations are also important to these parents inside the school, in terms of its instrumental order and thus the acquisition of specific skills and bodies of knowledge, especially for those who decide on, or can only contemplate, state schooling. Here the issues of setting and streaming become important. We have already seen the significance of setting or tracking as a policy issue in the UK, France and the USA (Chapter 3). Again, in a straightforward sense, parents see setting as a way of insulating their child from untoward influences – other students who are disruptive or work-shy or simply less able. They do not want their child dragged down or distracted. This is both a practical matter – time-on-task and level of work – and a social concern about learning bad values and habits. Several parents feared that in the wrong context their child would come under the influence of other children with the wrong attitudes and dangerous minds. But again the mix of values and self-interest here is complicated and ambivalences abound. Once more, guarantees are being sought and the obviousness of what every parent would want is invoked. Hierarchy and separation are 'legitimated by beliefs in achievement and excellence' (Sulkunen 1992: 19).

> I actually don't know what to ask ... what necessarily I'm going to be happy with, when they answer. I think what I need to feel confident about is if you have a bright child that they're going to be able to keep that bright child on task. Nobody's going to be stretched 100 per cent of the time, but equally, if you have less able children, if you don't cater for them they will become disaffected and a destructive influence in the class ... and that will indirectly affect your own child's education. I mean, I don't want anybody disruptive in my child's class, nor does any other parent.
>
> (Mrs Gosling)

> I wouldn't want them to set in the first year, I don't see how they can when they've got to see what the kids are like. I would like to see them setting earlier in what they call the hierarchical subjects like maths, and French and science ... very much. And I am concerned so many things are being aimed, obviously, at the average child, and I'm not sure that they're therefore stretching the bright child in the early stages of school, particularly in English ... I feel the able kids aren't getting that and they could be ... whatever it is that they've done because of finances and timetable and that, seems very sad, because its depriving the mathematical child or the linguistic child of that kind of stretching, and that's not personally for my children, it's for all children.
>
> (Mrs Mankell)

Arguments for setting are made both for individuals and for a more general good by invoking various 'abstractions' (Oakes and Lipton 2001). Pedagogical arguments about the greater efficacy of setted teaching were employed.

> I liked the fact that they catered specifically for children's abilities in subjects that I think are difficult to teach in a mixed ability group ... It was one of the points we thought were positive ... The fact that they set in specific subjects but the fact that they set in maths and languages straight off.
>
> (Mrs McBain)

However, again here there are forms of aversion and attraction related to ability and behaviour. Abilities are fixed categories which demarcate children off from one another; different sorts or types of children with different needs and capabilities or attitudes to work. These parents are primarily IQists (Gillborn and Youdell 2000), a stance they share with the UK's Labour government. Children are able, or less able; there are 'bright children' and there is 'the mathematical child'. The work of making up the educational subject is obscured by such fixity. Different types of children should not be mixed – another limit of exposure to 'all sorts'. Mix is opened and closed in the tension between social and academic learning. Nonetheless, these are not callous, illiberal or unthinking dogmas that parents are rehearsing, although clearly their sense of familial responsibility is to the fore, but structures of ability and distinctions between children of different sorts work to produce what Duru-Bellat (2000: 36) calls 'exclusion from within'. At a mundane level these are examples of what Bourdieu (1986a: 469) calls 'apocalyptic denunciations of all forms of levelling'.[8]

> I suppose I am a bit old-fashioned, I'd prefer them to be set and streamed, because the class he's in there's a lot like him that work hard but there's some who just don't want to do a thing and just want to make a nuisance of themselves.
>
> (Mrs Cody)

The use of setting then becomes a criterion for selecting schools and mixed ability grouping a matter of suspicion or grounds for rejection or at least, again, ambivalence. Indeed, as we have seen, parents work hard to prevent the erasure of markers, or boundaries, or press for their re-establishment. Again the exertions of social reproduction are woven into the minutiae of familial and institutional practices.

> ... the sort of thing we were particularly interested in was banding, setting or whatever it is called, whether children were distinguished from one another ... we think it's a good thing that children should be brought along as rapidly as is practically possible, especially in a subject like maths if all the children are lumped together ... and our two older boys, are good at it, and its a waste of time for them to have to drag along with the slowest children. One might think politically about sort

of elitism and things like that, practically ... for the progress of your own children it seems to be a good thing.

(Mr Parker)

We did ask about the setting, and it's different in all the schools, and in the end ... I think it ... was very confusing, I have very mixed feelings about setting and mixed ability, I don't actually know ...

(Mrs Gosling)

But we felt with Chileigh that the setting that was available and the choice of subjects ... indicated that the school was now much more interested in catering for the more academic pupils ... and setting does not take place in Fletcher except in maths and so if we go to Fletcher we won't get quite the same ability ... the feeling that Toby will be taught in a group of children who want to learn. Both Susan and I are suspicious about mixed ability teaching, which is what the majority of teaching at Fletcher is.

(Mr Simpson)

... somebody I know from work hailed me across a meeting and said 'they're going to stream at Milton, they're going to do something about the brighter child, you know, you must think about sending Todd there' ...

(Mr Marsh)

Whiteway I know are obsessed with setting and they set terribly early and for everything and I think in a way that works ... I thought it kept them on their toes really.

(Mrs Lovesey)

I made the point in Chapter 3 that the middle class are adept at taking up and taking advantage of policy innovations which can be used in the interests of their children. One recent example of this is the proliferation of gifted and talent programmes, both as school and government initiatives. Many UK, French and US schools have adopted such grouping practices as anticipatory responses to pressure from, or the expectations of, middle-class parents (Chapter 3). These thence become a 'target' for closure and internal exclusion (Lucey and Reay 2002). As Useem (1992: 264) describes, middle-class parents 'have a greater propensity to use of variety a strategies to ensure that their children are placed in more demanding classes'.

There is a further dimension to this, the related concern for what many of the parents called 'stretching' (see also Devine 1997). This can also be read as a form of differentiation but again has dual aspects to it. On the one hand, there is once more the responsibility to the child, making the most of the child, providing opportunities for self-development. A particular kind of individualism, embedded in the specialness and particularity of the child with the idea that it should be able to realize its inherent capabilities and

become a 'self-developing subject' (Charlesworth 2000: 8), a person of cate-
goric value. 'The parents wanted their children to fulfil their potential, to use
their talents ...' (Allatt 1993: 142). This is part of what Jordan, Redley and
James (1994: 5–6) call 'the pursuit of self-making'. These middle-class parents were able to talk in great detail about the particularity of their child in
relation to schooling and such particularities, as they see it, require certain
conditions, which would ensure that the child would flourish and realize its
potential. This often meant that the child could not be risked in state school
or mixed ability groups, or in contexts with lax rules of behaviour.

> ... to put him somewhere where they would expect quite a lot of him,
> because intellectually he's perfectly capable of it, but at the same time
> kind of cradle him in rules ... things that were expected.
>
> (Mrs Crichton)

> What I need to feel confident about is if you have a bright child ... that
> they're going to be able to keep that bright child on task.
>
> (Mrs Gosling)

> Parsons was the one we felt was most likely to push him, because they
> specifically said that they have an able pupils policy.
>
> (Mrs Crais)

However, the parents do not want or expect some kind of relentless utilitarian regime for their children. They do not want them 'force-fed but ...' (Mrs
Mankell) – the 'but' is interesting – the confusion of 'best interests' arises
again. A rounded general education, not too specialized, with plenty of
extra-curricular activity was what was envisaged by most. But whatever else
the important thing is that the child is stretched 'enough', kept on task and
not distracted.

On the other hand, and at the same time, this is one way of dividing the
child off from the average or the less able, those who are inherently less capable. Furthermore, stretching might be understood, in Bourdieu's terms, as a
'scholastic investment strategy' (Bourdieu 1986b: 244), an appropriation of
cultural capital, which involves work on and investment in the child. There is
a form of calculation here, a thinking through of those educational forms, or
conditions of acquisition, which involves 'deliberate inculcation' (Bourdieu
1986b: 245). Differentiation and development come together to underwrite
a 'specific logic of distinction' – which 'secures material and symbolic profits
for the possessors' of scarce cultural capital – having the right capital in the
right amounts. These profits are, in effect, held within the child. This is one
moment or a set of moments within a history of accumulation (see Chapters
5 and 7 on planning and futurity). It is also part of the building of a trajectory into the future and access to still more scarce opportunities, in
particular to higher education. In the 'icy water of egotistical calculation'

middle-class parents are accessing routes and preparing the next steps for their child: 'you want to make sure you're going to be able to give them a good education that will allow them to go on to do higher education' (Mrs Cody). Also embedded here is an inclination to competition. 'You start thinking that your child is going to have to cope with the real world, and the real world judges you by how well you do in exams' (Mrs Dexter). And all of this is set within a sense of 'entitlement' (Skeggs 1997) which is realized in demands that are made, on behalf of the child, of social institutions. Parents' 'repertoires of individualism' and their prioritization of the family are confronted in some instances by the more universalist aims of social institutions, which they seek to mould to their own needs and interests. 'You can do very well in the state sector with the right back up ... if you are prepared to work' (Mr Dexter). But if the state sector does not deliver:

> I think if we're not happy, we're not going to be happy about them being stretched enough, for various reasons, and if we do that I think we would both have to start looking at the private sector again more seriously ... but I hope we never will.
>
> (Mrs Mankell)

And, of course, middle-class parents do not always get their way. School policies and priorities do not inevitably serve the interests of middle-class families. A number of state school parents in the higher education study were critical of their child's school for not giving enough emphasis and support to entry to Oxbridge (see Mrs Summer in Chapter 5). This seemed to be a further example of the continual emphasis on differentiation, and a further stage of closure, and arguments for and efforts to attract priority and scarce resources to students, positioned by their parents as more able. Again such parents feel a responsibility to strive for privileges for their children and experience guilt when they fail. As elsewhere Mrs McCabe's use of 'we' here is significant and the emotional subtext to all this – guilt, anger, regret – is very apparent (this is taken up again in Chapter 5).

> I'm very angry about the school. And when Sian's finally left, and I feel positive about many aspects of the school, but I'm very, very angry about what they do in terms of academic support for the kids ... Sian had nine As, you know, seven A starred at GCSE. And several of her friends did, and they should have been, the whole group, the people who were coming in with these sorts of grades, should have been given a little bit of nurturing towards thinking about Oxbridge and places like that. And they never were. There was a meeting about applying to Oxbridge which you might or might not have seen which was just pathetic ... So we did make an application and I tried to support her, but it was very late. And we got books on how to go for Oxbridge and stuff like that, but I felt very angry that they hadn't nurtured those potential students and so she had a

very negative experience with her interview, and I felt very badly about that. I wished in a sense that I hadn't suggested she did it ... It was a very negative and very draining and quite humiliating experience for her and I didn't feel the school had done anything to help. And although they are supposed to make allowances for state pupils they didn't ... she hadn't had any coaching or grounding or been to a summer school. Whereas some of her friends had, from other places, because their parents were into that from the start. I did the application with her and fine-tuned it and stuff, and she did a good application, but she really hadn't had any preparation for the interview ... had she been prepared from the beginning of the sixth form that she was a potential Oxbridge candidate, she would have done the reading herself ... I think very few students from Maitland apply to Oxbridge and according to Sian they've nearly always come from private schools. So it wasn't until we visited that there was any kind of positive feeling about it.

Not surprisingly then forms of stretching, social context and mix, and matching the child to the institution also arose as issues for some parents in choice of university.

> ... when it came to the time of choice-making, it was quite clear she was choosing her universities in a way that I thought she would go somewhere and she wouldn't be stretched ...
>
> (Mrs Atwood: Hemsley Girls')

> I suppose my wife and I are a bit old-fashioned and snobbish in the sense that we would prefer him to go to a good university and we feel, I think, that some of the newer universities are perhaps not quite of the same standard as some of the older ones, we might be wrong there, I don't know. I'm not saying that he has to go to Oxford or Cambridge or somewhere like that, but some of the newest ones have perhaps not the same quality of teaching and of other students and so on, so we were keen that he should go to as good a university as he could get into ...
>
> (Mr Crispin: Riverway College)

When choosing a school, both setting and stretching are inter-related with parents' views about, and preference for, visible or invisible pedagogies. Indeed there is a certain abstract logic that relates the general concerns and strategies we have been addressing to the different distributions of space, time and control within these pedagogies. In spatial terms 'a visible pedagogy is based on the fundamental rule that "things must be kept apart"' (Bernstein 1990: 81), which is the thematic basis of this chapter. As Bernstein suggests, visible pedagogies may well be the necessary preference of middle-class families at secondary school level. It is at this time that structures of invisible pedagogy, with their 'relaxed rhythm' and 'less specialised acquisitions' (81) are out of tune with the urgent futurity of middle-class ambitions. However, it may be that the changing rules of exclusion and socio-economic conditions described earlier are forcing visible pedagogies earlier and earlier into the scholastic careers of the middle class (see Chapter 5). As indicated already these parents are worried about their children being held back by teaching in mixed ability classes within which 'statuses are relatively more weakly marked' (Bernstein 1990: 83). Particularly in so far as they perceive there to be a mismatch between mixed ability teaching and the temporal rhythms of externally imposed testing and examination deadlines which provide a template for the development of the child. Again Bernstein suggests that within each pedagogy: 'The child is developed in, and by, a particular construction of time' (81). Similarly these parents expect the 'rules of social order' within the school to be visible, that is 'explicit and specific' (82), a 'grammar of proscriptions and prescriptions' (83). Visible pedagogies are not 'necessarily authoritarian' (83), this is not what parents were looking for, but within them 'control functions to clarify, maintain, repair boundaries' (83). This grammar is complemented by high levels of surveillance by parents over child and school. The transcripts convey a sense of high alertness – looking for problems, failings or falling behind that may require 'strategies of retrieval' (83) (see Chapter 5 for examples). For some the visible pedagogy, and its reassurances were conveyed by the modalities of tradition: 'I like the fact that it still had the atmosphere of a grammar school' (Mrs Dexter). Logic and affect blend together to make the setting here seem familiar and safe. Others were less comfortable with traditional versions of visibility but progressivism was definitely out of favour.[9]

Mrs Marsh captures a sense of the unease of the middle-class parent when confronted with the relaxed rhythm of a comprehensive education, and its weaker boundaries of order: Milton, she said, 'very, very definitely had a reputation about being too laid back, it was too much like a club, it was too easy for the kids to get into the social scene rather than the academic scene'. Mr Christie was 'worried about' Milton because, it 'is very much the sixties ... the package doesn't seem to have changed'. Mrs Mankell chose her sons' school in good part because 'we felt the discipline was very strong ...'. Mrs Chandler wanted 'a degree of discipline, and bad reports from school carry a lot of weight'; and Mr Marsh found a more general problem, as far as he was concerned, in state schools:

> ... what we discovered in the state schools was that they were distributing sheets, work books and people working on their own, if you've got a problem then go to the teacher, and it's up to them to teach themselves new concepts in maths ... I don't see how somebody of 11, 12, 13 can suddenly pick up a new subject.

The majority of the middle-class parents interviewed indicated their preference for what Bernstein calls 'standard European pedagogic practice' (85), that is a traditional classroom arrangement which frames didactic teaching methods – a visible pedagogy. Often these preferences were accounted for in terms of what the parents knew and what they recognized from their own education. However, there were a few exceptions to this, such as parents seen as 'modernizers' who were looking for contemporary referents, who were put off schools which they saw as too familiar and too locked into traditional practices. 'It had desks rather than tables, I just didn't like the atmosphere there' (Mrs Doyle). Mrs Crais and her ex-husband and son visited the local ex-grammar, now private school, and found it 'archaic'. Mrs Crais asked her local private boys' school if they offered cookery – 'Oh no we don't do cookery [*posh voice*] and I thought up yours, and the pastoral part of the school seemed to be ignored'. However, within the whole context of any transcript such responses did not necessarily indicate unequivocal support for invisible pedagogies and seemed to represent an evaluation of the superficial aspects of the symbolic order of schools. Ms Turow, whose child has special educational needs, was impressed by Overbury school: 'it seemed a much friendlier kind of school, a more relaxed school, a school that seemed to have an ethos of caring ... less pressure on academic achievement'. Mrs Hillerman discerned the same quality in the same school, but for her this was good reason to reject the school: 'Orleans was a little more relaxed and laid back ... it was not quite as disciplined. I quite like the discipline of the uniform and the uniform being worn properly ...'. Dress and demeanour, as forms of embodied capital, are powerful signifiers, as noted already.

In looking at the pattern of responses to and preferences for pedagogy, this did not give support to Bernstein's proposition that: 'Those who opposed invisible pedagogies ... were likely to be those members of the middle class whose work had a direct relation to the production, distribution, and circulation of capital' (1990: 85). Such opposition was also articulated by parents like the Marshs, one a university lecturer, the other a clinical psychologist; Mr Christie, a college lecturer; the Mankells; an independent social worker and journalist; and the Mosleys, a systems analyst and advertising copywriter respectively. In part, for these parents, the attractions of a visible pedagogy are its very visibility. They are reassured by the obviousness of things, the clarity of boundaries, the possibility of evaluating practices and outcomes, surveilling school and child and measuring progress against fixed markers – 'The explicit rules of selection, sequence, pace and criteria of a visible pedagogy translate into performance indicators of schools' staff and pupils' (Bernstein 1990: 86). This visibility works to assuage at least some of the doubts and uncertainties which are inherent for them in school choice. As Ms Crais explained of one school she visited: 'I began to wonder how the kids there learned anything because the teachers and kids were just talking, messing about'. Invisible pedagogies can sometimes look to the outsider like 'talking, messing about' and not like teaching and learning at all. In all of this the stereotypical liberal middle-class parent seems an elusive social subject.

Conclusion

It is within the complex 'tapestry of practices' outlined above, in the inter-linking of the domestic sphere with public institutions that the work of social reproduction, closure and exclusion gets done. In the interaction between families and institutions, in struggles over scarce resources and valued trajectories, structural and cultural divisions are re-enacted. We can glimpse in these moments of choice the ways in which the structure of class relations creates 'forms of being through which its fundamental patterns of relations are realized by inscribing between bodies forces of attraction and repulsion that reproduce the structure' (Charlesworth 2000: 8). Boundaries are produced and maintained through attributions and judgements which are 'not so much means of knowledge as means of power' (Bourdieu 1986a: 477). Class-related resources and competencies are brought to bear in defending or asserting structures of division, of closure. In one particular form, that is evident here, is what Wacquant (1991: 52) refers to as the 'self production of class collectivities' achieved 'through struggles which simul-taneously involve relationships between and within classes and determine the actual demarcation of new frontiers'. As we have seen (and see also Chapters 5, 6 and 7), making choice decisions in education for these parents is a matter of drawing and redrawing (at different points in time) lines of demarcation, in terms of what is acceptable, what is necessary, what is in the interests of their child, and what is not. These parents are going about the business of creating or protecting 'exclusive schools' as 'class reproduc-ing institutions' (Pakulski and Waters 1996: 90).[10] For these families class continues to be a critical mediation of being, of who they are. They are doing what their class does in order to continue being what their class is. They reproduce themselves by strategically utilizing the capitals which define them.

Nonetheless within all this it would be wrong to suggest a complete absence of variability among the middle classes (Vincent 2001 points to some). The interplay of values and interests within families leads to the drawing of lines of closure in different ways and different places. Some par-ents are seeking firm and clear boundaries which cut their children off from 'others' and provide exclusive access to institutions and routes of social advantage – class enclaves. Other parents are happy to manage more fuzzy edges to closure and rely on 'exclusion from within'. In a sense the latter parents compensate for taking a principled, or necessary, position within comprehensive state schools or rather the new, increasingly fuzzy hierar-chies among state schools, by remaining more alert and more willing to intervene in their children's education. They are more active in monitoring and policing the fuzzy boundaries of setting, gifted programmes, high status courses, etc., and in providing 'add-ons' or remedial action, like employing tutors or paying for cramming at key moments (see Chapter 5). Intervention is nothing new. This was a phenomenon I recorded more than 25 years ago in my study *Beachside Comprehensive* (Ball 1981: 154–57). In that case several middle-class parents were able to challenge the schools' allocation of their child to CSE options and have them switched to the higher status GCE courses. As the year tutor in charge of allocations explained:

> Ten pupils have gone into subjects against the advice of staff. Two into Art were moved when their mothers complained. One boy in Mr Upland's form [band 3] whose father came up and the rest into Physics and Geography.

As I wrote at the time:

> If the school is considered as an arena, in which parents and children as teams compete for scarce rewards, then many pupils are seriously hand-icapped by the lack of knowledge and expertise, and of interest, of their parents.
>
> (157)

As we have seen some parents use mixed strategies, they are willing to keep their children in the state primary sector, and move them to private school for secondary education. Some then move back to the state sector for sixth-form education. Also as indicated here, but particularly in Chapter 3, middle-class parents in the state sector will also make choices and interventions to defend or assert the boundaries, or strong classifications, which are embedded in a particular 'culture of the pedagogic discourse' (Bernstein 1996: 75), a retro-spective pedagogic culture which makes certain 'ascribed' identities available to their children. Such identities are actively sought. Access to these routes and identities ensure the storing up of valuable cultural capital within the student. Concomitantly, invisible pedagogies with their weak demarcations of time and space are regarded with considerable suspicion. These cultural and calculative evaluations are part of the parents' reading of schools in the process of making choices between them. Furthermore, these suspicions and the interests of their child can lead them to dispute the process of the weaken-ing of classifications or to assert the need for stronger classifications, in Bernstein's terms they participate in 'a struggle over the nature of symbolic order' (1996: 30), or what Bourdieu (1986a: 477) calls 'the classification struggle'. All of these instances are particular ways in which 'social class is a major regulator of the distribution of students to privileging discourses and institutions' (Bernstein 1996: 11). The class cultures and attendant practices at work here 'act to transform micro differences into macro inequalities' (Bernstein 1996: 11).[11] As Pakulski and Waters (1996: 90) point out 'class is at its most real when it is experienced in day-to-day confrontations and strug-gles with members of other classes' (see Chapter 8). The confrontations here are in a sense symbolic, class struggle is displaced into a playing out of affini-ties and aversions, which underwrite and are intended to place a set of limitations upon daily confrontations across the boundaries of class. They are undertaken to maintain pure advantage.

Boundary making, and boundary protection, is one of the recurring themes in this text. These are the ways and means through which 'the *intrinsic* stratification features of modern education systems' (Bernstein 1996: 12) are re-inscribed and re-invented and the relationships between symbolic structures and social structures are produced. As I have tried to suggest (see Chapter 2) the strength and nature of the latter relationship may vary over time, and the urgency of the class interests of the middle class vary, more or less, in response. However, it may not be simply that current social and economic conditions bring into play a specific set of dispositions and vocabularies, but rather that these conditions re-emphasize or give particular legitimacy and necessity to existing aspects of middle-class sensibilities.

5 Social capital, social class and choice

> ... the network of relationships is the product of investment strategies, individual or collective, consciously or unconsciously aimed at establishing or reproducing social relationships that are directly usable in the short or long term ...
>
> (Bourdieu 1986b: 249)

Social capital is both a very fashionable and very slippery concept. Indeed it is in danger of becoming sociologically useless as a result of over-use and mis-use. It is one of those rare crossover concepts which has entered into public and political debate; 'a fad among non-academics ready to clutch at any term that might offer quick fix solutions for problems associated with the process of development and underdevelopment' (Wall, Ferrazzi and Schryer 1998: 103). In the UK it became a part of the Third Way lexicon of New Labour's first term in office (see Gamarnikow and Green 2000) and is popular with the World Bank and International Monetary Fund. The concept has at least three distinct points of origin and arenas of application but even in its academic usage it is not unusual to find social capital deployed without any acknowledgement that it is 'subject to a variety of interpretations reflecting different trends in dominant thinking' (Wall, Ferrazzi and Schryer 1998: 301). As Morrow (1999: 745–6) puts it, 'social capital is an elusive concept that is currently poorly specified ... the use of the term is inherently problematic'. However, in no small measure the difficulties which beset would-be users arise from the vagaries and slippages built in to the concept by its progenitors.

There are now a number of published papers which helpfully spell out the background and origins of social capital and critique these and their subsequent usage in various specialist fields (e.g. Gamarnikow and Green 2000; Morrow 1999; Wall, Ferrazzi and Schryer 1998). I do not propose to rehearse this background and the criticisms in detail here but it is important as Wall, Ferrazzi and Schryer (1998: 318–19) argue that 'those interested in employing the term should acknowledge the perspective from which their use of social capital is derived ... A more sensitive and cautious approach to invoking the idea of social capital will ensure that the term maintains some integrity'. I shall try to be both specific and sensitive.

As Gamarnikow and Green (2000: 98) explain there were three different 'sites for the production of social capital' – the work of Coleman, Putnam and Bourdieu; although the component elements of the concept can be found in Durkheim, Marx and Weber. For Coleman social capital has two main modalities. It is embedded within families, in the relationships between children and parents and the structure and organization of the family itself and family life. Thus, for Coleman 'non-traditional' or dual-earner families are deficient in social capital. The relationship between families and the community, their degree of embeddedness, is the other modality of Coleman's version, represented by such things as church attendance and stability of membership. Coleman relates low levels of social capital to infant mortality, under-achievement at school, youth crime, youth unemployment, etc. There are some clear overlaps between Coleman's and Putnam's definitions; although Putnam attempts to define social capital at a higher level of generality within communities and regions, initially based on work comparing north and south Italy. For Putnam, social capital inheres in three aspects of social and institutional relationships: networks, knowledge and shared norms. Where they are well developed these aspects underpin and are invested by trust or what Putnam calls 'generalised reciprocity'. High trust is fostered within communal relationships where networks are strong and dense, where obligations and expectations and sanctions are clear and participation in civic activities is extensive. As many commentators have pointed out, there is a strong normative edge to both Coleman's and Putnam's definitions, and as Morrow (1999: 749) notes they are also gender-blind and ethnocentric. Despite this, and despite the thinness and fragility of the indicators used in the initial studies by Coleman and Putnam, these versions of social capital have been taken up extensively both in work on communitarianism and in studies of the relationships between community characteristics and economic development and of student success in education.

To be clear, while I intend to take up particular aspects of Coleman's and Putnam's versions of social capital – the former's concern with social relationships in the family, and the latter's focus on networks and trust – my primary commitment here is to the third version of the concept, that articulated by Bourdieu. For Bourdieu, social capital plays a key part in his development of a 'general science of the economy of practices' (Bourdieu 1986b: 242). For him, it works within social groups and networks in the form of exchanges, social obligations and symbols, to define group membership, fix boundaries and create a sense of belonging. In this respect it coheres strongly with the themes of social closure and class collectivism which run through this study. It can thus 'provide actual or potential support and access to valued resources' (Bourdieu 1993). It is ubiquitous but is invested within class-specific forms of sociability. These forms are differentially effective in specific social 'fields' and differently articulated with economic and cultural capitals. Different social capitals are brought into play within specific fields as part of a struggle between classes and class fractions to maintain or improve their social position or advance and defend their interests. Bourdieu's notion of capital is a useful way forward 'because it is essentially a theory of privilege rather than a theory of inadequacy' (Morrow 1999: 760). But Morrow goes on to say, it is a notion that needs to be 'contextualised and empirically grounded' (760). Among many important differences between Bourdieu and Coleman and Putnam is this relational aspect to Bourdieu's formulation. The volume of social capital available to an individual or family can play a crucial part in their ability to mobilize their cultural and economic capital. As Gamarnikow and Green (2000: 98) say 'the most important way of generating social capital is to use it'. Social capital has to be worked at:

> ... the network of relationships is the product of investment strategies, individual or collective, consciously or unconsciously aimed at establishing or reproducing social relationships that are directly usable in the short or long term ... .
>
> (Bourdieu 1986b: 249)

Furthermore, in the deployment of their social capital on behalf of their children, parents demonstrate its uses and introduce the children to ways of creating their own (Allatt 1993). In this way, through the perceptions, practices and interactions of social agents, social structures 'in the head' are reproduced: '... privilege is not automatically transmitted but depends upon purposeful activity directed towards the maintenance of class position and the prevention of downward mobility' (Allatt 1993: 142). Again this is central to the general thesis outlined here.

All of this leaves researchers with the problem of operationalizing the concept and developing ways of identifying social capital in use. The main mode of measurement of social capital is quantitative, although the adequacy of these measures leaves much to be desired; see for example Levi's (1996) critique of Putnam's indicators. By contrast, Wall, Ferrazzi and Schryer (1998: 319) assert that: 'Virtually absent from any methodological strategies for social capital research are qualitative methods'. Now that is an exaggeration; some qualitative studies have been referred to above, but there are relatively few of these. Again, I shall draw on interviews with middle-class students and parents, in the first part of the chapter primarily those from the higher education choice study (see Appendix I), in the second from the secondary choice study, using both to explore the deployment of particular forms of social capital in relation to education. I deploy social capital as Morrow (1999: 757) suggests, 'as a tool or heuristic device for exploring processes and practices that are related to the acquisition of other forms of capital'.

I am less concerned with crude comparisons of the volume of relevant social capital available to different students, although this is of considerable significance in making and getting choice, and more with the activation of social capital – how it works! Although it is sometimes difficult to avoid conflating these two, I shall do my best to avoid doing so. As indicated above I will also consider the role of family relationships and of trust in the process of choice-making, particularly as this bears upon the role played by market information in this process. I shall suggest that this information has paradoxical functions. As a tactic in the analysis and presentation, and unlike other chapters, I will make some references here to differences between the middle-class and working-class families identified in the original studies from which data are drawn.

Two dimensions of social capital are crucial here. The existence and use of social networks; that is, group membership, contacts and shared identities, accumulated exchanges and obligations, and actual or potential support and access to other valued resources; and what Bourdieu (1986b: 250) calls 'the unceasing effort of sociability', that is, 'a continuous series of exchanges in which recognition is endlessly affirmed'. Particular skills and dispositions underpin these efforts. Some aspects of cultural capital are important in each dimension, particularly in its embodied forms – styles and modes of presentation; social etiquette and competence; and confidence and self-assurance. Social and cultural capital combine in various ways (particularly at key moments); for example, in generating decoding and management skills in relation to expert (or traditional cultural) systems, like schools and higher education. As we shall see, both of these capitals are intertwined and interdependent with economic and emotional capital. It is the combination of these that is often what makes the middle-class family so effective in the educational domain. Conceptually and empirically it is sometimes difficult to maintain a clear distinction between the different forms of capital in use.

The first point to make here concerns the social distribution of relevant social capital within this field of choice, and in relation to competition for places in higher education. There are two main points of difference to highlight – between middle-class and working-class students, and here the difference is stark; and between state school and private school students; here differences are clearly marked but state schools and their students are also different from one another. In the transcripts these differences were indicated by certain absences in the interviews both with working class and some of the state school students. That is, there were things that they did not talk about or mention which were well represented in the interviews with the middle-class and private school students, although not every one of these students talked about these things. The distribution of social capital, in terms of volume and type, was quite clear-cut. The social capital that was invoked by working-class students was almost exclusively very personal and familial and offered fairly limited descriptive information and bland recommendations and rarely involved other adults and certainly not adults who could be of use in choosing and applying to higher education. Many of these students did have friends or relatives who were in or had been to university but they had little to offer in the way of practical advice or support and certainly did not have relevant social contacts. This limited, low-volume social capital contrasts with what might by called effective or operant, high-volume social capital, that is, social capital realized through social networks providing direct support and relevant and valued resources. In all, twenty-five clear-cut[1] examples of effective social capital at work were identified in the 120 student transcripts; of these, thirteen came from the two private schools (Cosmopolitan Boys' and Hemsley Girls'), and twelve from the state schools, nine of these from just one of the contributory schools to the sixth form consortium (Maitland Union). All of these examples were articulated by middle-class students. Furthermore, with one or two exceptions, those offered by the private school students were much more elaborate and multi-faceted than those provided by state school students.

Now there is a degree of obviousness about this. The parents of working-class students were by definition unlikely to have completed higher education and would not normally have access through their work-based social networks to social capital which is useful and effective in relation to higher education. The parents of middle-class students, and middle-class schools, almost always had relevant social capital to hand. Let us look at some of these examples.

Dr:[2]   And what did you know about Imperial and UCL? Do you know anyone who has been there?

Lara: Well, I know some GPs who sort of teach there, I know one who teaches at Imperial and one who teaches at UCL, and they both recommended it. And then we went to the open days and I really liked them both. I really liked UCL and I went to a 'Women in Maths' day, at UCL, and that was really good as well. Imperial, I went to the open day for maths, so it wasn't exactly medicine, but I liked the facilities and everything, and I wanted to stay in London. I'd decided that was what I'd do. And in the end I said – no, actually I'll go for Cambridge. And so I applied there as well. Didn't get in.

Yeah, then there's the teacher whose daughter, she went to Cambridge and so I spoke to her about it, her course. My teacher arranged for me to talk to her.

Dr: She did medicine there as well?

Lara: Yeah, she did medicine, so she was just telling me about it. She thought it was really good and she enjoyed it. I don't think I've spoken to anyone else. Yeah, the two GPs, they just told me about how they found medical school and why they are GPs basically. And then on my work experience I got to speak to about four or five different GPs, because I was spending time with lots of them, so they all told me which one they would recommend

(Maitland Union)

And then there was a lot of pressure and I thought that I'd make a really good doctor, though. I was always divided because I changed my mind so many times and there would be lots of things that would change my mind, like, I mean, I did some work experience and it was great. And I really loved it, but also I've noticed, I did it in America with my mum's friend's husband. And I noticed that he spent so much time at the surgery and so much time doing what he did and he went to ... I mean, he'd wake up at six a.m. and go out to surgery. Then go to clinic, and then, I mean, I followed him around the whole time I was exhausted, and I thought to myself, I am so, I don't know, I am so changeable that I don't think I'd be able to do that. I do think I'd want a lot more out of my life than going in and doing surgery and going straight to that. I'd want more time. And I don't think I'd have got that if I'd gone into medicine. And my teachers, I think, were very happy about that choice, that I wasn't going for medicine.

(Dawn: Hemsley Girls')

I've been for a week at Oxford, following around my cousin, doing physiology. And a week at a vet's. A week in a doctors' clinic, which was really good.

(Lisa: Hemsley Girls')

I've got friends who know people who are lawyers. I know that once you've finished a law degree it's hard to get into practice, it takes a number of years, so I am not going to expect to jump into the big money, like, straight away ... I went to a law firm, and they didn't really give you any advice on unis to go to, but they gave advice on what area of law you should go in, you know, the solicitors said be a barrister, don't be a solicitor. And the barristers say – don't be a barrister, be a solicitor.

(Jane: Maitland Union)

Through the activation of social capital and participation in adult social networks these students come to see the relationships between school, higher education and work as a process, and in a time scale as a series of steps or moves. They also gain insights into the structure of professions and into how things work, the hierarchies of a career. Even at this early stage they become aware of choices to be made which will effect how things might turn out for them later or open up different possibilities for the future.

The main point here is that these young people are able to mobilize relationships and obligations which parents, other relatives and friends are part of or can access. This is an example of what Granovetter (1973) calls the 'strength of weak ties' or what Putnam (2000: 23) calls 'bridging' – a 'sociological WD40'. That is the ability to call upon and use relationships within extensive and loose-knit social networks: 'weak ties, often denounced as generative of alienation are here seen as indispensable to individual's opportunities and to their integration into communities' (Granovetter 1973: 1378). Such ties, encounters, links and networks work in various ways in relation to higher education choice and access. They provide important and useful advice and information about choice and careers. This is 'hot knowledge', direct and first-hand and means that the student need not rely on secondary or generic sources. This 'hot knowledge' can also function to eliminate possibilities, filter out unrealistic aspirations and narrow down career choices. In other words, again, this is about establishing boundaries, what is not worth considering. It is the management of aspirations or aligning of ambitions (Schneider and Stevenson 1999). Schneider and Stevenson (85) found that: 'In describing their life plans, adolescents with aligned ambitions demonstrate a knowledge of how the adult world works and thus are more likely to be seen as adult by others'. These experiences also make choices real, they enable the students to develop vivid and realistic 'imagined futures' for themselves, to put themselves in place, literally. There are also subtle aspects of social learning – forms of talk, presentation of self, dress, demeanour, modes of interaction. Skills of personal recontextualization are important, being about fitting in, being at ease – in return the young people gain 'acceptance and recognition' (Barbalet 2001: 87). They also provide experiential and informational resources that can be employed in making applications to higher education institutions, mobilizing resources of impression and enabling the students to present themselves as a particular kind of educational subject. They distinguish themselves from others who cannot so easily mobilize these resources, both on application forms and in interviews, in the form of cultural capital: they 'yield profits of distinction' (Bourdieu 1986b: 245). These weak ties are extensive in many cases, opening up for the students 'socioscapes' (Albrow 1997) which are national and global rather than, as in the case of working-class students, mostly local (Ball, Maguire and Macrae 2000). Through these links and processes students are becoming socially embedded in networks and exchanges that may well be of longer-term value to them in the labour market. This is part of what Allatt (1993) calls a 'critical transfer' which enables them to create their own social capital. In the process they are acquiring valuable skills and competencies, a form of reinvestment of cultural in social capital. The two interplay in providing for mutual recognition and boundary setting within social networks. And this interplay continues within prestigious higher education institutions.

> I've always wanted to work in the City [City of London, the financial centre] and I spent a week working in a merchant bank and they seem to spend the whole day on computers, and without computers they were nothing, and it wasn't just the basic use of computers, it is the programmes behind it that interests me, they take a lot of the work out ... speeds up transactions ... I've always been interested in money. I've wanted to be rich. And reading papers and articles it has always been things like "City bankers earn a million pounds bonus for a year's work".
>
> (Edward: Cosmopolitan Boys')

I've got friends who went to St Martin's [prestigious school of Art] for a foundation and then went on to Chelsea [another prestigious school of Art] and he does interior decorating, has done very well out of it ... these are professional people I've met through work experience, or I've met through my family but they are not actually friends of my family, some of them. But yeah, they were very helpful. In fact I think I've also asked a few people who have come to this school to do talks.

(Alex: Riverway College)

Again, the skills and resources deployed here involve activating both existing strong ties and accessing and making use of weak ties. Here, and in other examples quoted – McDonalds law firm in Chicago, a Harley Street doctor – there are indications of the dual profitability to be extracted from social capital, both material, in the form of specific advantage, and symbolic profits which accrue from association with prestigious groups or individuals.[3]

The schools themselves are also important in all this in a variety of ways. Some schools, especially in our research the private schools, were able to arrange work experience placements that put students in contact with well placed professionals in their field of career or higher education interest; although in some cases this is done, as above, through parents' contacts. The private schools were also able to draw upon their own resources of social capital through links with alumni and in particular with individuals or institutions in higher education, especially links with Oxbridge Colleges (see below). While virtually all students have work experience placements, here it is the type and level of experience that is important in offering advantages of access and advancement. Nigella makes this point very well.

When I did work experience, I spoke to a lot of doctors. And one of the doctors I did work experience for, I've kept in contact with, and he's helped me through my interviews, and advised me ... [he's] a private paediatrician in Harley Street, so it's very sort of the elite! But he's been brilliant and talked me through a whole lot of stuff, given me masses of advice.

(Hemsley Girls')

In effect when parents invest in private education for their children they are buying into a broad and complex body of social capital that is made available to the children and in relation to which the young people develop their own investment skills. As Coleman (1988: 98) points out 'Social capital is defined by its function ... like other forms of capital, social capital is productive, making possible the achievement of social ends that in its absence would not be possible'. Elite schooling is also an effective means to store value, which can later be released as surplus meaning – that is the 'metaphorical qualities of status and prestige' (Lee 1993: 33) – cultural capital.

While the tutors in all the schools in our study were immensely supportive of their university aspirants, some schools had particularly valuable resources embodied in their staff which could be deployed to considerable effect – to 'make a difference'. Geoffrey of Maitland Union explained:

> … there have been teachers like Miss Plummer who went to Cambridge herself and have kind of totally been really helpful and been right behind me and helped me out with my personal statement and my application and helping me for the interview and stuff, so, I mean, that sort of stuff makes a difference really. If you've got someone who is going to help you through and give you a bit of time and a bit of personal effort to help you with it then it makes it worth doing.

Here the teacher is able to offer a specific kind of preparation for the particular rigours of the Cambridge interview, a sharing of esoteric knowledge; the teacher acts as a kind of gatekeeper or legitimator, or, informally, what Bourdieu (1986b: 251) calls a 'mandated agent'. For some students, school and family capitals are mutually reinforcing and combine to scaffold aspirations and applications, as John, also from Maitland Union, explained.

> … my mum knows one of the people who works at one of the colleges in Cambridge and she spoke to them, and they gave her some advice and stuff. So she said it's probably one of the most difficult places to get in. And then I went to my history teacher Miss Plummer, who went to Trinity herself, and that's where I'm applying now, and she basically, she set me up to go on an open day there, and I went up and really liked it. And it just kind of worked, it's got a good reputation for history, and it's quite a big college, a rich college, it's a nice situation and they have actually got a reputation for having low numbers of state school entrants, but they are putting it up all the time, so there aren't that many applicants, and it's just kind of playing the odds really, a bit.

Here also the teacher can offer critical, insider knowledge related to the chances of success involved in making an application. Time and effort can be used effectively.

Schools can also foster social capital in other ways, for some students and again particularly for private schools' students, and particular Hemsley, social and cultural capital can also be accumulated in extra-curricular activities of various kinds. Such activities were rarely mentioned by state schools students but commonly mentioned by the private schools' students. And like work experience these activities fostered skills of presentation, leadership or teamwork experiences and in some cases social contacts which supported applications to Oxford and Cambridge. They contribute to the development of 'emotional energy' (Collins 1981: 1001). The reinforcement of experiences of success and inclusion through an educational career provides a resilience in the face of obstacles or challenges.

Amanda, who said she had given up most of her non-work activities to concentrate on her A levels, does drama lessons, used to do photography, cycling and swimming, and play the drums 'and piano quite a lot' as well as achieving the Duke of Edinburgh's Silver Award. Sheena, in contrast, said she had 'let her work slip' because she was 'ridiculously busy', that is, 'involved in plays and I'm editor of the magazine', and she was also involved in starting up the school's English Society. Miriam was a sixth form assistant, working with a teacher in the lower school and was a drama club leader, 'we produced a play with year seven students which was really hard work ... it took a lot of time and energy'. Alongside this, as reported elsewhere (Reay, Davies, David and Ball 2001), the private school students were less likely to have part-time jobs than other students and overall the length of time spent at work each week was directly related to the students' social class. The taking of a gap year before university was also an exclusively middle-class phenomenon, never once mentioned by any working-class applicants in our study. The gap year has certain economic costs, often uses social contacts and networks but can also in some cases be seen as an investment, a storing up of cultural and social capital for future use.

It is also evident in the various examples above that the self-confidence or what Morrow (1999) calls the 'self-efficacy' of the young people is being deployed and developed – as might also be the case in the working-class student's part-time work. As Barbalet (2001: 83–84) explains, confidence rests upon a self-knowledge which orients actions towards the future, the 'actor's own capacities to approximate what they set out to achieve'.[4]

> I was sort of stuck in two pathways. Either going to the business side or going to the diplomacy side ... it was more or less a year deciding which one was better. I went, for example, I went to King's College, to the War Studies department, and had a chat with a few lecturers and so forth and got more information about the subject.
>
> (Krystof: Maitland Union)

This kind of proactive confidence and direct engagement with higher education lecturers was totally absent from the working-class interviews. Indeed it is difficult to convey the sense of how alien this sounds in relation to the working-class students whose view of higher education was a distant and hazy one. They had little sense of what it would involve. They had yet to acquire the skills needed to decode its mysteries. For example, these students talked about subjects in general terms, with little sense of actual contents or differences between institutions, while the middle class and especially the private school students talked often in some detail about course structures, contents and organization and sometimes differences in teaching methods. When they did not know the middle-class students knew how to find out; whom to speak to, where to go for information, and the confidence to take up these possibilities directly.

This kind of confidence or self-efficacy becomes of particular importance at significant moments in higher education and beyond. Interviews at Oxbridge are a case in point. Indeed there is a kind of class homology embedded in these interviews – the sorts of intellectual presentations of self that appear to be valued and highly rated in such interviews are exactly those which are acquired and developed through the class-related social and cultural capitals addressed here. These are key moments of realization and reinvestment of social and cultural capital and of exchange of social signs. To understand the character of these moments, one needs to look at the context in which the capital is situated, the efforts by individuals to activate their capital, the skill with which individuals activate their capital, and the institutional response to the activation (Lareau and McNamara Horvat 1999: 38). There is a kind of mutual recognition and social exchange in these settings, between 'kindred spirits' (Bourdieu 1990): 'cultural value ... only becomes visible when the social sign within which it is stored exchanges with other social signs in the framework of a cultural code' (Lee 1993: 161). Geoffrey from Maitland Union, who applied to Cambridge, almost offers an explicit grasp of this, and certainly sees the relationships between his work experience and his ability to perform at interview, although he also recognizes that even his impressive credentials may not stand up to comparison with what can be offered by private school students. Here Geoffrey seems to recognize the way in which he is placed in a hierarchy of distinctions and his final comment is suggestive of Bourdieu's (1986a: 331) point that 'Culture is what remains when you've forgotten everything' or the gap between acknowledgement and knowledge.

> I've done work experience in the Treasury, in an MP's office, in a hospital, in business, two different business offices, so that's kind of the main stuff that I've got to go on, as far as that's concerned, and then I was hoping to get myself in on the history front. Because the two interviews are with history teachers, they are historians, other colleges do it with the Tutor of admissions as well, and I think if I had had one of those I would probably have had more chance of getting in, because I could make stuff up, but ... I mean, I don't think that many people do that much stuff. I don't know whether private school kids do, or whether they can just talk about them well, but I mean, I am not kind of totally lacking in culture, but I am quite lacking in culture, so ....

Geoffrey's accumulation of social and cultural capital is effortful and studied, volume seems important, and he suggests that his volume may be set in comparison against the relative value of the capitals of private school students. At these critical moments a condensate of capitals which have been accumulated and stored over time come into play, they are embedded in and realized or exchanged on these occasions. These are palpable class moments, Bourdieurian moments, invested with values and dispositions, modes of speech and gestures, demeanour, dress and forms of social discourse – embodied capital. Perhaps habituses can be glimpsed. Dispositions and structures are made visible in the validation of the former and the reinforcement of the latter. As the Oxbridge tutor, an Oxbridge graduate herself, at Riverway Tertiary College, saw it, college admissions tutors work with 'gut feelings' (see Chapter 4): 'your gut feeling is liable to prejudice you in favour of people whose body language you can interpret, who come from your social background ...'. Students like Geoffrey are able to 'form and sustain' a very particular, pragmatically situated identity (Cote 1996: 195) as part of a 'diversified portfolio of capitals' (195), which is deployed to good effect at these moments. Geoffrey also has a tactical understanding of the use of situated identities and a highly developed sense of 'self-monitoring' (Cote 1996: 195). As Bourdieu (1986a: 482) puts it: 'Social subjects comprehend the social world which comprehends them'. These moments are also points of closure, where the limits of membership are marked out and others are excluded.

Further to this, in the same way that parents find themselves responding intuitively and instinctively to certain schools (Chapter 4), so higher education applicants reported a sense of identification with particular universities. Again this was usually overtly or implicitly class related (see Reay, Davies, David and Ball 2001). As Anick, a Hemsley Girls' student, explained:

> I love it, and I visited a few universities, and also we've got friends there, so I've been to Oxford. And to be honest it's the only place that I felt I could be. I clicked with the place ... and it just happened to be Oxford.

My point is that it did not just happen to be Oxford. This clicking, this recognition, is a matching of an individual and institutional habitus. And, however obvious, it should be said that entry to Oxbridge is a further investment, another step on a trajectory of privilege and closure. Both points are made clear by the father of Nigel, a student from a state sixth form. Nigel's father had to work hard to convince his son to apply to Oxford; Nigel did not have a sense of place or recognition and thought that he might be out of place, and unhappy. The father thought not, but nonetheless sees what his son is attempting as 'very difficult' and he draws attention to further hierarchical divisions between types of schools and types of students (private and grammar rather than comprehensive):

> ... it isn't true. Of course there is an aspect of that, but there are plenty of people there who are from state schools, but not from comprehensives. They are all from grammars ... his friends at Oxford are all the grammar school people but he really enjoys the people who come from private school as well ... I think it is very difficult what he's doing, but

you know he regards it as not terribly difficult. He said these Oxford and Cambridge colleges are so well funded, compared with other places in the country, that if you've got an interest you can pursue it, you know, I just can't tell you how favoured they are, it's really amazing. Nigel hasn't taken up these options but some of his friends have, I mean some of these kids make films, put on a play a week, write a play, get a cast together, put it on ... in the science world they can go to people's labs, they get sent all around the world, it's fantastic.

Nigel's father is pointing up one aspect of what Bourdieu (1986b: 249) calls the 'multiplier effect' which arises from the 'profits of membership' of a 'rare, prestigious group'. However, Oxbridge also points up the minute complexity of social divisions, the limits of social capital and the mismatches than can arise in any portfolio of capitals. Frank, a student from a private boys' school, was offered a place at Merton College Oxford. His father had attended Merton and knew the admissions tutor. Nonetheless, Frank explained that:

I think I would have found it quite difficult saying – 'yeah my dad went here, and you want me, because I'm from the same stock'. Because I don't like that sort of idea of the way it works. And I did find Oxford a bit stuffy, all these sort of people sitting in their big armchairs with their notes saying tell me about this, tell me about that. And I thought the tutorials could be great, but on the other hand they could be awful ... I would have probably fitted in at Oxford even though everyone was earning ridiculous amounts of money, it was all sort of terribly higher income bracket than I was used to.

These fine distinctions, differences in social networks and cultural capital between members of different class fractions need teasing out in further research. They are pointed up even more starkly by some of the middle-class students from state schools for whom Oxbridge moments gave rise to different sorts of reactions, which led to rejection and alienation. In effect some students experience a grating or conflict of habituses, a stark non-recognition. Sian described her Cambridge interviews as 'just a miserable experience. They were such horrible people ... and then I was sort of worried that I'd get in'. Rebbeca from the Tertiary College had a similar 'not me' reaction.

When I went up to Cambridge, that was like, it was almost every body came from private schools. I didn't meet a single person like me, who came from a sixth form college. And I thought that might give me the edge. Obviously it didn't, thank goodness.

Greta, from Hemsley Girls' also 'didn't like' Cambridge; 'you need to feel comfortable wherever you are going, because if you don't enjoy the environment you're working in, it can be very tough'. Lisa, a Maitland Union student, applied to Cambridge but was having second thoughts:

> ... it has put me off strongly going there, because personal life, social life at university, is really important to me, and I think that Cambridge would be so restricting. I'm thinking if I do get in there, there's going to be no one I get on with, no one to go out with.

These are views from the other side of the us and them divide, for these students Oxbridge is a place that is not for people 'like us'. These students do not share with Oxbridge students a sense of common social history, they are alien. These are all forms of what Bourdieu and Passeron (1990) call 'self exclusion', boundaries that are drawn from the other side. Here there is a failure to recognize, a sense of discomfort, of moving outside of the natural limits of a social network.

Intervention

Another particular function for social capital arises at other critical moments. That is, those moments of difficulty or crisis in the educational career of the child; as Power, Edwards, Whitty and Wigfall (2002, Chapter 8) make clear some middle-class children find themselves with 'troubled and damaged educational identities'. Being middle-class is no absolute guarantee of success. What is notable at these moments of crisis is the ability of parents to mobilize various kinds of interventions in support of the child. These interventions are significant, when successful, in the construction of an educational trajectory that insulates the child from others who face similar difficulties but lack remedial resources. Lareau and McNamara Horvat (1999: 45) suggest that 'interventions provide a portrait of a series of moments of social inclusion'. Indeed, again a variety of kinds of capital come into play at such times. In particular, the ability to pay for specialist private services can be important. For example, the use of private tutors at particular times or as a routine addition to school teaching was common among the private school students in our higher education study. Emotional capital is also important at such times (see below). This and the other tactics, skills and capitals involved in such interventions were identified in Lacey's classic study of HighTown Grammar (Lacey 1970), they make up what he called psycho-social-cultural resources. As we shall see later, this is part of a general strategic infrastructure of support and middle-class parents are adept at knowing when to intervene and how to make best use of additional resources within this infrastructure. Again let us consider some examples. In the first, Anick describes the tactical support she receives as part of a more general framework of social capital.

> A couple of months ago I got a studies skills teacher and I started working, it's through my mum's friends, so I've been seeing this woman

weekly, and she's helping me, you know, how to work, when to work and actually getting down and doing it [Anick wants to be a lawyer]. Neither of my parents are lawyers, we have lawyer friends but I mean at school, my parents just saw me, because I argue, they said that would just fit a lawyer ... I think I am going to America this summer. I've got the opportunity of working at McDonalds law firm in Chicago. Because one of my Dad's best friends is head lawyer at McDonalds. So I could go there for a couple of months ...

(Hemsley Girls')

In the next three we can see the emotional dimensions to parental aspirations for their children and the role of the parents in supporting and managing the emotions of the child.

Well, I hope he gets in, I hope he gets the grades, he seems to want that very much, and I think I sort of changed my mind a bit, because I kept thinking he might not, and I don't want to be so disappointed, I don't want to make it seem serious. He is struggling, I mean, as we speak he's got the chemistry tutor here and it is difficult. It is not a foregone conclusion that he will get in, so I don't want to set my heart on it, on the other hand, if that's what he wants and he makes it then I am delighted ...

(Fred's mother: Cosmopolitan Boys')

... when it came to last Christmas and they had modules and she was in tears – why did we let her apply for Cambridge? Why did we let her do physics? She'd fail. She wasn't going to make the standard. All this kind of thing. She was hysterical. And we said ... I said to her – you've got six weeks, eight weeks before your modules, can't we get you a tutor? No, no, no, no, no! She was insistent. So the best we could do was to go to WH Smith and buy a revision book which she found very useful. Her sister said that she'd got to have a tutor. No, she didn't want one ... And we said – don't wait for the module results to come. Because that's another six weeks. We said – have a tutor now! Then you've got four months before your finals. She wouldn't hear of it and then when her module results came and she'd done so badly for her needs for university, then she really got a fright. And she said – OK, she would have a tutor. So she arranged a tutor. So she arranged a tutor herself, for three only, one-hour sessions. Then I started saying, you know, so and so said that some of these Easter revision courses are very good. And so she actually agreed to go and have an Easter revision course. Which was a week. But unfortunately, by the time she agreed to go to these various places, the best ones were all sort of full up and she chose to go to the nearest one, for least effort.

(Anthea's mother: Hemsley Girls')

... when it was put to the test the back up system wasn't there ... I supposed we believed them ... it is a white, middle-class college, we are white, middle-class parents and we thought these were people with the same values and attitudes as ourselves and of course they will support the students, but they didn't. If it hadn't been for his father and myself, he would have dropped out, we had to give him the help and support we expected from the college ...

(Mrs Collins: Post-16 study)

In the next we see the use of a private tutor as an alternative to intervention from the school.

... . yeah, but A level's beyond my field. A level maths. So sort of like, six months ago we got him a tutor anyway. And he was happy talking to him. So I think he sort of ... *[laughs]* ... overcame a lot of the problems. He didn't have many, I must say, actually. But anything he did have, the tutor sorted out with him, and he felt happier doing that than actually speaking to them. And I said – do you want me to talk to them? And he said no. So I thought I wouldn't interfere, especially as he seemed all right about it.

(Carl's mother: Maitland Union)

In the next two, interventions are aimed to respond directly to what are regarded as weaknesses in school provision.

I tried for Hendon and Hampstead and I tried for Henrietta Barnett but I didn't get through the exam. But I had a tutor to help me, because my primary school wasn't very good. So that's how I got here.

(Leonora: Hemsley Girls')

We got a study course in English, but it was really to support revision more than tuition, I think. But maths, we had to get her tutored to get over the lack of ... the poor system they used at the school, which was called Smile.

(Emily's mother: Maitland Union)

The last example emphasizes the normalcy of these kinds of bought-in support and the ready availability of financial capital. Such support is regarded as an inherent component of assuring a trajectory of educational success.

Yes, we got a biology teacher for extra tutoring and if he'd asked for ... they both knew that they could ask me for extra tuition, and perhaps I wasn't really on top of that and I should have insisted. And I know, I remember offering him a history tutor, and he said no.

(Rowan's mother: Maitland Union)

We can see the tight interweaving of economic, social and emotional capital in these examples. Middle-class parents are very aware that 'ability or talent is itself the product of an investment of time and cultural capital' (Bourdieu 1986b: 244). And the last extract is particularly telling – that is in the way that these students know that these possibilities are available to them. There are not only the practical aspects of support here but the sense of being supported, or having additional resources available should they be needed. These bought-in supplements work to fill in for the shortcomings of school provisions and ensure a surplus of performance which distinguishes this child from others, and they play their part in bolstering the matrix of expectations within which the child's educational career is assembled. In some respects, at these moments, economic capital is converted into cultural capital. This is very clear from Mr du Maurier's account of sending his son to a crammer.

> The school didn't support us, no, not very much. It was entirely off our own back that we found a crammer and you know, by that time he was absolutely up for it, we didn't have to persuade him to do anything, he wanted it, and so he had a few lessons, really in how to approach the Oxford entrance exam and then the interview.
>
> (Maitland Union)

These interventions, and those of a different kind examined in Chapter 3, underline the enormous amounts of time and energy devoted to ensuring social reproduction. For the middle class privilege requires continuous and intensive work. As Lareau and McNamara Horvat (1999: 38) put it 'reproduction is jagged and uneven and is continually negotiated by social actors'. The realization of advantage is not foregone and we can see the importance of constant monitoring and surveillance – parental vigilance. Nonetheless, a key factor in maintaining and developing the practical advantages and educational identity of the child, as bright or high-achieving, keeping the separated off from settings of failure or low-achievement, is the ability to supplement parental time and energy with professional support.

Participation and parenting

I want to look now at parental intervention in a different way. Already in Chapters 3 and 4 and above I have touched on some of the ways in which middle-class parents engage with schools to support and ensure the educational success of their children, by pushing for or opposing particular policies and practices, securing access to separated trajectories and intervening to avert or remediate difficulties. Another kind of intervention comes in the form of parents taking up representative or supportive roles within school. Other research has indicated the ways in which such roles have tended to be monopolized by middle-class parents (Deem, Brehony and Heath 1995), and in Chapter 3 I noted several examples of the ways in which such parents used the opportunities of these roles to exclude others and achieve privileged influence over, or access to, school personnel. McGrath and Kuriloff (1999) in their study of the Minsi Trail schools found that middle-class parents 'with school knowledge and resources pressured administrators for special services' (623) and also noted the 'passive exclusion of working-class and minority parents from the home and school associations' (617) leaving 'mothers and educators from similar backgrounds' working together (617). In the secondary choice sample to which I have been referring the number of parents involved within schools was high. Of the 35 families, 19 reported some kind of direct participation in their children's primary school,[5] a total of 24 participation roles. In all, 10 parents acted as chairpersons or members of governing bodies, 11 acted as chairpersons were on the committee of, or were actively involved in PTAs (Parent Teacher Associations), 3 others did volunteer work within schools – working in the school library or listening to children read. As Mrs Tey explained: 'we are part of a core of parents who are always doing things'.

The other factor which marks off those who participate from those who do not is gender. In all except one of the participation roles it was women, mothers, who were involved. Just one father acted as a school governor. As Mrs Smith put it succinctly, 'He leaves that to me'. Or as Mr Parker explained, 'She does it more, she's better informed'. Speaking generally about her involvement in schools in supporting and organizing her children's education Mrs Cornwell commented that 'I'm glad I wasn't working ... it takes up an awful lot of emotional energy'. The point is that most of the mothers in the sample were working. I pick up gender again below. Four of the parents spontaneously mentioned that there were some specific advantages arising from their participation. This was not asked about in the interviews. Mrs Mankell talked about being a governor and 'having quite close conversations' with the head teacher and other staff which were helpful in making the choice of a secondary school. Similarly, Mrs Simpson spoke of 'picking up quite a lot of information' about the local secondary school 'that's put us in the right position to ask the right questions'. Mrs Lovesey mentioned that her involvement in the PTA over a number of years meant that she 'got to know a lot of parents' and the primary head teacher. And Mrs Connelly made an explicit link between her parenting and her work on the PTA.

> If you go into the state sector I think you have to be a much more hands-on parent, you've got to be much more aware of what they are doing. I think you have to have a much stronger dialogue with teachers, say, than at a private school, there's more work there and a stricter environment in which the child has to work ... Again friends who have got older children have said, you have to be the one that keeps the finger on the pulse and a very good way of doing it is if you're on the PTA.

We can see a variety of things embedded here. Clearly, there is no clear distinction between the obligations which might underpin a sense of public service which is invested in these roles and a sense of self-interest or possible advantage accruing on behalf of the family – mixed motives in other words. There is also an indication of these roles, for these families, being an extension of good parenting. What we do not know from this data is the extent to which these parents are able to, or are interested in, influencing school policies through their participative roles. These different dimensions of parent involvement are taken up by Vincent (2001) in the 'Little polities' study. She identifies three forms and degrees of parental intervention – high, intermediate and low – in the study and notes that:

> The 'high' cohort are largely white, overwhelmingly home-owners, most are highly educated public sector professionals ... These parents shared a feeling of responsibility for their children's education. They were anxious to secure their future in the face of a congested labour market ... Having a relationship with the school overtly demonstrating your concern about your child's education, was to this cohort what 'people like us do'.
>
> (349)

This last comment indicates again the mixture of motives for parental participation in school. On the one hand there is a sense of good practice, good parenting in support of their child; on the other, a sense that such good parenting has to be registered with the school, that it needs to be seen to be done, demonstrating to the school their role as caring parents. Intervention is also a part of the surveillance of the school noted earlier. Vincent (2001: 349) again notes that: 'We characterised the high cohort as *risk managers*, they were not willing to leave education to the school and left as little to chance as possible where their children's educational prospects were concerned'. These parents were in contact with their children's school over a range of matters, some of these have been touched on above; '"high" parents initiated contact and conversation with school over achievement (e.g. assignment to ability sets, homework), welfare (e.g. bullying, teacher–pupil relations) *and*, especially at Willow, more general systemic issues (e.g. teaching styles and materials, pastoral care policies)' (350).

It is also worth noting one other feature of those parents from the secondary choice sample who were involved in participation roles; nine came from families where both parents were public sector workers, four where both worked in the private sector, and six from families with mixed employment, but of these, five of the mothers, those actually involved, were also public sector workers. Vincent (2001) in the study she reports, also points to class fractional differences which seemed to explain differences in 'parental voice and agency' (356), and in the general orientation of their involvements. The high intervening parents at Willow school, mainly public sector professionals, 'did give time and effort to discussing and supporting general school issues and events' (356–357) and also raised questions about teaching styles. On the other hand their counterparts at Carson school, an even mix of public, private and managerial professionals and routine white-collar workers, were much more 'firmly focused on their individual children' (356). There were other differences in attitudes to school between these two groups of parents.

Taken together with other kinds of involvement and intervention what we see here is middle-class parents using all and every opportunity to move their resources, their capitals, across the boundary between the private, domestic sphere and the public sphere of schooling. Through recent policies which emphasize parenting roles and empower parents in relation to schools, this boundary is being made increasingly porous (Walzer 1984).

Knowledge, norms and trust

Let us look at middle-class involvement in the education marketplace in a slightly different way by using the components of Putnam's model of the workings of social capital. As noted already, Putnam's mechanisms for the production, maintenance and growth of social capital involve three components – trust, norms and networks. These underpin Putnam's vision of a healthy community, a vision which Levi (1996) quite rightly labels as romantic. Further, Putnam's discussion of the components slips uneasily between the descriptive and the normative. Again, I want to use them analytically but heuristically, and not always in the way intended by Putnam.

Trust, argues Putnam, restating a sociological truism, 'is an essential component of social capital' (Putnam 1993: 170) because it 'lubricates co-operation' (171). The meaning of trust remains somewhat elusive in Putnam's work and its application is limited to the realm of civic and political affairs. In the social settings under scrutiny here the civic and economic are thoroughly blurred, in a number of senses. The schools, colleges and universities to which families address themselves are both civic institutions and competing businesses in the education marketplace. The families themselves, as we have seen, engage in the enterprise of education with a dual agenda; on the one hand are the developmental needs of their child and on the other their concerns about ensuring that their child acquires credentials for use in the labour market and thus the reproduction or enhancement of position and advantage. This duality is thoroughly interwoven, although one element of this, as part of the narrative of good parenting and of responsibility, may be given more emphasis at any point in time depending on circumstances. Trust in this kind of setting like any market takes on added complexity. In the simplest sense there is a basic tension between trust and self-interest, or between cooperation and competition. As a number of UK researchers have noted, the market form in education works against cooperation between participating institutions (Gewirtz, Ball and

Bowe 1995; Woods, Bagley and Glatter 1994). Indeed, Plant (1992: 90) argues that market relations are fundamentally opposed to civic virtue, but that nonetheless the market 'equally requires a sense of civic virtue without which the market cannot function effectively'. When applied to public sector institutions the market constantly threatens to 'displace the service ethic in society' (92). (I return to this in Chapter 8.)

We can see some of the side-effects of this tension in parents' confusion about the nature of educational institutions and whether they should relate to them as though they were businesses or as though they were public service organizations. Different kinds of relations may be appropriate in each case and recent education policy is schizophrenic in emphasizing both exit or choice, as though in a market, and participation or voice, as though in a partnership with school. In Plant's terms it is unclear to which 'moral realm' these institutions belong. Equally though, as suggested above, there are uncertainties among parents themselves about their interests-at-hand in their engagements with school. Martin and Vincent explore some of these uncertainties in their work on parental voice (Martin and Vincent 1999; Martin 2001; Vincent 1997; Vincent 2001). As noted already, the opportunities for voice may be exercised through a vocabulary of social good (see also Chapter 3), which is indirectly related to the interests of the child and the family, or through a more explicit register of social advantage. I return to these uncertainties in the discussion of values and principles (Chapter 6). Within all of this trust is made problematic. All the more so when trust in relation to educational institutions is placed in a more general social and political context. Putnam sees governments as both providing a backdrop for facilitating trust among citizens and as eliciting trust through their own policy performance. In most Western societies, and perhaps even more generally, neither condition has been met in recent times in relation to public sector organizations and public sector policy. Certainly in the UK and the USA successive governments have contributed to what I have called a 'discourse of derision' (Ball 1990) aimed at the public sector and public sector professionals. In effect these governments have asserted that teachers are not to be trusted, citing the problem of producer capture, and have introduced choice and performative systems to ensure teachers' responsiveness to parents and compliance with political objectives (Crozier 2000). These same governments have been judged as policy failures by their electorates in their management of the public sector and in the process education has shifted from being a political backwater to a headline election issue. More generally still Giddens (1991) asserts that we now live in a high-risk low-trust society. In Giddens' rather simplistic binary Putnam's civic community looks very much like a form of pre-modern society where trust in persons is focused upon 'personalised connections' and 'community and kinship networks' (Giddens 1991: 121). In contrast, high modern societies, according to Giddens, are denoted by social relations which are disembedded from local contexts and 'recombined across time–space distances' (53). The absence or fracturing of trust leads to the 'debilitating effects of modern institutions on self-experience and the emotions' (100) and the increasing plurality of values in this context again generates uncertainty and distrust of experts, like teachers (Troman 2000). To become re-established, Giddens argues, interpersonal trust must be 'worked at' (1990: 121) as a 'project' which involves the '*opening out of the individual to the other*' [emphasis in original] (121). The alternative, for Giddens, is a social world of anxiety and dread.

So how does all of this relate to our focus on the concerns of middle-class families in the education marketplace? In respect to the sorts of social networks and social capital described above, trust, for the most part, seems well entrenched in its pre-modern form, albeit with some updating. Weak as well as strong ties, local as well as distant relations, are in place. Social connections and networks are a key aspect of informal information gathering and social learning. This is evident from the displays of social capital presented above. However, interpersonally shared information is different in kind from that information which is generated by governments, local authorities or educational institutions about themselves. I want to go on to contrast the role of trust in relation to the different kinds of information which circulate within the education marketplace. I have written about this before (Ball and Vincent 1998). Information is a key dynamic in the workings of all markets and has been a particular focus and a powerful mechanism in the reform of education systems. That is the generation of judgemental and comparative performance information which is intended to allow consumers to make better choices between providers (Ball 2000). As indicated, there are two main aspects to trust within this social grid of information: formal information provided by or about schools, colleges, universities – cold knowledge; and informal, interpersonal information that circulates through social networks around them – hot knowledge. It is clear in the interviews with parents and students that the latter is almost always privileged over the former; thus in choosing a university and in choosing a school, 'a lot of my opinions about where to send my child have relied entirely in playground gossip' (Mrs Rankin). Again within the process of choice these parents seek to activate an excess of social capital and a range of social skills, and the use of networks. Again this illustrates the strength of weak ties. 'We spoke to teachers in the schools, spoke to other parents, and spoke to my friends who were scattered across the borough and where their children went and what they felt about it' (Mrs Gosling). 'I know people who have taught there, and I know parents of children who already go there' (Mrs Miles). 'We watched others and saw what they went through ... there's a lot of discussion around the playground' (Mrs Crichton). First-hand accounts of institutions and their foibles are considered infinitely superior to the second-hand or artefactual information provided in reports or tables and to promotional information like brochures and open days. However, this is not a simple story of the mistrust of expert systems set over and against much higher levels of trust in interpersonal relations. Just as Giddens (1991: 7) suggests, trust, 'pragmatic acceptance, scepticism, rejection and withdrawal uneasily co-exist in the social space linking individual activities and expert systems'. The school choice transcripts convey a general sense of anxiety and uncertainty. Parents have doubts about their own judgements ('you forget how to judge schools') as much as those of friends ('you hear so many conflicting opinions': Mr Moseley), and formal documents were regarded as particularly unreliable; 'I'm cynical about advertising – the whole truth is never told' (Mrs Rankin). Generally, brochures and open evenings were regarded with suspicion: 'It's all a front really' (Ms West). Kenway and Bullen (2001: 149) concur and suggest that the world of school marketing 'celebrates surfaces, encourages conformity, hypocrisy and repression'. The insertion of consumption/capital relations into state education in the form of quasi-markets and their paraphernalia produces paradoxes. The promise of greater transparency and responsiveness through the mechanism of market information may actually make things more opaque (see Ball 2000).

Several of the parents expressed their dismay about, and difficulty with, the slippage between information and promotion in the education market, which contributed to their general sense of uncertainty. One father found the open evening presentation at a local City Technology College particularly objectionable, describing it as 'detestable sort of late 80s entrepreneurial glib and without any content at all' (Mr Marsh). This parent and others seem to want to keep apart the moral realms of market and civic institutions and are perplexed when the boundary between them is blurred. The form of representation derived from the former was generally mistrusted and contrasted with a different kind of civic discourse. In contrast, the head of another state school he visited was applauded by Mr Marsh because 'he was prepared to sit down with small groups of parents, in a room, and talk and answer questions'. In such a setting the father's own social skill could be directly brought to bear but also an interpersonal dimension is reintroduced. Somewhat in Giddensian fashion the head teacher was prepared to 'open out' his school and his values to parents, to 'work at' establishing trust; although, as it turned out for Mr Marsh even this school remained too much of a risk and he chose a private school for his child (see Chapter 7).

In one sense, there is a frustration of reason here, a reiteration of the lack of perfect and complete information, a sense of not knowing how much is enough but also a sense of knowing too much: 'I've been inundated with information' (Ms West). Choice has its downside: 'We have such a vast choice, we are lucky. I think it just clouds the issue, if you have too much choice, you just get confused' (Mrs Hillerman) and 'there's a lot of flux ... you tend to have to rely on friends' (Mrs Gosling).

It was a whole new world and we hadn't any close friends who'd been through that process so there wasn't that sort of modelling procedure to know what to do next, so it was all rather hand to mouth.

(Mrs Collins: Post-16 study)

These parents are very aware of the models of rational consumption which are embedded in published school and university guides and rating systems and local league tables but they constantly bump up against the limits of their own rationality. There is a tension between rationality and reaction. In their accounts affective response is almost always privileged over the careful evaluation of information. There is a final reliance, for most parents, on emotional reactions to institutions: 'it's a question of the feel of it' (Mrs Mankell) (see Chapter 4).

... we went to look at those three on an ordinary day, just to get the gut reaction ... the feel of what the places were like when they were full of kids ... doing ordinary things, not set up with special ... from there we shortlisted Overbury and Lockmere, at that point we'd have been happy with either ... I actually felt more comfortable ... in Overbury. Joseph felt more comfortable in Lockmere ...

(Mrs Hammet)

As Gorard (1997) found, people strive to be 'rational' but usually fail. Norms of parenting and parental responsibility are at work again here and, as noted previously, parents' accounts of their choosing behaviour are over-lain with a sense of obligation and often tinged with guilt. Here their failure to be rational, to be an ideal consumer, to live up to the expectations of the consuming subject discursively embedded in guides and tables leaves them with a sense not being good parents. There is also, obviously, a high level of effort involved in all this, the networking, visits, collection of materials and information-processing. These are some of the transaction costs of choice, which Szeter (1998: 11) argues are one source of social inequality arising from the insertion of markets into the public sector.

As ever perhaps, the closer one gets to the site of social action, the less clear-cut things become. This is not Giddens' 'run away world', filled with anxiety and dread, but uncertainty is certainly rife and parents frequently referred to their sense of panic in relation to school choice. Trust in schools as expert systems is unstable; although the private sector retains, for the most part, a bedrock of confidence. But parents are also uncertain about their own judgements. As Mrs McDermid put it, 'I don't know what I'm looking for'. In good part this may relate as much to values conflicts as it does to doubts about perception or understanding (see Chapter 6). There is then a degree of lack of 'confidence in the reliability of' (Giddens 1991: 34) persons and systems. Nonetheless, there are also indications of the impor-tant role of extant social networks, which rest upon trust in persons and face work commitment. 'We knew some people that had already gone there anyway, and we know one of the teachers there ... and we know a couple of people through the local branch of another organization, local members whose children went there' (Mrs Doyle). Communal perceptions, hearsay, gossip and reputation are all valuable and influential and point up again the middle-class duality of independence and the importance of self-reliance and influence, or individualism and collectivism. On the one hand, these influences and the establishing of school reputations are the basis for norms, judgements about good schools or the right sort of schools for 'people like us', what is appropriate or at least acceptable education. A damning remark by a reliable source can exclude a school from further consideration (see Ball 1987). There is a local excitement of opinion around these issues. On the other, there are well established class norms about making your own judgements, coming to an independent view. These parents sit somewhat uneasily between the two. As Mrs Dexter explained:

> though you try not to be, you are very influenced by the parents and what you hear and coming up to making a secondary school choice, in fact the phone rings all the time.
>
> (Mrs Dexter)

> I know a lot of people with older children ... I started ringing round, what did people think of the schools that their children were at, and what were the plusses and minuses. In fact I got Brian to organize a sort of questionnaire.
>
> (Mrs Crais)

Formal, social and personal views are set against and alongside one another; 'you hear things from people and you want to make up your own mind' (Mr Pelecanos). Both strong and weak ties, bonds and bridges are involved here and considerable volumes of social capital are used (Bourdieu 1986b: 249). According to Putnam, bonding reinforces exclusive identities and is 'inward looking' (Putnam 2000: 22) and bridging works 'across social cleavages'. Here both sorts of ties seem to rest upon forms of homogeneity. 'We sought people out and spoke to people who aren't close friends' (Mr Parker). Being a good parent, a responsible parent means taking all of this very seriously, collecting all the information available, exploiting all sources of information, striving to be rational, organized: 'Doing your homework ... Building up a dossier on a school ... Probably I should have spent a week there, but to be honest with you, you cannot do it' (Mrs West).

It is important to remind ourselves that these networks and the social capital that they generate are strongly classed. Their scope and boundaries and the substance of social interaction within them, especially in relation to school choice underpin a communal reproduction of class and class demarcations; 'recognition is endlessly affirmed and reaffirmed' (Bourdieu 1986a:

25). The social capital in such networks rests on a mutual habitus, a sharing of perspectives and of a sense of common self-interest and therefore confidence in the opinion of these significant others. While both Putnam and Coleman rely heavily in their accounts of social capital on notions of solidarity and belonging, they fail to relate these to any sense of class identity and class or other social divisions. Their norms are singular and uncontested. Clearly though there is no one seamless social network in play here, rather a myriad of separate and overlapping networks based on a variety of kinds of second-order relationships, although primary schools do provide one focal point which was often referred to. Neither do all these networks share the same evaluation of schools. Reputations are unstable and affective responses vary and can be swayed by fairly minor incidents or observations. And as addressed in Chapter 4, the particularity or uniqueness of the child makes different characteristics of a school more or less significant for any family. And for some, distance, transport and geography play their part in the overall evaluation of schools.

> There's a good strong drama department at Overbury. I was very impressed with the drama teacher ... the year she started ... then she left and went to Singapore ... and so ... although they got somebody else ... you do seem to latch on to certain teachers going round, and they give an impression ... and the head is very strong there, she gave a very good impression ... especially the first time when we heard her. There is slightly ... he would probably fit in more easily, he's a bit more outgoing than Adriana ... we tended to look at a slightly more warmer, cosy environment for her ...
>
> (Mrs Doyle)

Nonetheless, within these variations, again as indicated in Chapter 4, there are firm lines to be drawn in certain places. For some that is between the state and private sector. For the rest choosing within the state-sector, as we have seen, certain schools are revealed as being beyond serious consideration. For example, not one of the Riverway parents mentioned the possibility of sending their child to the local ecumenical school, Saint's, which mainly attracts students from Northwark and has a high proportion of minority ethnic students.

> ... obviously some schools in the area that are less well thought of than others ... and I presume that a lot of people don't want to send their children there. You see nobody I know of was even thinking of looking round at Saint's or something, nobody's looked round it, so I'm presuming that's a no no school. Nobody looked round Overbury which ... I know people that went there, I don't know why they didn't look round Overbury but they didn't ... and maybe it's to do with the tradition ... to do with the [primary] school you're at ...
>
> (Mrs West)

> I wouldn't send her to Saint's whatever happened, I would probably chain myself to the railings of Borough House.
>
> (Mrs Lovesey)

Putnam's social capital analysis is, as noted already, 'gender blind' (Morrow 1999: 749). Yet these 'choice networks' are strongly gendered, as one widower respondent realized: 'it's very much a female-led process' (Mr Christie). As is often the case, social ties and social relationships related to family life, 'the unceasing effort of sociability' (Bourdieu 1986b: 252), become the responsibility of the mother. Further, in so far as cultural capital is primarily transmitted within the family, its accumulation depends heavily on the family's 'usable time (particularly in the form of mother's free time)' (Bourdieu 1986b: 253). This is typically reinforced by the division of child care responsibilities within families. While families varied, in the overwhelming majority of cases it was the mother who dealt with the process of choosing school or university for that matter. Mothers were the main gatherers of information, of all kinds. They were the ones who were participants in the school gate communities at primary school – delivering and collecting children. There were only a few exceptions to this, as noted above.

Likewise almost all of the middle-class mothers in the higher education study were involved in visiting universities with their children. They also telephoned higher education institutions on behalf of their children and collected brochures and various kinds of 'hot' knowledge. Mothers and daughters, less so mothers and sons, represented choosing as a joint exercise (see David, Ball, Davies, and Reay 2002). They acted as 'composite choosers' (Foskett and Hesketh 1997).

> Mark never really discussed it properly, he just wouldn't and we did try, but Susan is 'what about this mum or so and so's mum says this what do you think' and we go on like that ...
>
> (Mrs Haggard: Post-16 study)

Some of the mothers work, and the nature of social relationships within the middle-class families, particular as these are focused upon achieving and assuring forms of educational success and distinction for their children, and the processes of sculpting aspirations and expectations, can be glimpsed in the following long extract. This also indicates something of Mrs Summer's expectations of her daughter's school, expectations which in this instance they failed to fulfil. The sense of responsibility of the parent, and the attendant guilt are clearly evident (see Chapter 4). And there is some indication of the tension that Reay (2000: 580) draws attention to between emotional wellbeing and educational success. Reay suggests that: 'If emotional capital is to be viewed as inextricably linked to educational success then it sometimes appears to be at the cost of both mothers' and their children's well-being'. The expressed as opposed to inferred interests and needs of the child may not be the same (see Chapter 6). This extract also relates back to the central theme of this study – middle-class anxieties around social reproduction in a congested labour market and various forms of capital are in play here. If you only read one of the extracts quoted in this chapter, read this one.

> Anyway we just went for the open day at Cambridge and she just felt she was against it. She also, I don't think had a great deal of confidence. She said other people had been chucked out and so on, hadn't got in who should have got in ... I pressed her and she got upset about applying to Cambridge. She wouldn't be happy there. So I thought I'd drop the issue. And I asked her from time to time – when has your UCAS form got to be in? And she said plenty of time, plenty of time ... So when she started filling in the UCAS form, I said why don't you put down Cambridge. And she said no I can't do that, it's closed. It closes two weeks before everyone else. I sort of really felt annoyed about this because the school had not told me what the timetable was. They never sent anything out ... over the road, at the Catholic school I noticed that they had a schedule of visits on the board for girls to go to Oxbridge colleges ... If Maitland had done this Catherine might well have had a different attitude ... I mean, she was clearly Oxbridge material. I mean she is fluent in French. And I am quite happy with her at Nottingham in one sense, but you see I have been around and I have seen the realities of the situation in the employment market. However much people say – Oh! it doesn't really matter where you go – the facts are that an Oxbridge degree is, in many ways, better than say, a Leicester degree, which is what I have got. So I felt very upset about it. I felt I'd let her down by not going on about it, but I did not know you see. I am not opposed to redbrick universities, but I am concerned about the level of standards falling ... I think this is bringing down the reputation of universities. So I hope Nottingham is not like that. I mean you can be sure with Cambridge but I am not sure about Nottingham. I think it's terrible she gets me going on at her about Cambridge and then when she gets around to thinking I may have some good points she then finds the door is bolted anyway ... I just feel I let Catherine down, really. Because I had arguments with her about Cambridge at the beginning and we both got stressed out about it, then I dropped the whole thing for a long time. And unfortunately that was the critical time that I should have been pressing it ...

All of this involves what Bourdieu (1986b: 253) describes as 'the gratuitous expenditure of time, attention, care and concern'. And invested in and underpinning the use of social and cultural capital is, as noted, another sort of capital, emotional capital (Reay 1998a).[6] The support and encouragement, and 'warming up' and 'cooling out' of the child, the sculpting of family decision-making (Hemsley-Brown 1996), making the child feel involved but nonetheless clear about what is important and possible and what is not, by rehearsing cultural scripts, are all aspects of emotional labour mostly undertaken by mothers (see Reay and Ball 1998). Blumin (1989: 191 quoted in Savage, Barlow, Dickens and Fielding 1992) goes as far as arguing that 'middle-class formation [is] women's work'. Also, as we have seen, some middle-class families are able to supplement their own emotional capital and extend their time budgets by buying-in commercial forms of practical and emotional support. This begins with child care (Vincent and Ball 2001) and extends to commercial play and development activities (Tumbletots, swimming classes, music and dance and so on, at a cost of £4 per half-hour, see Chapter 7) and to the use of tutors, advisers and counsellors. These experiences provided by parents for their children, even from a very young age, can be seen as part of the process of making up the child as a certain sort of educational subject. These experiences both develop basic skills and capabilities which constitute the child as able, and have a more direct practical relevance to school work. They are also investments in cultural capital, particular in the form of music and art skills and appreciation. Some sense of the complexity of this making up is evident from the following extracts where Mrs Deighton and then Mrs Fleming, from the child care study, describe some of their children's extra-curricula experiences.

I go to the playgroup with her on Friday mornings, and she gets that in addition to the nursery school, and the music group, we do a music group as well on Tuesday which we've just this week started, the same place, for half an hour, well to call it singing would be a little bit of an exaggeration ... we felt quite strongly that Seven Steps had been very good for Harriet and had been very fair to us too, and we always felt treated like a valued customer, and we were comfortable with the routines, with the regimes, the staff, there's a lot of extra curricular activity, they go swimming once a week, and when they're a little bit older a lady comes in once a week to do music and movement with them, they can have French lessons, I mean French at the age of two and a half is a ridiculous concept, but I think it's the concept of other stimulation and exposure to other things, and also I guess, there's a little bit of being disciplined there, you know, they have to sit around the table and spout French words for half an hour or something and soon enough they're at school and they've got to get used to it ...

Larry goes to Tumble Tots, although he, that hasn't been an enormous success, he doesn't really like it, I mean Brenda takes him, and according to Brenda he just took a dislike to the ladies that were standing on the equipment, and as I say, they're not groupy children, so just because other children are going on things, my children don't necessarily do it, so yes, he's done a term of Tumble Tots, no two nearly, and he really doesn't do much, so he's changing to something else which is called Tin Pan Annie, which is a music group. Frances also did, erm she did Blueberries which was a music group at the contact centre, and she did Tumble Tots, erm she did ballet for a while at the contact centre, but got bored with that, I think she found it a bit much when she started school ...

For mothers the commercial sessions were also an investment in the development of social capital, places where they would meet other mothers like them and share and exchange ideas about child-rearing and information about nurseries, courses, schools, etc. Mrs Baron conveys a sense of careful deliberateness to this, and an intertwining of her social capital with that of her child.

I hope even more as time goes on at this new nursery, to meet other parents who've got children exactly the same age, where I don't necessarily have to do that networking myself, although I do as well, but it's another additional aspect of her friends that we're building now.

This is where Coleman's notion of social capital within the family is also relevant. In his terms such capital accrues to the child from the *knowledge, support* and *expectations* provided by parents. Or, in other words, for Coleman the success of children in school and society rests upon the parent's ability to build social capital within the family, in the form of communication, trust and a sense of shared responsibility. This is not all that far distant, albeit in a different lexicon, from Bourdieu and Boltanski's (2000: 905) point that:

... the owners of diversified capital, with a strong cultural component, have everything to gain by maintaining the family ties which allow them to pool the capital possessed by each of the members. Thus, the network of family relations can be the locus of an unofficial or even clandestine circulation of capital ...

Again the interweaving and inter-relationship of different forms of capital is crucial. Knowledge takes a variety of forms but the understanding of and ability to manipulate expert systems, however limited, is a crucial resource. These are field-dependent tactical resources. Support and communication is both emotional and practical, both care and concern and time and energy, but also rests upon the ability to mobilize, when relevant, formal support or remedial systems, as we have seen. In these respects, as Walkerdine, Lucey and Melody (2001: 126) argue: '"Fighting" for your child is something that middle-class parents are far more emotionally and materially equipped and discursively positioned to do'. The communication of expectations also embed the child in an imagined future, in a sense of what they could and should aspire to, in the form of a normal biography. This is important in linking the here and now to a possible and realizable future and the planning of the steps, the trajectory, which can realize the relationship between the two. The once fashionable notion of deferred gratification plays its part here. The important thing is to have options, possibilities. Not to have routes or alternatives closed off. This is a matter, literally and figuratively, of positioning the child so that advantage can be taken of different possibilities. As Mrs Rendell, from the Child Care choice study, talking about her three-year-old, explained:

> ... the school around the corner, one of the best primary schools in the borough, that was a big reason for moving ... the primary school. About a third of the children at that school go on to competitive private secondary schools ... not as if we necessarily want to do that but it's quite nice to have the option.

The middle-class orientation to what Prout (1999) calls futurity is fostered by and feeds into the fears and anxieties of the middle class in relation to social reproduction and underpins a sense of needing to plan and anticipate, and is also key to the notion of investment in the child. Again the duality of emotions, confidence and anxiety, which run through the parents' narratives have, as Barbalet (2001: 89) puts it, temporal states as 'their very objects'; they are 'anticipatory emotions' (see Chapter 7).

In some ways this chapter has covered a lot of ground and yet in other ways it has only begun to scratch the surface of the complex and sophisticated uses of forms of capital by the middle class in the fields of education. I have concentrated on social capital (I have more to say about economic capital in Chapter 6) but I hope that it has become clear that the different forms cannot be separated out in their deployment nor in some respects conceptually. The use of and investment in social capital requires and produces cultural and emotional capital. Social capital requires emotional work and emotional capital can be supplemented by economic capital and so on. Any deployment of these concepts must involve some heurism; they are a way of simplifying and formalizing class practices and the work of achieving class advantage for the purpose of analysis. Nonetheless, they do useful analytic work and begin to fill in some of the multi-faceted ways in which social reproduction is achieved by agency and application and the adept deployment of relevant capitals by families. We begin to see the jagged, uneven and negotiated aspects of reproduction. We can also see the points at which reproduction may not be achieved. Bourdieu and Boltanski's (2000: 903) point that 'the educational system depends less directly on the demands of the production system than on the demands of reproducing the family group' seems from this perspective to be very apt, as does Wilkes's (1990: 127) comment that families 'should be the units of study for class analysis'. There are also some indications here, again, of different distributions of capitals and different volumes of capitals across the middle class. At points here the differences between state and private school middle-class families and between middle-class and working-class families in state sector schools are stark, certainly with respect to forms and volumes both of social and economic capital. The gendered nature of reproduction is also absolutely clear, the invisible work of mothers as 'status maintainers' (Brantlinger, Majd-Jabbari and Guskin 1996: 589) is crucial to the development and knitting together and activation of different forms of capital.

6 Values and principles
Social justice in the head

This is not, on the whole, a pretty story, but one marred by prejudice, delusion, and even, at a deeper level, self-loathing.

(Ehrenreich 1989: 11)

Overwhelmingly, the existing literature on parents and school choice either excludes consideration of values altogether, or relegates values to a subordinate role. In a sense this is one of a number of ways in which this literature is 'captured by the discourse' (Bowe, Ball and Gewirtz 1994) it seeks to explain. Both advocates of choice and choice theories tend to rely on narrow rational and utilitarian conceptualizations of the chooser. There is an emphasis on the functional role of self-interest. As noted in Chapter 2, Goldthorpe's work is one example where pre-eminence is given to calculation, and Hatcher's (1998) critique of this was quoted. Altogether little attention is given to values in research into choice and this is part of a more general neglect of the ethical dimensions of social arrangements like the market within social research – Johnathan (1989), Bottery (1992), Halstead (1994), Grace (1995 and 2002) being notable exceptions. It is worth reiterating Morgan's (1989: 29) point that an over-emphasis on rational calculation can lead to a 'diminishment of our moral understanding of human agency': it is sociologically inadequate. As Jordan, Redley and James (1994: 4) suggest: the 'denizen of the marketplace – homo economicus is somewhat emaciated'. Attention to the role of values and principles in decision-making disturbs the neat simplicities of homo economicus.

The personal aims, interests and desires of individuals are, as Nagel (1991: 14) puts it, 'the raw material from which ethics begins'. This chapter works with some of that raw material and is about the ethics of the education marketplace as enacted through the principles and practices of middle-class families as they attempt to realize their desires for their children in the immediate and for the future within various social and ethical contexts. In previous work I began to explore how the education market calls up and legitimates a certain sort of ethics in the practices and perspectives of education providers (Ball 1997; Ball, Maguire and Macrae

1997; Ball 1998). I argued that a shift is 'taking place in schools and colleges from ... "professional" values or the values of "professional community"' (Grace 1995) to the values of the market (see also Gewirtz, Ball and Bowe 1995 and Gewirtz 2001). That is, where there is competition to recruit, non-market values and professional ethics are being devalued and displaced by the need to sell schools and colleges and make and manage image in the competitive education marketplace. In other words, the incentives of the education market encourage commercial responses and marginalize professional ethics. The discourses of policy which animate and infuse the market work to provide a climate of legitimation and vocabulary of motives which make new ways of action thinkable, possible and acceptable and old ways seem less appropriate. Thus, within the educational context the pedagogy of the market teaches and disseminates 'a new morality' (Ball 1998). One part of this shift, I suggest, is the articulation of a market ontology producing new kinds of moral subjects and changing the ways in 'which we think about ourselves, the criteria and norms we use to judge ourselves' (Rose 1992: 161). The result is 'an attenuated creature' (Cohen 1992: 183). This chapter considers just how attenuated that market creature might be.

However, the education market does not invent or import an entirely new values system, rather it draws upon classical liberal views underpinned by a political and economic individualism which is deeply embedded within modern Western societies. This individualism hails and celebrates independent and rational beings 'who are the sole generators of their own wants and preferences and the best judges of their own interests' (Lukes 1974: 79). Choice, then, is a key concept in the political articulation of these beings. The idea, as Bauman (1993: 4) puts it, is of individuals with 'identities not-yet-given' which in their construction over time involve the making of choices. These values stand over and against those of the fragile discourse of welfare, wherein the state represents collective interests, supports universalism and manages politics to support all members of the citizen community. These embedded values are given new impetus and a new kind of discursive validity within our contemporary market society – 'the horizon within which more and more people live ever-larger parts of their lives' (Slater and Tonkiss 2001: 203). This market society entails ' ... the privatist dissipation of normative self-obligations and institutional ties' and displays 'unmistakable tendencies towards social closure' (Berking 1996: 190). Thus, 'social protectionism' presents itself 'as a promising strategy in the competitive struggle for material and symbolic advantage – all of these phenomena conjure up the image of a society whose assets in solidarity and legitimacy are exhausted' (Berking 1996: 190). Bourdieu (1986a: 369) addresses these changes in a rather oblique way when he refers to a transformation in the mode of social reproduction, which means that 'scholastic errors tend to count more than moral errors, with academic anxiety, previously a more male concern, replacing ethical anxiety'.

However, despite the pessimism of Berking and others, the ethics of the market are not, as I hope to show, hegemonic. They are contested or struggled over in the head or at least in some heads, in the 'profound complexity and disparity' (Cohen 1992: 184) of what Cohen (1992: 183) calls 'empirical pragmatics', that is, as set within the practices of liberal individualism (Johnathan 1989). Here I want to extend my previous examination to focus on the consumer in the education market. In particular, the decision-making related to choice between state and private schooling provides a rich nexus of personal conflicts within which ethical positions are formulated or tested in relation to practice. Again, I will be picking up themes introduced in previous chapters – those of individualism, responsibility and guilt, and in relation to these the contradictory role of the middle-class collectivity, what Jordan, Redley and James (1994: 77) call the 'microcommunities of mutual commitment' – the 'other side' of privatism and independence.

There are, embedded in the literatures on class and on choice, two distinct themes: one which portrays middle-class families as, *sui generis*, decidedly self-interested and calculating; the other, reinforcing this, points up the various effects and consequences of the market ethic as contributing to the destruction of collective social relations and commitments.[1] In other words, the generation of a 'consumer ethic' which 'produces consumers who are isolated' and therefore 'untrammelled by the constraints and brakes imposed by collective memories and expectations' (Bourdieu 1986a: 371). This literature is supported more generally by recent work on individuation within high modernity (Giddens 1991; Beck 1992).

Nonetheless, as I have suggested this is only half of the story, the individualism of the school consumer is, in particular locations, mediated and encouraged through collective and familial memories and expectations. I will explore this further. I shall also take up again a tricky issue which is embedded in some of the earlier discussion. I have argued in previous chapters that the strategies of social advantage pursued by middle-class families have untoward, exploitative consequences for other social groups. These others find themselves closed off or excluded from certain advantageous roles and routes, and often confronted as a result with services of a poorer standard. I want to consider how it is that middle-class families 'prioritise their commitments to others, how they reconcile conflicting demands arising from these priorities, and the extent to which they recognise the wider social relevance of their actions' (Jordan, Redley and James 1994: 4). Jordan, Redley and James (1994: 12), drawing on their interviews with middle-class families, are unequivocal; they find that 'when there was a clash between their political principles and the best interests of their children, they should put the family first'. The picture here is not quite so clear-cut, and perhaps the simplest and best position from which to start is Pahl and Wallace's (1985: 106) point that family choices and strategies may well be invested with 'a mixture of rationalities'.

I would like to make two further points of clarification here before I move on. First, there are problems of tone and standpoint in discussions of this kind. I shall not make facile claims about even-handedness but I will attempt to maintain a healthy level of reflexivity in relation to my presentation. Second, I am using the terms values and principles somewhat loosely, but I shall try to reserve values to refer to general, embedded beliefs and principles to refer to commitments which are related to the impersonal standpoint – matters of social good or civic virtue.

I have tried to indicate that strategies of social closure are both informed and driven by a degree of reflexive knowingness but also firmly shaped by the dispositions and practical sense and inventions of habitus. The question is, as White (1994: 83) puts it: 'Can one be a good parent and a bad citizen?'. To what extent are these families aware of the effects and consequences of their actions, or should we simply accept the dictum offered by Dreyfus and Rabinow (1983: 189) that 'people know what they do; they frequently know why they do what they do: but [very often] they don't know what what they do does'. In the simplest, and maybe on this occasion the most useful, sense, we need once more to slip away from a binary, either/or position. That is, it is neither the case that middle-class families are cynical individualists who recognize that they contribute to, and indeed are motivated by, the creation of social inequalities; nor are they merely trying to do the best for their own children without having any real sense that their individual actions might have large social consequences. Rather, we all act within unclear and contradictory values systems which are complexly and unevenly related to our social practices. Our ethics are socially situated and realized within a variety of material and discursive contexts and often involve 'delicate balances' (White 1994: 92). In other words, 'We see things from here' as Nagel (1991: 10) puts it, from an individual point of view, or more appropriately for our purposes, from the point of view of the family but at particular times and in specific places. Over and against this is the issue or challenge of seeing that what is true for us is also 'true of others' (10). This is the problem of recognizing others as ourselves. In practice class and race identities rip across this possibility, as we have already seen. Running through the processes of schooling and choice for middle-class families is a strong sense of boundaries between 'us' and 'others' – a sense of 'other' families as not 'normal', as not intelligible in terms of our values, attitudes and behaviour. The whole point is that these others are not easily recognizable or understood, what is there for 'us' does not seem to be true for 'them'. Nonetheless, against this, principles have their part to play within the liberal social identities which many of these families claim for themselves. Without any sarcasm intended, they are caring people and people who care. Within all of this, in making decisions about the schooling of their children, the families represented here are engaged in a complex cobbling together of values and principles, all a part of what van Zanten and Veleda (2001) call 'ethical bricolage'. However, the value of putting the family first, in one way or another, remains the centrepiece of this decision-making. In philosophical and common-sense terms this is all very proper. Morally, parents have a right, even a duty perhaps, to do their best to get an adequate education for their children. Action taken to benefit a child is not strictly self-interested. We are not required to treat our intimates in the same ways as we treat or think about others. These are 'sound motives' (McLaughlin 1994). Again, in philosophical terms, there are actions we are entitled to take even though they may not lead to the best of all possible overall outcomes. It would be difficult to lead a normal life otherwise. However, clearly for some parents, as we have seen already, their concerns go beyond adequacy to a commitment to achieve maximal positional advantage for their child. This is not easy to defend on moral grounds, particularly as it involves an explicit awareness of, and in effect a condoning of, inequalities of provision. However, Johnathan (1989: 334) does suggest that arguments can be made that parents have a duty to secure the interests of their child 'even (or especially) in circumstance where they are in competition with the interests of children in general'.[2] There is a further difficulty enmeshed in all of this, something that was flagged in Chapter 5; that is, how do we know what is the best for the child? Is it simply what parents say it is? Is 'best' a singular notion? In particular is what is best now the same as what might be best for their child in the future? This is the basis of deferred gratification. It also raises the question of the child's role in deciding what is in its best interests. All of this means that within the interviews the parents are frequently engaged in sophisticated processes of reworking, recovery and *post hoc* legitimation. They are also inconsistent or contradictory at times. Also some are simply unsure that they are doing the right or the best thing and are torn between doing their best and doing right – in their own terms. Let us see!

So I want to run three arguments together here: first, that middle-class values privilege certain sorts of selfish, or at least short-sighted individualism; second, that the market feeds and exacerbates this to produce attenuated beings. Third, neither of the previous are adequate in all cases to account for the complex, situated values which are involved in decision-making about schooling. In effect this is a story that can be told in more than one way – more or less sympathetically or cynically – again, though, I shall try to elude the temptations of the simple binary and steer between the two. I certainly will not be offering a simple answer to any of the questions asked above and my own emphasis in terms of sympathy or judgement shifts over time.

Some writers, like Kohn (1998) and Brantlinger, Majd-Jabbari and Guskin (1996) take up a strongly cynical position. Kohn describes parents who opposed detracking reforms in the US as 'in effect sacrificing other children to their own' (571). That is, they are locked absolutely within the personal standpoint, within which self-interest and aggregative principles predominate. Their concern is clearly with advantage rather than adequacy. These self-interested parents might be seen in Barber's (1994) terms: 'oblivious to that essential human interdependency that underlies all political life'

(25). Brantlinger, Majd-Jabbari and Guskin (1996: 590), reporting an interview study of US mothers, point to a simple contradiction between what their respondents say and what they do. They conclude that: 'Results indicate that educated middle-class mothers, perceived by others as well as themselves as liberals who believe in integrated and inclusive education, often support segregated and stratified schools structures that mainly benefit students of the middle class'.

A glimpse of the seedier side of the education market and its particular ethics is offered through examples of what Williamson (1975) calls 'opportunism'; that is, 'the incomplete or distorted disclosure of information, especially calculated efforts to mislead, distort, disguise, obfuscate or otherwise confuse ...' (47). On the demand side of the education market in the UK, there are two fairly common examples of opportunism which have been reported in the press. One is the use of false addresses by parents attempting to get their children accepted in schools which are over-subscribed and operate with residence qualifications for admission. (Van Zanten reports the same tactic used in Paris.) Another is the tactical deployment of religious affiliation as an entry qualification to over-subscribed faith schools. In an article in *The Guardian* (22 April 2002: 5) Catherine Bennett, under a headline 'A cheat's guide to getting into a good school', discussed the example of a Birmingham family who 'have devised a plan' to have their daughter adopted by her aunt, who lives in the catchment area of their preferred school. *The Sunday Telegraph* in an article (2 July 2000 – www.telegraph.co.uk) reported that: 'the leader of Britain's independent school bursars has accused middle-class parents of cheating the tax-payer in an attempt to gain cheap private education for their children'. Mike Sant, Secretary of the Independent Schools Bursars' Association was reported as saying 'Assisted places were designed for bright children of poor parents who had no money. I'm sure some deserving children got through, but the reality was that it was hijacked by the middle classes' (see also Chapters 3 and 4). On the supply side there are matching distortions and obfuscations. A recent example is the Coopers school in Essex, a school which is committed to a Christian ethos, which according to a government ombudsman had illicitly used interviews with prospective parents, which were intended to probe religious commitment, to ask questions about children's hobbies and other things, as a means of social selection of applicants (*The Independent*, 9 March 2002). The Labour government had prohibited the use of interviews in this way. Such behaviours may well be increasing; by definition they are difficult to access and they give support to the general thesis being developed here, but my main focus is on the rather more ordinary ethics that are embedded in choosing, and getting a place, in school.

The ethical dilemmas and embedded values invested in school choice are pointed up particularly well, particularly sharply, as I have suggested above, when it comes to choosing between state and private schools. I will use this as a focus for the major part of this chapter. I shall employ two different presentational and interpretational devices to illustrate and develop the issues adumbrated above. First, I will outline an heuristic model or map of choice which attends specifically to values issues. I will then work through two case studies of family values and choice – those of the Simpsons and the Goslings.

I want to propose a map which will allow us to look at the ethical dilemmas of choice in an orderly way. This map is drawn from and based upon the analysis of parents' accounts of their choice-making. It is a dynamic relational model; the elements are not free-standing categories, they are interacting dimensions in the empirical pragmatics of choice. Only rarely does one element predominate; more typically they interplay to produce analytic complexity and individual doubt and confusion. However, there are particular interpretational difficulties embedded in this kind of analysis and discussion, more than is usually the case when working with qualitative data. How far can we accept these accounts and the motives and rationales presented at face value? To what extent can we read off or read into these accounts value rationalities? Indeed to what extent are these respondents ever clear themselves of the reasons for their choices when values are set in relation to other sorts of more practical concerns? What I would suggest here is that rather than seeing the examination of values-in-use as indictments or critical accounts of individuals or families, they be regarded as different possible 'types' of decision-making; although, as we shall see, there are some examples where the role of values in relation to choice seems absolutely clear-cut. As noted with respect to other issues the narratives vary in the extent of reflexivity that they display. It also has to be borne in mind, as Jordan, Redley and James (1994: 6) point out, that the interview situation, from which these data were elicited, requires the respondents to produce a morally adequate account of themselves. This is done through their 'management of accounts' (6). Some parents were keen to establish, within the interview, a 'liberal identity' (Brantlinger, Majd-Jabbari and Guskin 1996). However, this management is not always convincing.

While some aspects of the map may seem straightforward, overall I want to stress the messiness and the difficulties which are involved in plotting the work done by values rather than come to any clear-cut resolutions. However, Jordan, Redley and James (1994: 141) make the point that in their study it was in the context of choice of school 'that the concept of "putting the family first" was most explicitly deployed'. In effect the various elements of the map are contextual or contingent factors within which, or in relation to which, principles operate. The work done by principles in decision-making varies in terms of possibility or significance accordingly (see Figure 6.1).

Cost produces the first contingency here. For some parents their inability to afford private school fees means that they avoid the values dilemmas that might arise in choosing between state and private. But in the accounts given there are ambivalences even here. Different sorts of values are in play – personal and impersonal standpoints. Parents who appear to be both unable

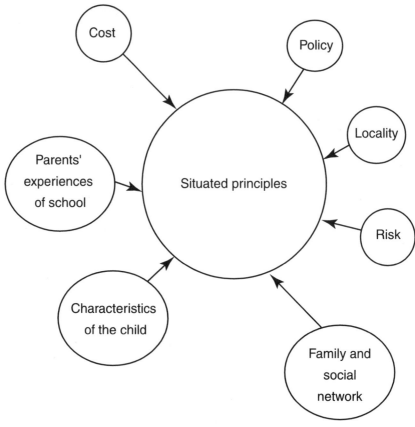

Figure 6.1 An heuristic map of choice of school

and unwilling to send their children to private school often give consideration to the private sector. In part, as noted previously, this arises from their
sense of obligation to take choice seriously, to give due consideration to all
the options, in the best interests of their child. All possibilities need to be
considered even if some possibilities are unlikely or indeed unwelcome.
Jordan, Redley and James (1994: 142) note the same thing. Mrs Rankin for
example explained:

> ... we looked at the glossy pictures, then we looked at our bank balance
> ... and we couldn't possibly have afforded it anyway, I think we knew
> all along that he'd go to Milton, but we felt we ought to go through the
> motions, so that he felt he hadn't just been shoved into the sausage
> machine, like his brothers ...

As Mrs Rankin indicates, this is in part to do with recognizing the individuality of this child, and not treating choice for him as foregone. The

ethics within the family, to which we will return, mean treating each child as of equal worth. But as Mrs Rankin says, the family did look at their bank balance. It is unclear what would have followed if the family's finances had been different, but then they 'knew all along' that he would be attending a state comprehensive. Nonetheless, choice brings with it obligations which need to be attended to, and these are reinforced, as we shall see, by more immediate expectations and pressures. This is one small example of the interpretational difficulties involved here. We will return to the Rankins. There is perhaps an element here of what Bauman (1998: 58) calls 'the public manifestation of connoisseurship'. The need to be seen to exercise the right to choose and celebrate visits to the marketplace, and the gratifications of choosing such that an object 'freely chosen has the power to bestow that distinction on its chooser which objects "just allotted" obviously do not possess' (58–9). Bauman goes on to conclude that: 'Consumerism and the welfare state are therefore at cross-purposes' (59).

The Fyfields, both teachers, chose a state school for their son, but were certain that they would have tried for a private school if their financial position had allowed. Mr Fyfield was clear that 'what we couldn't do for both we wouldn't do for one'. However, 'if we won the pools, before he's in the fourth year, then we would see about the private sector'. The Graftons, who also chose a state school for their child, also indicated the way in which private schools had been part of their exercise of due care in choice-making. They also illustrate the costs and time involved in gearing up for private school. Again various cultural and social capitals and financial resources are required in order to position children favourably in relation to choice – to make certain choices possible. Choice here is not free-floating; it involves costs or investments. In effect there is a complex chain of decision-making which occurs over time. Planning and futurity are again central to the making up of the child in relation to educational opportunities. The Graftons did not want to feel 'rushed':

> ... if we wanted Angus to go privately he would have to be tutored, and it takes about two years really ... for them to get used to the idea of having to sit exams, doing things within a time limit, and they are just taught in a different way in the private sector, so if you really want to do that you've got to give your child a fair chance ... so we thought we wouldn't feel rushed in our decision that's why we started looking two years ago.

The Graftons also display an ambivalence between values and costs, an absence of ethical closure, and again we see the role of ethics inside the family. They also have uncertainties about the state sector. Here there is a variety of un-joined-up and pragmatic principles at work.

Well first I think state education should work, should be a viable option and also that it's very nice to have local friends. Apart from that ideologically we are pro state education ... but ... and also it's a huge amount of money. Perhaps one could afford it for one child but you can't offer all your children ... and private schools are probably around 5,000 a year ... so it actually shouldn't be worth it, in my view, the state should provide a good education.

The language here is unresolved – coulds, shoulds and buts. Costs reinforce values but there is no absolute principled dismissal of the private possibility. However, in contrast, for other parents the private sector was the only option. Costs had to be borne, even if sacrifices had to be made, and impersonal principles play no real part, if the state sector is deemed to be not good enough.

I resent the fact that we were forced into the private sector. Money won't be easy, we're not confident that our work will give us enough money to keep both of the children in private schools throughout secondary school, and we will be missing out on holidays which would have been very nice for the children ... holidays abroad. But we are making sacrifices in order to go to a private school. But really the state schools should be good enough, that we don't have to send them to private schools.

(Mrs Bellingham)

I don't know that I would have wanted there to have been actually selective schools, I don't know that I would ... I think that does, to some extent, go against the grain ... although we were looking at that when we were looking at the private sector. I wouldn't want them to have the kind of rigid education that is offered in say Marshalls Grammar, I wouldn't want them to have what we had. I think the world has moved on from what we got.

(Mrs Mankell)

In the second extract, the abstract opposition to selective and private schools sits fairly unproblematically alongside a serious consideration of both possibilities. Somehow the principles and the pragmatics get separated off from one another. In the end, despite concerns about size and a lack of diversity, the Mankells chose a state comprehensive for their son. Nonetheless, the private sector remained a fall-back, and Mrs Mankell intended to remain vigilant for signs that her son was not 'being stretched' (Chapter 4).

I think if we're not happy we're not going to be happy about them being stretched enough, for various reasons, and if we do that I think we would both have to start looking at the private sector ... again, more seriously. But we hope we never will, we are impressed with what they can do ... .

As Jordan, Redley and James (1994: 146) found, the 'carefully reasoned' accounts of choice offered by parents work as 'generalised guidelines, and that actual decisions are often taken in the wake of events or developments that are inherently unpredictable'. Even so these parents do not intend to be taken by surprise. There are very few examples of clear-cut, once-and-for-all principles at work in these parents' accounts (see case study families below). Mrs Rankin believes 'passionately' in comprehensive education. But this does not mean that any comprehensive will do. She perceives comprehensive schools to be different and some to be unacceptable. What is not clear is whether such unacceptability is based on educational or demographic criteria or some combination of the two. School choice allows her to put her commitments into practice. It allows her to choose a comprehensive and not to have to accept any comprehensive. This is one way of retaining middle-class commitment to the state sector (Chapter 3). Thus these principles are situated in a particular way within policy. And in stark contrast to other parents, even if the academic progress of her children is not what she would wish, Mrs Rankin sees other social benefits of a comprehensive schooling. On the whole, parents' expectations of schools are primarily utilitarian (cf. Woods, Bagley and Glatter 1998), although issues of social mixing, the relationships between school and the real world, are of importance for a small minority of parents.

> ... really that's a lot to do with my politics and my husband's politics, that I passionately believe in comprehensive education, or in state education ... and I think it holds a lot of very good things for children, I wouldn't want them to be closeted away from the real world, I'd rather they went out and saw ... what life was really like for a lot of people ... and understood it. I can see there are faults in it, I think the first two years at the school they wasted their time ... both of my two elder ones. They back-pedalled a lot ... and they didn't get on with work, but I still wouldn't change my mind, I still would want them to go to a comprehensive school, even knowing that ... when it came to the time to send Tim there ... knowing that he would probably back-pedal for a couple of years, I still saw advantages we well had two things very strongly on our mind, one was we wanted co-ed for him, because again three sons ... and so I do believe that boys benefit from being taught alongside girls ... and we both very strongly believe in comprehensive education, so we wanted a comprehensive school ... co-educational school. And there wasn't an awful lot of choice in Northwark in those days. There was a school which in fact was nearer to us, which now I probably would have sent them to, because it's changing, it's getting a good reputation, it has a strong Head, and its reputation is improving a lot, but in those days it was a pretty grim place, with a lot of fights outside the

school and ... a not very attractive building, so that was off the list. I think we looked at an all-boys school, just so that we didn't make our decision without at least having looked at something else, and that absolutely horrified me, it was just like a seething bed of aggression, I didn't like it at all.

Mrs Archer and Mrs Hammet illustrate what Jordan, Redley and James (1994: 146) call the provisionality of decision-making. Both mothers rehearse their fears about the risks of the state sector, over and against their principles. Mrs Archer also talks of the value of mix (see below) and Mrs Hammet is uncomfortable with the expressive culture of the independent school she visited. In both cases these families are 'putting their principles first'. They have not entirely lost the 'vocabulary of association' (Jordan, Redley and James 1994: 43) but we do see the tensions between public principles and private obligations. Again the state sector is seen as full of risks. It could be said that this makes their decision all that more laudable. The Archers and the Hammets, husbands and wives, are all public sector professionals.

> ... both of us feel quite strongly about all children having equal opportunity till school-leaving age at least, and so ... sometimes you have a quandary, cos both of them are reasonably bright and I think that both of them could have got into Trinity or Madeley High [private schools] ... you wonder sometimes if when you're sending them to a comprehensive school, you know, if they get in a bad class it can affect them, but no, we've been happy with that, the choice seems okay. There's a range of ability which is what we wanted, and a good range of background, not just the privileged background you'd predominately get in the independent sector.

> We looked at Highway Grammar and we agonized over it, it was more a fear of letting our principles get in the way, feeling in ten years' time, would we wish ... would they have suffered for our principles, do you know what I mean, it was this kind of niggling doubt. So we went to look at it. But I didn't feel as convinced as I thought I might have done. I didn't like the way it felt ...

Mrs Archer expresses the dilemmas of personal and impersonal principles, the moral obligation to the child and family as against an abstract social good very clearly. An adequate education is basic and necessary but not the only consideration. Certainty and closure are elusive. She 'agonized', is left with 'niggling doubts' and 'didn't feel convinced'. Bersteinian ambivalences abound. The Symons' commitment to state schooling is in part based on their own experience of state schools. But here again things are not as clear-cut as they might at first seem; selective schools were considered as a possibility, and what starts out as a complete objection to paying for school becomes something to be considered if circumstances made it necessary – 'we weren't on principle opposed to paying'. Indeed, the Symons seem to privilege a set of calculative and utilitarian concerns. Impersonal values and principles are hard things to pin down when it comes to making difficult decisions and can very quickly become sidelined when set over and against other values embedded in putting the family first.

> ... so this is our kind of general approach ... and it's been true for both kids. We really wanted state schools, our general feeling is we did very well at state schools and we're blowed if you should have to pay extra ... because it is paying extra, you pay for state schools, so therefore you pay extra for fee-paying, and we on principle, were ... if you like, not against grammar ... we have friends who are ... and who would never ... therefore quite a few years ago we knew that Sutton had never stopped their grammar schools, and although that's not completely on our doorstep, it's not a crazy distance, so we've always had this in the back of our minds. The Northwark schools ... on balance again we'd rather have kids in borough, why go out if you don't have to ... we knew the Northwark schools had changed up and down and around, over a period of years ... so we just kept an open mind. And I did actually get some very general information about fee-paying schools ... way back, really, because we thought again ... we preferred state, but we weren't on principle opposed to paying if we couldn't get a good education, other than that way, but we've always taken the view that they go to state schools unless there's reasons why not, and so for our son, we looked at a number of the local and not so local Northwark schools ...

Mrs Highsmith represents the *ad hocery* of most of the families, and the justification of public and private values, very precisely when she explained that: 'you will do what you want to do, even if it isn't really what you want to do'. The deployment of principles might best be described as fuzzy, and in relation to school choice they are certainly situated. In part, as several of the parents made clear, they are situated in the literal sense. It was, more or less, possible to take up particular principled stances towards the schooling of their child, given the sorts of schools available to them in their locality, and in relation to the sort of child involved. Some respondents were frank enough to indicate that their principles might not have operated in the same way in a different locality: 'the effects of our actions are altered by the context and because we ourselves are transformed by our place in it' (Nagel 1991: 17). This is also linked in some of the accounts to the targeting of a particular locality when house-hunting, seeking out a locality in which certain actions then become possible. This is the point often made by critics of allocative school systems – that some parents can use their financial capital to choose a state school by buying a house in the catchment area of their preferred school. Again this highlights the strategic approach of middle-class families to the education of their children. Recent research by Gibson and Machin reported in *The Guardian* (15 April 2002) found that a 25 per cent difference in school performance increased house prices in London by between £37,000–45,000. Other researchers reported in *The Times* (20 April 2002: 15) found that some middle-class families were moving to unfashionable areas of London to buy bigger houses at lower prices, and using the savings to pay for private schools – local schools in these areas being unacceptable. School choice policies in fact change the logic of selection very little for these parents. As we have seen, choice of school is to a great extent choice of school clientele. Choice of housing location is in part a choice of neighbours. If school places are then filled by local choosers, the school then becomes closed off to non-locals, unless other forms of selection come into play.

> ... we knew about Overbury Secondary School obviously because it's just across the road from here, so you can't actually miss it ... it was something that we had sort of thought about, but neither of the boys had even started school then, they were only three and 18 months when we came here ... and we had thought probably then that they would go on to St Bartholomew and then after St Bartholomew, that's when we thought ... that's when we might go private, if we went private. And from here there are quite a lot of private schools, so we thought we're sort of getting the best of both worlds really.
>
> (Mrs Connelly)

As it turned out, as Mrs Connelly explained, choosing a state school from where she lives was 'easy'; dilemmas of principle are avoided. She also suggests below that the costs of a mortgage can be seen as an alternative to the costs of private schooling. This is a useful reminder of the argument made by Savage, Barlow, Dickens and Fielding (1992: 59) that 'property costs ... are becoming more integrally tied to processes of middle class formation. We suggest that increasing numbers of the middle class can draw upon both property and cultural assets'. That is certainly evident here (see Chapter 7).

> ... people move in, and then they start to have children ... they like the local schools, and then you find that where they might have moved out they tend to stay and really only move within the area, to stay within the state sector because they either find that they've got a large mortgage so they can't afford to pay the fees ... for private education ... .
>
> (Mrs Connelly)

Mrs McBain was also able to save her principles, although obligation and ambivalence again play their part.

> ... we sort of vaguely thought should he sit the Highway Boys' exam for a scholarship because, I mean, we could afford to send them privately

and ... in some ways we're not keen on the private sector, I think they actually get a more rounded education going to the state school here ... I think we're actually well served.

Again the point is that it is easier to maintain a liberal identity and position that is defensible in relation to the impersonal standpoint in some social settings. However, choice is also situated socially and historically within families. Mrs Cornwell rehearses a number of issues: the role of the parents' own schooling, and the way in which assumptions about schooling become embedded in family histories (see below); the link between choice of locality and choice of school, and the way that this interplays with private/state choosing, and thus the different mechanisms of closure involved; the influence of social networks; and the privileged access to information and social capital provided by her husband's job.

> Well, as it happened, because my husband is a local doctor a lot of the children that he sees obviously go to local schools ... so that was a decision because I'd gone privately and all my family have been educated privately ... my husband's haven't, they've always been state-educated, so ... we weren't thinking about them going privately, and he said well all the children that I treat ... most of them go ... and it was actually to the junior school, St Bartholemew, that was the one that he knew, and he said they are really nice children, and they seem to be very well behaved ... they asked interesting questions when they come to see him, they don't just walk in the surgery and open their mouths, they often ask about what's happening ... then if we move over the bridge and we buy in this little area here, that would be the junior school that the two boys, as we had then, would go to. So that was an influencing factor on us moving round here, in the area called St Vincent's, it was, yes.

Mrs Bellingham also set moving house as an alternative to choosing a private school: '... we thought of perhaps moving house to a different area, putting them in the local school for a year but then moving, I don't want my children to get a second-rate education'.

What begins to emerge from these examples is the interplay between a calculative orientation, investment in the child, and various impersonal values which have different degrees of strength, according to circumstances. Jordan, Redley and James's (1994) 'individualist repertoire' is, for most families, firmly embedded in school choice decision-making. Ms West gives a very good account of the sort of interplay of factors referred to above. Calculation, strategy and closure are all evident and values are very difficult to pin down.

> I've seen a lot of people who've had an awful lot of money paid on their education who've ended up really doing nothing with their lives, and equally well I've seen a lot of people come from the state system who've

done extremely well. So my feelings about both systems are I don't like having to pay for it but I'm not married to the fact that the state system should or could be the best, and I've actually been a teacher too in the state system, so I've seen both sides of it. I would be very concerned if I wasn't in this area, about the state provision I have to say ... I've taught in priority areas and there's no way I would want any of my children to go through that system, not because I don't think the teachers have done a good job ... but because of their peer group, and it's as straight-forward as that, you look at the peer group, the children they're with, the stimulation they're going to get, the ability of the teacher to teach ... relies an awful lot on your catchment area ... and Riverway has an extremely good catchment area, and I presume a large majority of people adopting the state system ... and that influenced me a great deal ... I felt I had a choice, it could be that if I didn't feel I had a choice, it could be if I had been for instance living in Northwark for instance, I may not have felt I had nearly as much choice as I have in Riverway, which is one of the reasons why we moved from Madeley to Riverway, not because of the state system *per se*, but because I was looking for a state school and I was very dissatisfied with the one I had, in Madeley, and I found what I thought was an extremely good one in Fletcher, and hence we moved, I mean it was as simple as that ...

The relationships between closure and principles are quite difficult here, as I have tried to suggest the deployment of principle is situated rather than absolute. For those families who acknowledged an issue of principle in the choice of private schooling, and I must be clear that not all did, there was typically both a deliberate setting aside of principles in the face of circumstances and, in some cases, an attempt at what were referred to by some as liberal compromises. The moral obligation of parents to their children excluded bad schools from any serious consideration. Principles were displaced rather than abandoned entirely and as we have seen some families held on harder to their principles than did others. The Marshes, both public sector professionals, chose private secondary schools for their children, although they recognized that their children would probably flourish virtually wherever they were schooled. Advantage is deliberately privileged over adequacy. This points up the strategic nature of choice as a means of social advantage. The Christies were also committed to providing an education that was more than adequate and which would set their children apart from others. Nonetheless, they wanted in effect the advantages of private schooling without the attitudes – the instrumental without the expressive. They also felt that the schools they had chosen were relatively mixed compared with other private schools. This points to an awareness of middle-class fractioning to which we will return. Mr Marsh also points to a particular sense of responsibility towards an able child, he says:

My conscience still pricks me about paying ... and I therefore ... would actually prefer the private system to be abolished ... but I also don't want them to have that sort of attitude that some of them have ... in terms of money buys everything, and they're superior ... because ... my ones are able, therefore in terms of academically ... they could ... I think they'd probably be alright in most systems ... so I try and help them with that, but I don't want them to come out with some of the attitudes that some of the people have ... schools ... I want a mix of people as much as they possibly can, although it's biased I know ... it is restricted, I know ... so ... the chances of them going to see people council houses ... but I mean that sort of background is more likely to be in Alleyns than it is in the others.

Local knowledge

There is a further dimension to the situated nature of principles and values. Principles are situated in a locality, as above, and also in relation to a more general social or political context and in relation to the realization of the comprehensive ideal, as parents saw it. That is, there were a number of parents for whom comprehensive education would be a real choice, in the best possible of all schooling worlds – that is, if comprehensives were what they were 'supposed to be'; although what they are supposed to be was not always clear. And it is also unclear whether, if they *were* what they were 'supposed to be', they would be comprehensive. Part of this non-realization is brought about by the existence of the private sector and its creaming-off of other children like their own, thus creating a social and academic mix in the comprehensive school which is deemed unacceptable. Here we can see some glimpses again of a link between individual choices and a more general social good. Here principles are suspended until circumstances change. They do not come into play because the circumstances in which they would or should operate do not pertain. Here government policy towards private schools and school choice generally creates a situation in which it is possible to avoid state schooling. Nonetheless, the effects and consequences of policy come about from the aggregate of choices made by individual families. These parents believe that their individual choice otherwise will make little difference overall and their obligation to their own child weighs heavily. Choices are made within the options available. Successive governments have been uninterested or unwilling to take action to produce socially mixed comprehensive schooling and only some parents are able, in various senses, to avoid those comprehensive schools which are unmixed.

It's the problem of taking a chance with your child, throwing them into the state sector ... and the dilemmas that that creates, I dream of having good comprehensive schools that I could send my child to, and I'm very aware of the creaming effects of private and elite schools of various kinds.

(Mrs Crichton)

Well the choice unfortunately is veering away from comprehensive school ... we happen, because of money left to me when my mother died, to be able to pay for ... and we may be going that way, which personally I regret, but the other things don't seem to be met, at least for a boy, from the local state education.

(Mrs Tey)

I think they tend to get lost in the system, and also because ... if comprehensive education was really what it's supposed to be ... if all the children went, then that would be okay, but the cream is all going somewhere else. And so therefore when they go, they haven't got the competition, they haven't got the children at the top that they should have ... it isn't comprehensive education ... it's only those ... in this borough ... .

(Mr Highsmith)

Then again, for some parents, as explored in Chapter 4, there are particular structural characteristics of the comprehensive system, as they understand it, which make it 'impossible' to contemplate, and raise concerns which again seem to emphasize advantage rather than adequacy.

I mean there was non-streaming ... I mean you cannot teach non-streamed GCSE, it's just not possible. And at several of the schools ... and Lockmere was one of them, there were non-streamed GCSE classes.

(Mr Highsmith)

Values and principles are situated in a third sense; that is, values systems are constructed, or influenced, or inflected within families, social networks and local communities. They become part of the taken for granted response to decisions, what people 'like us', in this place, do. This is where, again, the collectivity, the awareness of a collective identity, comes back in, and is a basis for the values of individualism, the putting of the family first; although these are not always as 'explicit and unambiguous' as Bernstein (1975: 127) suggests. These social contexts constitute a moral community within which the necessity of an attitude, toward family, schooling and parenting, is formed and maintained. Specific versions of the good parent circulate within this community which both provide a repertoire of meanings through which to account for actions and which constrain or judge those actions.

That's the way it is here ... everybody who can afford to, sends their children to independent schools, especially in this particular part of the borough.

(Mr Highsmith)

... from the way the family operates it will probably be the line of least resistance which is ... if we can afford it then you go to Alleyns as well ... yes, I mean ... or we will afford it somehow and he will go to Alleyns as well ... .

(Mrs Symons)

Primary school events and social activities and the school-gate network of mothers, together with children's own reporting back to parents, are all influential in establishing a sense of normal trajectories for children like 'ours' and appropriate choices for parents like 'us'. Norms and expectations circulate through networks of talk and through the use of pointed questions and comparisons in school-gate conversations. According to the parents themselves, norms and expectations become embedded over time in the parental cultures of particular primary schools, making some choices obvious and others perverse; although most London primary schools will encompass some diversity of parental cultures. These vocabularies of expectation produce a framework of possibilities which need to be taken into account when decisions are made.

There's a great sort of ethos in many of the primary schools to go on to private education, so you have to actually apply yourself to what you're going to do with your child quite early on because they're all ... a lot of them have been tutored since the age of seven or eight to get into wherever they want them to go, either by nine or 11, so I suppose in all honesty I must have started thinking about it about four years ago. But I didn't know anything much about the actual state provisions because that wasn't a consideration I had to actually take into account at that point ... I had to actually make a decision whether I wanted to tutor her to go into the private system or not.

(Mrs West)

... but even now they're all talking because a lot of the children are taking exams for the private schools ... are you going here, are you going there, and then for all the other children to know where they're going and your child ... well I don't know, we're waiting for appeal ... .

(Mrs Connelly)

For many families the extended family is a further source of norms and expectations, despite the general assumption in most contemporary literature on the middle class that the extended family is a thing of the past. Private or selective or state school traditions become embedded in families. Halsey, Heath and Ridge (1980: 39) report private school attendance by parents as the best predictor of a child's attendance. Power, Edwards, Whitty and Wigfall (2002) found the same pattern:

... we've come from a family where the tradition has been for the boys to go to the local grammar school, which is now an independent school. So brothers, uncles, cousins are all there and have been there. So there's a very strong inclination for the first son to go to the independent school Highway. And if he failed that our only other consideration was a local church school, out of borough.

(Mrs Smith)

Nonetheless, in this sample, not all parents accept family expectations as common sense or as in the best interests of their child. In these circumstances family expectations are experienced as pressures which have to be withstood in order to make a choice 'otherwise' (more of this later in the Simpsons' case study). For Mrs Mankell, who chose a state school, looking at, giving consideration to, the private sector is still the obvious thing to do in her social milieu. Again the pressures she mentions are part of the construction of a good parent in this social setting. And some parents in choosing a comprehensive school for their child were aware that they were going against the grain in relation to the majority of their peers.

we obviously looked at the private sector, as well, so it wasn't automatically our first choice, though it was the one we went for and it was the one we liked best ... in an area like this there is pressure on you to look at private education ... it's very very strong ...

However, set over and against tradition and expectations was, for some of the parents, their own none too fond memories of private or selective schooling. These negative experiences seemed to provide a firm basis for a principled choice of comprehensive education. Principle and the child's best interests seemed to coincide. The idea of an obvious advantage to private schooling was not so obvious to these parents. Indeed of the 25 sets of parents who had both attended private or grammar schools, 18 chose state schools for their children; of the 15 sets where one or both had attended private schools, ten chose state schools for their children. These choices, as indicated already, have to be related to the locality of choice; nonetheless there is an interesting counter-discourse around private schooling here.

Samuel, my husband, was at a direct grant school in Manchester, which he didn't really have fond memories of.

(Mrs Hammet)

I found it fairly boring, except perhaps the last two years, from the age of 16 to 18, but apart from that I was fairly uninspired by it.

(Mrs Leon)

I started off at a private school until I was ten, then my parents had the sense to move me to the local primary, where you did actually learn things other than good elocution and dance and things like that and so I went there for a year and loved it.

(Mrs Rankin)

My husband was a failed 11⁺ student, who then went at 13 to the local grammar school, and was very unhappy.

(Mrs Smith)

Well, I liked having a very broad-based education, I liked mixing with a lot of different sorts of people … and I do think that I've benefited more from my education than my two sisters who went to a private school.

(Mrs Rankin)

I want to take a moment to reiterate my purposes and my claims here. As I have tried to make clear I make no claims for the general representativeness of these parents. They do not stand for all middle-class parents. And as a sample group they are internally diverse both in terms of the narratives they offer and their demographic characteristics and the metropolitan intensity of the education markets in which they find themselves. I have already pointed to some exceptions to the predominant pattern of values and will explore others in more detail below; although in many respects the exceptions are not as exceptional as all that. I have also given emphasis here, and in other chapters to the situated specificity of aspects of the middle-class culture portrayed here. My primary purpose is to begin to understand the lifestyles and actions of the middle classes, and the consequences of these actions in relation to social policy and social justice, and for class analysis; that is, to try to expand and develop the existing paraphernalia of description and analysis.

Recovering principles and the science of division

As indicated already, for some parents there is, at least at face value, an absolute contradiction between their espoused values and their actions. This is what Brantlinger, Majd-Jabbari and Guskin (1996: 586) refer to as 'The dissonance of class epistemology and liberal identity'. In a harsh condemnation of their own middle-class respondents Brantlinger, Majd-Jabbari and Guskin (1996: 587) argue that 'liberal verbalisations served mainly to solidify a liberal identity'. In effect there were disjunctures between how the respondents wished to present themselves in terms of a public moral identity and their morality in action. Like the parents represented here, Brantlinger, Majd-Jabbari and Guskin's mothers worked hard to establish boundaries between the schooling of their children and the schooling of others. Jordan, Redley and James (1994: 190) found some of their respondents caught within the same disjuncture when they attempted to use a 'collectivist repertoire' in some kind of relation to their family decision-making; 'the use of these repertoires does not give those who deploy them an easy way to link accounts of their decisions and actions with discourses of active citizenship or democratic participation'. They go on to argue that collective issues 'do not construct means of acting to be effective in relation to these issues' (190). This is the problem of the ineffectiveness of individual choices noted above. Indeed, Jordan, Redley and James (190) suggest that use of the 'collectivist repertoire' can be understood as 'a temporary shift from narratives of self and family'. All this is evident among the families discussed here; nonetheless I have already indicated some of the ways in which respondents attempt to repair their liberal identity with accounts of the necessities and impossibilities of choice. A further tactic of repair occurred for some of those parents who chose private school, but emphasized the choice of a particular kind of private school. These may be read as attempts to achieve a resolution between an individualist and some kind of collectivist repertoire. Of course, as should be apparent, this was not a need for all families, many of whom are happily grounded within the values and actions of individualism. There were no difficult resolutions required.

Like Mr Christie quoted earlier, Mr Bellingham explains that his preferred private school has a good social mix. This is an issue which recurs in the interviews and has to be understood, I would suggest, within the particular imperatives of choice that are articulated. Social mix sits uneasily with the emphasis on boundaries and distinctions examined in Chapter 4. Some parents saw mix as important to their children's social development, as part of learning to be in the 'real world' (see the Simpsons below). Jordan, Redley and James's respondents made the same point, but underpinning this was a concern to control or determine the specific mix that their children would experience. This is most obviously the case in private schools. In effect, like other terms deployed in these accounts, mix is, as Jordan, Redley and James (1994: 146) point out, 'indexical', that is remaining 'indeterminate until put into the context of everyday life'.

> There's quite a few drawbacks to City of London ... except it seems to have a very nice mix of pupils as well ... That's the other thing that worries me slightly, in a private school ... that he's going to mix with a far narrower range of kids, and I think City of London has really sort of got pupils from everywhere, all walks of life ... Again we have to wait and see, we don't know if they're going to accept him, we'll worry about that when it happens ... and ... ask him, he's got to be in on the final decision. I'm not happy with any private school that is selective in sort of social class, which basically they've got to be, given that they're going to charge thousands of pounds a year. I think Bob has had a wonderful time at Merrybush because it's been so mixed,[3] and I'm very ... I regret a lot that he'll only start to mix with different kids. Having said that ... I think ... that Merrybush and certain children ... find it just not cool to work, and he's been influenced that

way ... so I don't regret it completely, but I ... just want him to be surrounded by all sorts of people, which I ... that's why I like City of London
because I think that's very very different, there's a lot more scholarships ...
and bright children from any background can get in there.

(Mr Bellingham)

Mr Bellingham's account is full of 'skilful improvisations' through which 'a
sense of order and obligation is created' (Jordan, Redley and James 1994:
8). But there are no clear guidelines for action here. This is an example of
what Jordan, Redley and James (1994: 147) call 'cobbled together reasoning'. Mrs Cornwell offered another kind of orientation to mix, as awareness
rather than direct experience, when she explained that she wanted a private
school but she also wanted 'a lack of snobbery, that's what I mean by a similar outlook, the acceptance that there's a wider world than the privileged
group of children who happen to be at that school'.

The other point that emerges indirectly from these 'repairs' of principle is
yet another kind of boundary making. That is, an awareness of and response
to the use of different private schools by different middle-class fractions. As
in Chapter 4, the parents reacted differently to the expressive cultures of the
different private schools they visited. The degree of mix was one element, Mr
Marsh below also notes an ethnic difference between schools, the values dispositions of parents – 'dozy *Guardian*-reading middle class' – is another, and
the pedagogies and rules of social order are also important. Mrs Simpson
below notes that an 'old fashioned grammar school' would not suit her son,
whereas this was exactly what other parents were seeking. Mrs Cornwell,
above, wants a 'lack of snobbery'. This is a further iteration of the role of
class fit, and divisions between 'us' and 'them', between different class fractions and class cultures within the middle class.

> Funnily Alleyns is ... and I don't know why this should be, but Alleyns
> is kind of whiter than Dulwich ... I don't know why, I don't know what
> that reflects and that certainly didn't matter a damn one way or the
> other, although it's interesting to speculate why ... whether it's because
> the dozy *Guardian*-reading middle class tend to be white, I don't know
> ... this is awful stereotyping now ... whereas people who are trying
> much harder to get their children on in the world ... there are more ...
> I suppose more Asian families who are hoping that their children will
> improve their lot, and what you've got at Alleyns certainly is an awful
> lot of soggy middle-class people who've had a reasonable education
> themselves and now aren't trying very hard, which is ... probably
> damning the next generation. I don't know.

(Mr Marsh)

As noted above, the relationship between principles and the practice of
choice is also mediated by the characteristics of the child. In some cases this

makes private schooling an imperative, in others either unnecessary or inappropriate. Furthermore, the child's own wishes and preferences can intervene. Families differed to the extent to which the child's views carried weight (see Reay and Ball 1998). Here more personal or familial values are in play, related both to the treatment of the child and to the extent to which the child is viewed as having the right and the competence to make decisions about its own future. In a sense, there are principles here which occupy a space between the personal and impersonal – an ethics within the family. Below are a variety of examples; in some it is the child's characteristics which are decisive, in others the child's preferences.

> Highway is more like an old-fashioned grammar school ... we also felt that that probably didn't suit Michael ... we felt that was not a climate in which he would flourish, so we'd sort of knocked that on the head really by the time he was in the fifth year, so now we were just really concentrating on the state schools and I think once we'd decided that for us that was the biggest issue really ... not which school he went to, but whether we went state or private.
>
> (Mrs Connelly)

> ... again, that's the school he wanted [a state school] ... we felt very strongly that he did have to be a part of the decision making ... .
>
> (Mrs Connelly)

> Um ... I think if she'd been highly academic, which she isn't, I think I'd have thought very seriously about whether the state system was going to offer enough stimulation. I've found the whole system into private education was a rat race ... and that people became very emotive about it. I didn't want to be sucked into it and we took a choice about ... I suppose about 18 months ago ... we decided that to put pressure on her to take the necessary exams would hamper her, I mean it was as straightforward as that. It wasn't financial, I mean we could afford to send her to private education ... .
>
> (Ms West)

> No, because I didn't want him to think that one was any better than the other ... that ... because it was a private school ... obviously the fact comes into it, can you afford to pay the fees, and I didn't really want him to think that just because you paid for an education that it was better, so we just said ... it's a school ... he was not very keen on them because they were single-sex schools ... he didn't like the idea of that, and Kingston Grammar is actually co-ed but he doesn't know anybody there, whereas at Highway Grammar he would have known quite a few boys, and by this time he was showing a very strong preference to go to Overbury.
>
> (Mr Connelly)

out of the private schools I think Ned would be just as happy at Dulwich, because he's a much tougher, more competitive person ... I think he would probably thrive there, so if he passes both then I'll put that to him, because it wouldn't be essential for them to go to the same school ... if they're going in the same direction and having more or less the same holidays, then these arguments wouldn't be a problem.

(Mr Marsh)

We considered it but Laura doesn't want to go to a private school, so we didn't pursue it.

(Mrs Leonard)

Familial ethics was also a factor in the treatment of different children. Unless there was a very good reason, like the child's own preferences, it was the case that parents regarded equal treatment as a basic principle.

I mean on the balance of probabilities, if he passes, then we'll try and afford to send him to one of the same schools as his brother ... because ... I think he would feel mortified if we seemed to believe that he wasn't worth spending money on, which is what it comes down to ... you know, if his education somehow wasn't as important, so unless we were very convinced that the local state school could deliver the same quality of education, same degree of education ... .

(Mrs Crichton)

because the other two went to it, and that was the big choice that you make for the first one ... if you do it for one you have to do it for all of them, so ... it's not fair ... otherwise it becomes divisive within the family ... .

(Mr Christie)

... since his older brother has gone into the private sector ... Ned has exams coming up ... we don't know what will happen with that ... I suppose we had assumed that having made the decision for the one we would do the same for the other, although not necessarily. But in this particular area, in the Streetley area, within reach ... the state provision certainly for boys is, I think, chronic.

(Mrs Crichton)

I have indicated a number of times already that within the limitations of the small interview samples upon which I draw in this study I have not been able to identify clear fractional differences which rest upon different forms or levels of employment but there are clusters of values or stance differences which relate in a patterned, if not absolutely systematic way to state versus private school parents. This, though, begs the question as to whether the differences produce the choices or the choices give rise to the differences, or a bit of both. But here we also see differences between choosers of private schooling and this points to the need for a more nuanced approach to private school types (see Power, Edwards, Whitty and Wigfall 2002).

Table 6.1 shows the distribution of private/state choosers related to parental employment – but remember these are families which, for the most part, are choosing private education at eleven and not at five, which may already indicate some equivocation. Halsey, Heath and Ridge (1980) also found that parents in some middle-class occupations, particularly self-employed professionals, were more likely to choose private schooling than others. These patterns are then in no way conclusive. They are indicative; they raise issues for discussion and for further research.

Let us also look at the relationship between parents' school experience and their choice of school for their children (Table 6.2). It needs to be borne in mind that a large number of parents attended state grammar schools, an option no longer readily available in these localities. I have included these with those who attended private school (in italics).

Table 6.1 Parents' employment and choice of school

Parents' employment	Private school	State school
Private sector employment	Crichtons, Forsythes, Pelecanos, Moseleys	Wests, Graftons, Parkers, Grishams, Crais
State/ voluntary sector	Marshes, Christie, Teys	Hammets, Archers, Doyles, Dexters, Codys, McBains, Highsmiths, Fyfields, Simpsons, Connellys, Turow
Mixed	Cornwells, Francis	Rankins, Mankells, Goslings, Leonards, Hillermans, Leons, Smiths, McDermids, Symons, Chandlers, Loveseys

Table 6.2 Parents' schooling and choice of school*

Parents' schooling	Private school	State school
Parents attended private or grammar school (italic)	*Cornwells*, Crichtons, Teys, *Pelecanos*, *Marshes*, *Forsythes*, Moseleys	*Goslings*, *Rankins*, *Wests*, Mankells, Symons, *Graftons*, *Doyles*, *Leonards*, Simpsons, *Francis*, Hillermans, Cody, *Loveseys*, Chandlers, *Hammets*, Fyfields, Smiths, *Parkers*, Crais
State school	Christies	Highsmiths, McBains, Leons, McDermids, Turow
Mixed		Dexters, Grishams

* Data are missing from two families here, the Connellys and the Archers

As noted already, what is interesting about this table, as far as choice of state school is concerned, is the number of parents who had private or grammar school educations themselves who end up choosing differently for their children.

I now want to take a slightly different analytical tack and get even closer to the work of 'ethical bricolage' by taking two families as case studies of choice and ethics in practice. Now you might well wonder why it is that both these case studies are of families who end up choosing state schools rather than private. There are two main reasons. First, they serve particularly well to illustrate the complexity and dilemmas of choice. Second, in contrast to the majority of private school choosers they go beyond the obviousness of choice in their narratives. First, there are the Simpsons and then the Goslings. Mr Simpson is a senior civil servant and Mrs Simpson is a teacher in a private secondary school; they both attended grammar schools and a high status university; they have three sons, at the time of interview aged three, seven and eleven.

The Simpsons started out thinking about their children's schooling in terms of sending them to private school. However, Mr Simpson presents two reasons for eventually choosing state schools for all three sons. The first reason displays careful rational calculation, in the literal sense. The costs are too high, at least that is the opportunity costs. Nonetheless, the Simpsons' thinking displays strategic care. The family's material capital will be deployed to fund an educative infrastructure within the home and to provide back-ups and interventions in order to assure success and insure against failure.

> A long time ago we put Toby's name down for St Jude's school ... because St Jude's is the local school ... a private school, of very high standard ... very very expensive, and when we had two children we wondered whether to put the second one down and when it was the possibility of three boys going to a private school because if you add the fees up, and income ... and we could just about afford it, but when we had three we realized that we had no intention of sending them, we would be spending a fortune, and we do have a reasonable income, it would mean a stretch in terms of other things ... so on the basis of finance we thought it would need to be a pretty special school that would require us to give up as much as we would have to give up ... and ... in terms of making any financial decision you should look at what else you could buy with that same amount of money ... and we decided that we could do more for our children by spending on computers and books and ... other resources at home, and if necessary later on ... buy coaching and remedial teaching, if that was necessary ... than by committing to the private system from the start ... and so we didn't take up the invitation from St Jude's to send Toby along for the tests at age seven, and we've no intention of trying at age 13. So that would be the first reason.

The Simpsons' second reason for choosing the state sector is articulated in a different discourse and Mr Simpson displays a considerable degree of reflexivity in relation to the 'strength' of the family's principles. There are two related elements to these principles. One, identified previously, expresses a belief in educating their children in a setting which reflects the social diversity of the world at large. This includes a rejection of single-sex education and the studied traditionalism of a grammar school. Neither are considered relevant to today's world. The other indicates a link between the family's choice and the general social consequences of choice. This was certainly not common in the data set as a whole. Here what is acknowledged is the 'creaming' effect in the state sector of choice of private school.

The issue of diversity or mix crops up again below and has an interesting and rather complicated relationship to the themes of boundary and closure which also run through the analysis as a whole. If I can indulge, for a moment at least, in the safe simplicities of binarism, the families who appear in this chapter display either one of two tendencies, a preference for absolute or relative closure.

> The second reason for not going for private education was really on a matter of principle ... everybody's principles I think have a certain degree of strength, and I'm not sure how strong ours would ultimately be, my wife has taught for ten years in the private sector, and she therefore has an awareness of what qualities there are in a private school as distinct from the qualities you get in a state school ... and we all have to live our lives in a world with a mixture of all sorts of other societies around us ... with other people in society around us ... and I think that's probably what ... on a matter of principle ... would persuade us not to use a private school now ... and because we see in this area how much quality is already being deprived of the comprehensive schools, by the number of children who are driven off each day to the private schools around, and we would prefer not to contribute to that, but to bring up our children in something which represents a small slice of the world that they're going to have to live ... I had forgotten what it was like in an all-boys school, and when I got there I remembered what it was like in an all-boys school, and for the reasons I gave in not choosing private education, I don't actually think you get a cross-section of society ... in a single-sex school, and I would like Toby to grow up in a society which was peopled almost equally by women, and so the last thing to do is to cut all his experience of the opposite sex out ... during his school years. That was ... I think one of my reasons for rejecting Marshalls Grammar. The other reason was that it was just so old-fashioned. It reminded me of what education was like 25 years ago. I don't want to put Toby through that, I want to put Toby through the education of today ... I'm sure that education has to be very different today than it was when I was at school.

While the Simpsons knew what they would be getting in the private sector they were much less sure about quality within the state sector. As we have seen before they believed that having chosen to remain in the state sector, they would have to take choice of a particular school very seriously indeed. They ended up comparing in detail two comprehensive schools and somewhat less seriously a state grammar school, and developed a checklist of indicators they considered important. These mainly concerned the quality of teaching and the subjects and activities on offer, in effect both the instrumental and expressive order. What they end up with is a messy calculus of issues, of very different sorts, both big and small, more or less important, resting on both instrumental and expressive values. For example, the Simpsons, unlike some other families, are not willing to send their sons long distances to find the right school. Like the working-class families reported in Gewirtz, Ball and Bowe (1995), the idea of the school being an extension of the local community is important to them.

> ... we also have set down a checklist I suppose, because we found it very difficult to make a final decision as to which school to opt for. The quality of the staff is a very difficult thing to judge, but I think is actually one of the critical things ... how much the teachers are going to stimulate the children to want to learn ... and ... in every subject it's quite difficult because there are so many subjects that you can't start to get a grasp of ... so we ... have ... at both Fletcher and at Peyton ... been to the open evening when you can go round and look at the school facilities ... talk to the staff, talk about how teaching is done in particular subjects, and we've also been on a tour of the schools ... looking at the schools in normal working hours. So we've been looking primarily for the quality of the teaching and the choice of subjects offered and taught. So one of the factors for example that makes Peyton particularly interesting is that they offer a slightly wider choice of subjects that are taught, they don't for example ... group all the humanities together quite as much as they do at Fletcher ... They offer the option of doing Latin should a child want to do that. Toby probably won't want to do that but nevertheless it's nice to be in a school where you know that that choice is available. Another factor which has influenced us is the quality of the IT equipment on display and the IT which is apparently used in teaching. The reason for this is that we believe that schools which are using IT in this way are more likely to be up-to-date with other aspects of teaching too, so that we would judge those schools to be up-to-date, reflecting the current requirements and understanding about subjects taught ... Another factor I think is the sports facilities ... in particular because Toby loves playing football and ... neither Sara nor I were at all sporty when we were at school ... and we want to encourage him to be what we weren't, because when you come to be part of a team in any organization, I think it's extremely valuable that you've been part of a team in some sort of sporting activity ... so we've

been very keen to encourage Toby in that, and so we've looked at sports facilities ... but not only sports facilities, but the encouragement of children to take part, and so therefore we've been impressed by the range of clubs, extra curricular activities, the sorts of things that children can opt into. So I think those were the key things that we were looking for ... Another thing that's very important to us is that the school should be accessible to where we live, in some ways I rather regret that there is a choice of school at all because we've sent Toby and Issac to the local primary school, because it's the nearest school and because we felt it would offer a satisfactory service. There's an awful lot of time and energy wasted in bussing children to schools that are some distance away ... both in the private sector and in the state sector, and so what we were looking for was a school to which Toby could walk ... a school at which other people would be going from this neighbourhood to that school ... in other words a neighbourhood or a community school, and that's why we haven't looked at schools further away from us in this borough, even though they might offer a perfectly adequate product. And in some ways we realized that that could leave us vulnerable, because we know nothing about the other schools in the borough and should we fail to get Toby into Fletcher, we would have no basis on which to judge whether what we were being offered was at all satisfactory.

The Simpsons were also influenced by things they did not expect to find, that is, impressions which they accumulated during their visits to schools. The effects of how the schools looked, as well as how they presented themselves – impressions 'given' and 'given off'. The importance of these has been noted in earlier chapters. The vibrancy and inclusiveness of the open evening presentation of one of the schools also made an impression. Nonetheless, in relative terms, the Simpsons' processing of choice is highly rational. They would be good exemplars of Goldthorpe's (1996) rational actors, knowledgeable about their society and the constraints and possibilities related to the achievement of goals.

Other factors that have influenced us that perhaps we weren't looking for ... when we went to Peyton ... the presentation at the open evening ... was headed by the head teacher, but sitting alongside the head teacher was the chairman of governors, who happens also to be a parent ... also on the stage was a representative of the parent/teacher association ... each had their say. It was as if the various parties involved in management of the school and the governing of the school, and participation in school events ... were demonstrating that they were co-operating and being as one ... whereas in the other two schools that we've been to, Fletcher and Marshalls Grammar, the presentation was entirely by members of the staff and was actually rather less vibrant, and was rather less convincing as a result. So that was something which we didn't quite expect. The quality of work on display and almost the colours of the corridors were also factors which influence you in one way or another. We came away from Peyton feeling that the school was terribly cluttered, but afterwards we discovered it's because they offer every child the opportunity of using a locker ... whereas at Fletcher school the children have to carry round their own books and coats, all day, wherever they go, there's no base to come back to ... there's nowhere to store books, and knowing how reluctant people are to carry round things ... that led us to believe that perhaps children were going unprepared into lessons. Small factors like that, which are quite difficult to rank in any form, but nevertheless are factors that we would take into account.

The third and final source of choice data is the 'objective' cold knowledge provided by school results. Here the Simpsons are able to deploy a considerable range of skills and judgements. They see these data as requiring interpretation, both in terms of the intakes of the schools and their current as opposed to previous policies and practices. They also find the schools' own interpretation and presentation of results to be confusing (see Chapters 5 and 7). We can also see here the way in which choice-making at 11 is seen as part of an overall educational trajectory and in terms of thinking ahead to future choice points.

The results and presentation of the school ... I haven't mentioned, partly because they require a great deal of interpretation ... the way in which the government statistics were recently received gives a good indication. We were quite surprised ... well we were not surprised, because we were already aware that the results at Peyton school are nowhere near as good at the moment as the results at Fletcher school, nevertheless we believe the quality of the teaching there that's being offered there at the bottom of the school and the product when those years come through to taking their exams will be very different from what they have now and that's partly because the school has turned itself around and become very much more successful. And so ... in looking at the results ... everyone wants to present their results in their best light. In fact the results were presented in an extremely confusing light, and I think it's actually very difficult indeed to judge how effective a school is, and in particular ... I think it's difficult because you have no idea what the quality of the intake was that the output should really be compared with, you can't work out the added value. But ... we felt with Peyton that the setting that was available and the choice of subjects ... indicated that the school was now much more interested in catering for the more academic pupils ... and setting does not take place in Fletcher except in maths and so if we go to Fletcher we won't get quite the same ... ability ... the feeling that Toby will be taught in a group of children who want to learn. Both Sara and I are suspicious about mixed ability teaching, which is what the majority of teaching at Fletcher is. And then … I realise I'm adding a number of … supplementary points but … there is a difference that Fletcher is a school that effectively caters for first to fifth years, there is no sixth form. There are no sixth forms in any Riverway schools, but Peyton school is a school which includes a sixth form and again we felt that that would influence the quality of staff, because with a teacher in the house, we know that staff are more interested in going to schools where there is a sixth form, so that they get a share of the most challenging teaching, as well as the ability to influence children right at the bottom of the school, and perhaps steer them towards the specialities at the top of the school.

As discussed in Chapter 4, grouping practices are viewed as being of major significance in providing contexts for 'more academic pupils', those 'who want to learn'. In other words, again there are lines to be drawn within social diversity and there are limits to community and social mixing. These are not matters of principle in the general sense, and they are not seen as such by the Simpsons. These are matters of necessity, which make choice of a state school possible. What this highlights is the way in which different things become issues of principle for different families, and the different points at which principles give way to practicalities or the embedded values involved in putting the family first. This also indicates something of the effectiveness or accuracy of New Labour's opinion testing; although it is difficult to know to what extent the government's overt commitment to setting reflects or moulds opinion.

The Goslings are a mixed couple in the sense that Mrs Gosling is a public sector professional, a speech therapist, and her husband a private sector professional, a civil engineer, who had been made redundant a couple of weeks prior to the interview. Both parents had been privately schooled. Neither had enjoyed or rated very highly their own school experience. As Power, Whitty, Edwards and Wigfall (1998: 47) note 'even high academic achievement does not generate loyalty to a particular form of schooling'.

> He didn't enjoy his education at all, he didn't think it was a very good education. I went to an all-girls private day school and didn't enjoy my education at all, either. Having said that we both went to university so, if you like, it gave us whatever that required. But I felt that my education was very unchallenging … very very unchallenging, very dull, and I had so much to learn when I left school and went to college. I had to learn to live … .

Again here the private system is seen as unworldly, as not offering a proper preparation for the real world. For Mrs Gosling the real world is a social world. As I have tried to make clear, for parents who choose private school, it is also often because it does prepare their children for the real world. But this real world is an economic or utilitarian one. There are two different educational modalities here. The Goslings also have a clear-cut principled position toward private schooling. But they also recognize the tension between public principles and private pragmatics and did look at and consider private primary schools. They found these schools inappropriate for their son. Mrs Gosling also points up a set of tensions between an educational, child-centred and principled decision-making ensemble and a more instrumental set of concerns. There are compromises to be made on either side. Either choosing the guarantees offered by the private sector but forms of teaching and learning inappropriate to the child, or going for state school which is deemed more socially appropriate, in a variety of ways, but which does not offer the same educational/instrumental guarantees. Indeed, the Goslings perfectly encapsulate the basic moral tension between on the one hand legitimate parental partiality, and a special duty of care towards their own child, and on the other an awareness of the social injustice of the private system. Again in this calculus of obligations and principles the best interests of the child are also somewhat unclear. The Goslings' orientation to the private sector is inflected by the concern that it is inappropriate for their son. Here again we have the tension between a personal and a positional interpretation of the child's best interests. Like some other parents they are struggling with this tension.

> ... both of us are very pro state schools ... And I have a lot of problems philosophically with even coping with the fact that independent schools exist. I do feel that every child has the right to a good education, and I really don't think you should get it just because you've got more money than Joe Bloggs next door. Having said that, when it comes to your child, we did go and have a look ... we looked at actually at every level, we looked at the infant level and did not like at all what they were doing, it was far too heavy ... far too formal ... and then we looked at junior school level and felt that Ibworth was better actually than any of the private schools we went to look at ... depending on what you're wanting. If you want them to go to Westminster you have to send them to a prep school, but that's not what we wanted anyway. Rodney particularly is the sort of child ... who doesn't necessarily go down that formal road ... he learns in a very erratic sense ... and there was no room for that sort of ingenuity and individuality I felt, within the prep school system ... you either did A, B and C and you came out with D or you didn't make it. So I felt that that would actually totally inhibit him. And we did go and have a look at Highway Grammar, which is the independent ... but in fact ... the only reason I would have really considered it was because of ensuring ... if you like, like an insurance policy, that if he went there, he was very likely to come out with good results. And I suppose when you send your child to a comprehensive, which is not the system that we knew as children, you have less of a guarantee. However ... I would have found it very difficult to make that decision, given my own thoughts about state education, and all of that.

Bernstein's analysis of the new middle classes, which I have deployed at several points already, suggests that these tensions, dilemmas and contradictions are representative of the structural ambiguities embedded in positioning and perspectives of the new middle class. He says: 'The contemporary new middle class is unique, for in the socialisation of its young there is a sharp and penetrating contradiction between a subjective personal identity and an objective privatised identity; between the release of the person and the hierarchy of class' (1975: 136). This is also a further aspect of individualism and what Jordan, Redley and James (1994: 94) refer to as 'the discourses of a developmental self'. These parents feel a strong sense of obligation to enable their children to make the best of themselves, but as I have tried to suggest, via Bernstein, it is not always clear whether this is a 'release' or a programme of differentiation. While perhaps not an ideal-typical new middle-class woman, Mrs Gosling seems very aware of this contradiction and her choice is for release rather than hierarchy. She chooses between the personal particularities of her child and the trajectory of advantages offered by private schooling. However, the alignments between principles, person and advantage differ from case to case, as we have seen. Brantlinger, Majd-Jabbari and Guskin (1996: 589) suggest that when it comes to the relationship between liberal principles and practice the mothers' role as 'status maintainers' puts them 'in a contradictory or dissonant position'.

The son's own preferences play a key role here but are set over and against the expectations and pressures of the extended family. Choice of state school involves taking a stand against norms strongly embedded within the history and practices of the family. The Goslings are like the 'non-conformists' described by Power, Edwards, Whitty and Wigfall (2002) who had to resist considerable pressure from family, schools and peers to get their way. The cultural script of the family becomes very clear here and the Goslings have to work hard to rewrite the script for their child. In effect they are interrupting an embedded trajectory of class reproduction and its attendant expectations and obligations and are striking out on their own. A non-decision, the obviousness of the private sector is rewritten as a decision; whether to send their son or not.

> He said he'd pay us back his pocket money every week, if we promised him we wouldn't send him to an all-boys school where you pay fees, and that rather clinched the deal. Also I said would he like to take the exam just in case, now maybe that was just a reassurance for me to say, well alright, he would have a place in grammar school, he's bright enough for that, but we turned it down ... and he said, if I don't want to go there, I don't think I'm going to be trying terribly hard in the exam, so I might fail, so I can't see any point in sitting it ... and I'm really not sorry. But equally, because he's in contact with both my brother's children, and my husband's children are both at independent schools, both very expensive independent schools ... and so we very much had to strike out on our own ... and to put this whole conversation in context ... it has caused

me a huge amount of personal anguish ... going down the road that we go, and we've come under huge pressure from parents and in-laws and the rest of the family. And a lot of persuasion that we ought to be sending our children to private school ... .

In contrast to the Simpsons, the Goslings' account does not touch upon the more specific social consequences of their decisions. Their principles are primarily abstract and emotional rather than grounded in any strong sense of a common good. Even so, though different, neither of these families are simply 'unencumbered' individuals, nor entirely 'separate self-contained, motivated by the pursuit of private desires' (Sandel 1982, quoted in Martin and Vincent 1999). There are some faint glimpses here of what Rikowski (2001: 15) calls 'the class struggle within the human' or the *psychology of class*, a 'clash of forces and drives' which recur 'in and through our everyday lives'. A clash which Nagel (1991: 1) describes as a 'question about each individual's relation to himself'.

So what, if anything, can we conclude from this examination of the values and principles of the middle class. I have tried to avoid a one-sidedly grim picture, a dystopic view of some aspects of a more general de-socialization and de-moralization of society (Fevre 2000). I have not sought to over-emphasize the role of bourgeois individualism, 'an idea of society as a neutral area within which each individual is free to pursue his own development and his own advantage as a natural right' (Williams 1959: 325) or ignore the growth of what Berking (1996: 195) calls 'solidary individualism'. Berking puts forward a balanced view, wherein the tendencies of individualization in modern society also involve 'learning, at all levels of social intercourse, to deal with paradoxical demands on one's behaviour, controlling one's affects without ceasing to be natural, utilising the chances offered by an increasing informalisation without casting conventions to the winds, demanding authenticity, and steering clear of the constraints of depersonalisation'. In fact this is a reasonable rendition of the sorts of tensions and dilemmas of 'between-ness' that I want to capture as a common, although not universal element, of the perspectives and orientations of these families. To greater or lesser extents, they feel very responsible for their children but still recognize themselves as living in a complex and diverse social world, within and towards which they also have some sort of responsibility. Again it is tempting to want to reduce this complexity and variety to a binary – a separation between those more clearly typified by bourgeois individualism and those who might be said to be solidary individualists. But that fails to capture the struggles and tensions that are embedded in at least some of the families, or the different kinds of relationships between principles and actions. These are not simply calculating, uncaring people, but they are very desperate to do the best for their children. They typically work within and make decisions in a mass of contradictions which set pragmatism and love against principles and the impersonal standpoint. It is not the individual choices of particular families that create social divisions and inequalities, it is the aggregate of the pattern of choices, the hidden hand of class thinking, if you like, the repetition of certain decisions, views, perspectives and actions – that is, what Bourdieu (1990b: 79) would call 'a system of dispositions to a certain practice ... the regularity of modes of practice'. Where dilemmas are recognized these dilemmas capture 'the dialectic between alternative views, values, beliefs in persons and in society' (Berlak and Berlak 1981: 124), but what we see is a particular 'pattern of resolution' (132), or 'dominant modes of resolution' (133). Certainly these families see themselves as autonomous decision-makers in a contradictory but all too real world, however much they feel constrained by their sense of a responsibility for a future which must be planned for. The decisions to which this responsibility gives rise are made within a particular framework of possibilities, which at least some of the families are uncomfortable with (but see Chapter 3). This often means having to privilege necessary interests over right or preferable values. When it came down to it 'commitments to the welfare of others ... were not part of the respondents' primary accountability' (Jordan, Redley and James 1994: 197); putting the family first was. And, as I have stressed, this is entirely defensible morally, at least as far as ensuring an adequate education is concerned. Furthermore, impersonal values do play a part in school choice for some and these are not simply attenuated individuals; indeed there are some families for whom principle is certainly more important than advantage. This is not a simple story of self-loathing. Nonetheless, the material presented and discussed here does confirm Jordan's account of the predominance of the 'personal standpoint'. Where it exists, their support for, or willingness to trust their children to, comprehensive education rests upon being able to find comprehensive settings in which certain kinds of social relations and forms of distinction are available to them. Again this is entirely defensible in terms of ensuring a high probability of an adequate education for their children, but as I have tried to demonstrate previously adequacy is often conflated with the search for a distinct and advantageous education. This relates back to the argument in Chapter 3, which suggests that increasingly comprehensive schooling or state schooling more generally is being recaptured and reworked by the needs, real or perceived, of the middle class. Even so, for some, as we have seen, the risks to their child or the imperatives of social advantage make any kind of comprehensive education unthinkable. For these families ethical considerations may impinge upon the calculus of school choice but are subordinated to both calculation and the values of individualism. That is to say, most families regard the choice between public and private school as having ethical connotations but principles are not adequate in themselves as guides to action. 'Without any ill-will toward others, the logic of their choices must always tend towards giving their offspring a head start ...' (Jordan, Redley and James 1994: 222). But I have also tried to raise questions about whether this logic should be seen 'simply' as a representation of the child's best interests.

Also I do not intend to pretend that these parents are, or should be viewed as, unified or stable moral subjects. Like the rest of us, they make sense of their lives and actions within different, often discordant, narratives using different repertoires of meaning; although currently certain meanings and narratives have discursive privilege. At times liberal identities are displaced by the empirical pragmatics of choice, and the moral imperatives of good parenting. I have not attempted to erase the complications that arise from the analysis but I do suggest that the displacement of values captured here, and the actions and choices which this displacement makes possible, fit back directly into the analysis of differentiations and boundaries outlined in previous chapters.

7 Risk, uncertainty and fear

... modernity ... brings uncertainty to the very mode of existence ...

(Giddens 1998: 102)

... risk is a way – or rather a set of different ways of ordering reality, of rendering it into a calculable form ...

(Dean 1999: 131)

It is almost obligatory these days that any text which addresses contemporary social and political issues has a chapter on risk. So here is mine. This chapter revisits some of the themes and issues addressed previously. It does so from the perspective of risk and illustrates the interwoven social and psychological complexity, for the middle class, of the contemporary education enterprise. The dualism of risk and fear in the *conscience collective* of the middle class, as related to the problematics of social reproduction (see Chapter 2), is at least one reason for the massively increased role of education within politics and the media. As Douglas (1994: 3) opines, 'it is hard to maintain seriously that the perception of risk is private' and Giddens (1998) asserts that we now live in a 'risk climate'. The risks in play here lie somewhere between global and everyday risks. However, while Beck (1992) and Giddens have written the sociological headlines of the risk society, their representations of risk have a number of weaknesses and limitations (see Dean 1999; Crook 1999). In particular, 'Beck's approach to risk can be characterised as totalising, realist and relying on a uniform conception of risk' (Dean 1999: 131). While I would not demur from his realism, Beck's portrayal of risk as an ontological condition of all humans fails to take adequate account either of the social differentiation of risk or of the existence of different regimes of risk and risk management. Therefore the discussion here draws to a greater extent on the more nuanced work of Crook (1999), and to a lesser extent Douglas (1994), rather than the 'super-realists' Beck and Giddens. Crook's conceptual framework provides a language for thinking about the relationship between risk-regimes and different forms of risk management behaviour.[1] In other words, it creates a theoretical space in which it is possible to think about both the role of the social actor and the role of the state. I shall get back to the role of the state at the end of the chapter but can do no more than make some theoretical gestures here to what needs to be a more thorough and extended theoretical and empirical exercise.

In an unintended restatement of Parkin's (1979) thesis of class and social closure, Ehrenreich (1989: 83) makes the point that the 'barriers that the middle class erected to protect itself make it painfully difficult to reproduce itself'. The individualist mode of social reproduction (see Chapter 4) is fraught with difficulties and beset by anxiety and 'the fear of falling'. To put it another way: 'Utterly dependent on market and state, the social fate of the many is becoming the particular fate of each individual' (Berking 1996: 191). The regime of choice and individualism threatens an equality that was unthinkable within collectivist modes of social reproduction. Demarcations cannot be taken for granted; they have to be maintained and achieved. While the middle class enter the education market with considerable advantages, tangible and otherwise, with 'resources to at least attempt to live [the] dream of order' (Crook 1999: 186), as I have sought to demonstrate, there are no guarantees, no certainties of a smooth and uneventful process of social reproduction. Middle-class parents, like all parents, can only do their best – deploy their capitals as strategically as they are able and 'through careful molding and psychological pressure ... predispose each child to retrace the same long road they themselves once took' (Ehrenreich 1989: 83). In particular, as we have seen, these families rely heavily on 'the domestic transmission of cultural capital' (Bourdieu 1980: 244). (This is very evident, for example, in the way middle-class students have the necessity of higher education inculcated into their thinking – see below.) In other words, social reproduction is a risky business. 'There are fewer and fewer unquestionably given paths of life conduct available' (Berking 1996: 195).[2] This sense of risk in the enterprise of education interplays forcefully with the strong sense of responsibility which is so central to middle-class individualism, what Jordan, Redley and James (1994) call 'putting the family first' (see Chapter 6).

In effect, risk theorists like Beck and Giddens now see the whole of society and social life as dominated by the kind of strategic morality I have been seeking to adumbrate here. 'In the individualised society, the individual must therefore learn, on pain of permanent disadvantage, to conceive of himself or herself as the centre of activity, as the planning office with respect to his or her own biography, abilities, orientations, relationships and so on' (Beck 1992: 55). Risk constantly reinforces responsibility and the values of the developmental self. And this touches upon the central concerns of this treatise in two senses. First, this book focuses upon one sphere of such planning work within families – their education strategies. Second, the book rests upon the premise that the skills and orientations of, or dispositions for, such work are unevenly distributed across societies. This gives rise to a new form of inequality, that is, 'the inequality of dealing with insecurity and reflexivity' (Beck 1992: 98).

Perversely then, given my argument that the market form privileges middle-class families, the sense of risk and uncertainty experienced by the middle classes is almost certainly heightened by the market. The market has a degree of openness and unplannedness which constantly threatens to overwhelm the orderliness, planning and futurity that denotes many middle-class households. It is often not clear what the right choice is. Choice of school is often, for these families, a matter of uneasy compromise. That is to say, there is 'risk anxiety inherent in neo-liberal over-production and under control of risk' (Crook 1999: 181). Risks in the achievement of educational success and accumulation of credentials, as a result of a combination of neo-liberal policies and the concomitant individualization and privatization of social reproduction that results in part at least from this, have increased significantly (see Chapter 4). Indeed, there is a kind of moral panic around schooling and school choice, particularly in metropolitan settings. An ephemeral example:

> Having put my seven-year-old son, Nicolas, through the ordeal of an entrance examination for two massively over-subscribed schools that would take him through to 18, I am distressed at the selection process. Just before the deadline for registration we were told he was borderline in terms of maturity. Did we want to gamble and enter him nonetheless? We all take gambles throughout our lives, but not usually on behalf of our children.
>
> (Debbie Beckerman, 'Private lottery: Opting out of "bog standard" schooling can be a harrowing process', *The Times* 1 March 2001)

Families are expected to take responsibility for choosing. Rose (1996: 57) goes as far as to suggest that the new advanced liberal regime of choice, the enpowerment of the citizen–consumer, is in fact a yet more sophisticated means of government: 'It has become possible to actualize this notion of the actively responsible individual because of the development of a new apparatus that integrates subjects into a moral nexus of identifications and allegiances in the very process in which they appear to act out their most personal choices'. Within the regime of choice the failings of the system become lodged within the shortcomings of individuals or families. Douglas (1994: 321) argues that the culture of the market, of individualism, 'is so organised that incompetence and weakness cannot be compensated for'. There is too much choice, and yet always a possibility of wrong or unsuccessful choice-making in the education marketplace. Choice of school and schools chosen both require assiduous and careful attention if the risks of social reproduction are to be minimized: 'Individual agents must become risk monitors and risk calculators' (Crook 1999: 171). This is very clear in the choice narratives of the middle-class families with which we are concerned – 'we knew we could get my son into the local school and the question is whether there's something better' (Mr Simpson).

... you think of the happiness of your child for the next five or six years, of course it's a big decision, you wonder if you are going to make the right one, cos ok, you can change, but you don't want to unsettle them.

(Mrs Wall)

Two very different forms of risk and risk management are juxtaposed. On the one hand there is the modernist, welfarist, one-fits-all, organized risk management solution of comprehensivism and neighbourhood schooling which is perceived as engendering its own risks for the middle-class project of social reproduction and differentiation. The continuing political and media critiques of state schooling generally and comprehensive schooling in particular (see Chapter 3) emphasizes their riskiness, rightly or wrongly, in these respects. As I have tried to illustrate, the construction of an educational career by middle-class parents for their children is denoted by planning and thoughtfulness. Lupton (1999: 3) suggests indeed that 'risk is an integral feature of a society that has come to reflect upon itself, critique itself'. On the other, there is the privatized and more open post-welfare, choice solution which has been the focus of the foregoing chapters. And again risk is an inherent characteristic of the market form, an essential part of its dynamic, a quality that is celebrated and set over and against the conservatism of bureaucratic systems. The market form rests on responsibility, skills and resourcefulness and an absence of certainty. In the interviews there were occasional yearnings for less choice and the older simplicities of the welfarist system of local schooling. Part of the riskiness of the post-welfare, choice system, as explored in Chapter 5, inheres in the importance and elusiveness of useful and accurate information.

Trust/distrust of professional and expert systems

The respondents also talked of not enough choice and too much. Schools were too alike, or simply there were not enough schools available to choose from. Too much choice reflected both a response to the stresses of choice-making and a sense of having too much information to process and assess. That is, you can never know enough but often know too much, and it is difficult to know what is important and what is not. Thus, 'for the educated middle classes of the advanced societies, at least, risk communications merge with problems of consumption and lifestyle choice in a general information overload that is more likely to provoke anxiety and insecurity than a sense of safety and control' (Crook 1999: 180).

... I'd like to be able to pick up so much more, it's this thing that you can't pick up until you get into the classroom, how good are they? And I don't mean when they're on display, that means you want some kind of independent judgement system ... I'd rather have too much than too little ... a whole variety, capital rate of spending, floor space of gyms whatever. If we're not too careful we're going to concentrate on one aspect of it, that is, examination results.

(Mr Marsh)

Again this highlights what Bourdieu (1986b: 253) describes as 'the gratuitous expenditure of time ...' on collecting more and more information, which leads to more and more discussion within the family and the family's social network. The Cornwells reported that they had been 'thinking for four years' about the choice of a secondary school. The Mankells talked of an 'ongoing discussion since they were born'. 'This overload connects with the arbitrariness and necessary incompleteness of even the most assiduous individual risk calculation' (Crook 1999: 180). Again these may be close up aspects of more general social changes. Distrust, self-interest and the over-supply of information within market societies are a heady and unstable combination. This may be a paradox of reflexive modernization, the idea that information provides control, but that all information is potentially unreliable. Indeed, Douglas (1994: 32) suggests that 'knowledge is falling apart' and that 'no one offers us certainty'. In a way that parallels Parkin's analysis (Chapter 4), Douglas suggests that the move from 'hierarchy' to 'market' or individualism removes certainty. Or in Crook's terms this replaces an 'organized' risk management regime with a neo-liberal one. One of the paradoxes of choice then is that the market itself (applied to schools, as elsewhere) 'undermines the communicative conditions of intersubjective trust' (Berking 1996: 1997). Market systems produce a particular genre of communication which is not to be trusted (Chapter 5). There is a frustration of reason, the lack of a perfect science of choice, of complete, accurate, robust information.

Spatialization of risk and class – strategies and concerns are localized

Over and against the generalized sense of anxiety which besets the middle-class project of social reproduction it is also important to acknowledge that risks and the perception of risk vary. They vary, to some extent, according to the resources available to the family. Some families minimize risk by deploying their economic capital to buy educational advantages in the private system (see Chapter 5). This is a fairly sure and certain way of doing your best for your children in terms of ensuring a high probability of social advantage. Also we saw in Chapter 5 that some families are able to use economic, social, cultural and emotional capital at moments of crisis or key moments of transition to ensure access to privileged trajectories or avert calamity. Interventions of various kinds are a key tactical device in managing the 'uncertainties' of schooling (see Vincent and Martin 2002). The risks, or perceptions of risk with which we are concerned here, also vary according to where you live and who else lives there. This was certainly evident in marked differences between the two localities from which the secondary school parent sample was drawn – Northwark and Riverway. The class and ethnic composition of the two localities is very different. As regards minority ethnicity, only 5 per cent of the Riverway population were so identified in 1991, compared with 22 per cent in Northwark. In 1998 only 23 per cent of secondary school students were in LEA schools in Northwark and only 15 per cent achieved five or more A to C grades at GCSE, compared with 87 per cent in LEA schools in Riverway and a 51 per cent GCSE score. At Key Stage 2 in national tests 62 per cent of Northwark students were level 4 or above; in Riverway the figure was 77 per cent. Total net spending, per head of population, was the lowest of all the London boroughs in Riverway in 1998; Northwark's spending was 18th of the 32 boroughs; but spending on education was almost identical in the two authorities.

Beyond, or embedded in, these statistics there is a variety of cultural and lifestyle factors which distinguish the middle class in Northwark from that in Riverway. Riverway is the 'white highlands', it is a middle-class enclave, healthy, wealthy and safe and mono-cultural. Riverway has a stable and long-established middle-class community. Northwark is more multi-ethnic and class-diverse, with some parts having been recently 'regentrified' and with what Butler and Robson (2002b: 15) describe as a middle-class community that is 'highly bounded and inward looking'. The gentrified areas of Northwark, in which the respondents quoted here lived, were fairly 'atomised' and the 'actors motivated instrumentally by the requirements of their households and jobs' (Butler and Robson 2001: 27). Butler and Robson (2001: 27) also refer to a low level of 'active mutuality' and go on to say that:

> It is the strength of the local markets in education, housing and leisure and consumption that satisfies the needs of middle-class residents. The cultural capital stored in this community being highly variable, the educational success of children and the infrastructure of social interaction can ultimately be secured through the deployment of economic capital.

Both impressionistically, and from the figures quoted above, Riverway has a stronger sense of mutuality, a higher investment in collective cultural activities and, obviously, a higher level of trust in local state schooling. The newness of the Northwark middle class and the changing local social structure was emphasized by Mr Marsh.

> More people like me are moving in. We were originally advised not to move into the area, because it was too rough, so yes it has changed tremendously, particularly the City people moving in, whereas before there were very few, and it's now socially acceptable to be in the area.

Gentrification is not a unitary phenomenon and needs 'to be examined in each case according to its own logic and outcomes' (Butler and Robson

2001: 29: see Butler and Robson 2002b for a full discussion of such differences in various London settings). These differences give rise to different local class cultures, infrastructures and histories. There are different sedimentations of class and what Butler and Robson (2002a: 21) call different 'narratives of the areas'. Different engagements between class and locality. Particular classes and class segments are attracted to and are able to afford to live in these localities, and within the localities class is realized differently. The directing and socializing effects of the local social networks also differ in relation to stability and integration. Classes and class fractions are realized in subtly different ways in interaction, in participation in the lifestyle of the locality and its social networks. These are different spaces of subjectivity. Class then takes on an emergent, localized quality.

The school markets in these two localities also differ. They differ by virtue of who attends the schools. In terms of the organization and history of provision and in relation to local politics – Riverway is a Social Democrat authority, which has a commitment to comprehensive education; Northwark is Conservative and the LEA is decidedly against comprehensivism. There are large numbers of private schools in both locations. In Riverway there are several long-established private schools, some ex-direct grant. In Northwark the private sector is for the most part more recent but there are many established, high-reputation schools near at hand. Access to state secondary schools in Riverway was 'organized' and in Northwark 'open' – more like a free market. (See Gewirtz, Ball and Bowe 1995, and Bowe, Ball and Gewirtz 1995 for a fuller discussion of differences between the two education markets.)

It seemed to be the case that suspicion of the state sector among equivalent families was at much higher levels in Northwark than in Riverway, although the samples were not matched as such. As a part of this the state sector in Riverway was seen as more uniform than that in Northwark – which is certainly accurate and reflects the class make-up of the two localities. These give rise to different 'situated risk logics' as Lupton (1999: 6) calls them. Mrs Connelly makes the point very nicely:

> I mean this area, which is St Vincents, is a very odd area, cos what happens is ... people move in ... into it, and then they start to have children ... they like the local schools, and then you find that where they might have moved out they tend to stay and really only move within the area, to stay within the state sector because they either find that they've got a large mortgage so they can't afford to pay the fees ... for private education or they want to support state education and actually it's very easy if you live here. You know it's easy to really support state education because if you look at the results they're pretty good ... and having said that ... the type of parents that live in Riverway and Tidewell ... they should be good. I mean I think everybody that I know has got a degree ... so the chances are that our children will go on and at least do A levels,

so I think if you're dealing with that type of parent, whether they go privately or state, the results should be good. And there's a lot of those types of people living round here.

I didn't think it was necessary within this area to send her to a private school. The only reason I would even consider an independent school would be is if I was living in an area where I felt the schools were appalling.

(Mrs Dexter)

Here the schools are seen as a reflection of the locality and of the parents who send their children to them. This provides a sort of guarantee, an assurance of success. The school is not represented as an independent variable here with qualities of its own separate from its intake and this gives a general indication of the way in which perceptions of schools and perceptions of risk are constructed. In effect a school can only be as good as its intake. The logic of this is that in another setting, as Mrs Dexter says, the evaluation of the state sector, as a whole or locally, might be very different. In contrast, in Northwark, Mr Turner cannot quite bring himself to trust the state schools, but again evaluates the schools by their intake of other children like his.

There are more bright kids going into the state sector this year for a mixture of ideological and other reasons, if we were really starting again we might have taken a risk with Fletcher.

The choice between state and private schooling has to be understood as socially situated, as discussed in Chapter 6 on values and principles. There are further aspects to the class logic embedded here. Mrs Connelly suggests that a further dimension to choice of state schools, again as discussed in Chapter 6, is the messy tension between affording private education and valuing in principle state education. Mrs Connelly hints that despite the quality of the state sector, if more parents could afford private schooling they would chose it for their children. As suggested already, for some parents private schooling is always preferable simply because it is not state schooling and because it offers inherent advantages to their child. In all this risk is not a stable category. Rather: 'Risk is a way – or rather a set of different ways of ordering reality' (Dean 1999: 131).

State sector as a risk

As noted already, for some parents entrusting their children to the state sector was one risk that they were unwilling to take. Mrs Crichton explained, very simply, that she was 'nervous about the state sector' and the 'problem of taking a chance with your child and throwing them into the state sector'. For such parents private schools provided environments and opportunities and forms of provision which would simply not be available, as they saw it, to their children in the state sector. These 'class enclaves' (Teese 2000) offer 'long term protections from potential risk in an increasingly uncertain world' (Sedden 2001: 139). Concomitantly they regarded entering their child in the state sector as putting their child and their child's future at risk. As Devine (1997: 37) puts it: 'they were not confident that their children would realise their full potential in a state system and they were not prepared to risk their children's future especially if they had the capacity to increase their children's chance of success'. Such a position is both moral and strategic: 'the process of decision-making is regarded as a specialised technique for connecting belief, desires and actions' (Devine 1997: 11). As such 'the class project feels like good parenting' (Sedden 2001: 139). Private schools offer a cultural milieu, 'a communicative order of self-recognition' (Teese 1981: 103–4), which is coherent and undiluted, and constitutes a 'protected enclave for class formation' (Sedden 2001: 134). As Teese (2000) concludes, private schools are fortified sites within diverse school systems which represent class projects and 'renew middle class culture and collectivity in predictable ways across generations' (Sedden 2001: 136). They transform or reinvest economic capital into cultural capital. In effect these enclaves work to export risk of failure to state schools. They protect and reproduce 'communities of destiny'. They discipline students into academic success.

> Everyone I know either went to a grammar school or a private school … so it's something … comprehensive to me is a complete unknown quantity, so therefore it's alarming, only based on ignorance really. And also you do have to be able to handle those … varying degrees, you are not in an environment where everybody wants to work.

Here Mrs Grafton is willing to take the risk of sending her child to state school but she does this reflexively and her language of 'panic' and 'alarm' gives some indication of the emotional underpinnings of the decision. Indeed Barbalet (2001: 41) suggests that 'emotion provides appropriate or enhanced goals for self-interested action, enlarging its rationality' – fear, panic and alarm must be assuaged. As we have seen, this kind of mix of rational and affective responses runs through all of the narratives of these parents. Here the comprehensive school is an unknown, and Mrs Grafton is anticipating difficulties in 'an environment' where not 'everyone wants to work'. The 'not everyone' is the 'other', those children who are not like mine. These are the risks of social mix, of boundary crossing, of going outside of grid and group (Pakulsi and Waters 1996: 118). Indeed, Douglas suggests that risk works to maintain cultural boundaries (Lupton 1999: 4). In the case of schooling these are risks that have to be managed or handled by the family. Again there is a clear sense of the perspective of planning that underlies the enterprise of education within the family. Indeed there are glimpses here, and throughout these accounts, of what Crook (1999: 175) calls 'a hyper-reflexive ordering'. This is particularly evident in the 'over-response', the hyper-responsibility, of many middle-class families in their management of the problem of choice. They appear in their own accounts, and indeed may be concerned to want to appear, 'as responsible and calculating prudentialists' (O'Malley 1996: 199). Again this is particularly the case in relation to the use of information. Within neo-liberal risk-regimes the state takes on a role of information and advice provision (see Ball 2000), for example through the publication of league tables and inspection reports, but again there is a paradox here. Crook (1999: 180) argues that 'the provision of advice and information means precisely the "production" and communication of risks in greater numbers'. And indeed it would be irresponsible simply to leave the collection and provision of information to the state – and can this information be trusted? Responsibility must be played out, taken seriously. 'To rely on the state to deal with the harmful effects of known, calculable and individually manageable risks appears feckless and culpable' (O'Malley 1996: 202). Parents' narratives of choice were full of detailed accounts of the collecting, shifting, checking and rechecking of information, and of the use of perceptions, experiences, advertising and hearsay. In a sense, all information was considered but none, or almost none, was trusted (see Chapter 5, Ball and Vincent 1998 and below). Let us look at some extracts from interviews here. These illustrate several of the issues discussed and also pick up on themes introduced in previous chapters.

> Yes, we went to open days in the private sector, we went to Overbury and Tideway open days … the year before we chose for Todd … we went to them the year we chose for Todd … we went round in the day and we also made an individual visit to Tideway, when we looked and made the decision about whether we chose the private sector or not. So yes, we must have gone round Tideway four or five times.
>
> (Mrs Mankell)

Again Mrs Mankell illustrates the ever-presence of the private sector and the comparisons between state and private schools and the time and effort devoted to ensuring that the chosen school is the right school. The Crichtons were particularly assiduous, careful and reflexive choosers and information managers. Here we get a sense of the timescale of choosing and the ways in which choice is part of a collective effort and part of the management of a whole school career and orientation to education for children. There can be no doubts about the Crichtons' sense of responsibility:

> Thinking about her specifically … I would say we've been generally thinking over three or four years. Detailed thinking and asking really over the last year, and visits, prospectuses, this term, but it has to be

said that ... given that she's our second child, quite a lot of the thinking and the tramping round and tapping the local grapevine that we did ... we started doing a couple of years before our son, who is two years older, was coming up, and some of the tramping round ... that we did with him, for us eliminated some possible co-ed schools, locally. So the process we've gone through this autumn with her, has been helped, and I would say shortened, by some of what we did for him two years ago.

Here a key part of the process is elimination, drawing lines and boundaries around the acceptable and unacceptable (Bagley, Woods and Glatter 2000). One form of risk management, as noted already, involves the maintenance of cultural boundaries. The process is long, measured and organized around talk within the family (see Reay and Ball 1998). Hasty decisions are definitely avoided. These are families at ease with talk, families that have a certain 'distance from the world' (Bourdieu 1986a) that permits planning and reflection, relatively unencumbered by 'material constraints and temporal urgencies' and freed from the 'submission to necessity'.

> Yes, there was always a point ... because there has to be if nothing else ... there's a time deadline that you're working to. Each time it has been ... when we've done all our visits, we keep an open ... say we've done all our visits, and we've looked at the written material, and we have what I would call our final conversations with our children, we've talked with them all the way along ... and have ... with both of them kind of tried to put to rest any immediate leaping in. For both of them, I think ... our daughter ... having heard these conversations with our son.
>
> (Mrs Crichton)

All information is considered, but not unthinkingly; there is a degree of scepticism about the information required from schools by the state. Expert systems have to be dealt with skilfully. This information does not stand up on its own and has to be supplemented by the immediacy of the visit and direct questioning by the family themselves.

> Yes, especially now that they have little choice but to include exam results and truancy rates and all the rest ... I'm fully in favour of public information, so yes, I would say ... you know, any organization, and schools are stupid if they don't ... again present themselves as best they can, so if anybody didn't take care of a prospectus I'd wonder what on earth they were up to. The little bits of paper shoved in the back are usually what we pored over because that was exam results, details about how they split up the curriculum, list of staff and what qualifications they'd got ... so it did matter, yes, and we did look very carefully at them ... and that was often out of the prospectuses, that we got our kind of hit list of three or four key questions ... that we wanted straight answers to ... when we visited.

Mrs Grafton reiterates the local context of choice, the use of social capital resources, the need for 'loads' of visits, the role of talk, and the basic concern with finding the school that matches your child. The child is also the object of careful reflection in this process.

> Well Riverway as you know has very good state schools, so it has a reputation for that and that's one of the reasons people move into this area. How did we go about deciding ... we talked to other people, we went to that talk on choosing your own secondary school, where I think you were, we visited loads of schools ... we talked to each other, you think about your child.

Mrs Connelly's description begins by emphasizing the normativities that are embedded in 'good parenting', what the good parent does and taking responsibility. Again appropriate social capital is a vital component of decision-making. That is, as Crook (1999: 175) suggests, hyper-reflexive ordering 'operates through networks rather than institutions ... It is associated with individualism and the reflexive monitoring of the self'. The Connellys feel rushed, but will not be rushed. To be responsible, like the Crichtons, you must take your time. You are 'bombarded with information, again there is too much and not enough' (see Mrs Crichton below). The problem is to get 'a true picture' of a school; 'you visit one school after another'. Your own impressions are important but cannot always be trusted. The social network is vital but cannot always be trusted either. Yet again the private sector is a possibility. You have your child tutored for entrance exams. Time and planning and taking the long view are basic to the management of risk. The bottom line and the responsible thing to do is 'to give your child a fair chance'.

> Well obviously, if you're in a school, and you're fairly active within a school, you know parents who've got older children and younger children ... The ones who have got older children who are coming to the decision that we've come to now, have said that what happens is that you go into the last year of primary school, you just get back to school and then suddenly you get these forms from the council, saying ... your child is now going on to secondary education, here are a list of open evenings for all the schools, but then you have to have made your mind up by November ... and you visit one school after another, sometimes on consecutive evenings ... you don't really get a chance to sit down and think about the school that you've seen, you're just bombarded with information, bits of paper to read, and it's not really long enough to sit down and really think about it, and also if you go and visit a school on one day, they could be having a bad day or you could be having a bad day and you don't really get a true picture of that school. So it was really friends who'd got older children, who felt that they really

didn't have long enough to make that decision ... plus if we wanted Alex to go privately he would have to be tutored, and it takes about two years really for them to get used to the idea of having to sit exams, doing things within a time limit, and they are just taught in a different way in the private sector, so if you really want to do that you've got to give your child a fair chance ... so we thought ... so we wouldn't feel rushed in our decision that's why we started looking two years ago ... .

(Mrs Crichton)

When it comes down to it information may not be enough. Indeed as suggested earlier, the more you know the more doubtful you can become. And in this arena of choice, for these parents, mistakes may be 'low probability' but 'high consequence'. Their child's whole future, as they see it, is at stake.

... the only reason I would have really considered it was because of ensuring ... if you like, like an insurance policy, that if he went there, he was very likely to come out with good results. And I suppose when you send your child to a comprehensive, which is not the system that we knew as children, you have less of a guarantee.

(Mrs Gosling)

In effect choosing the private sector, as a response to the risks of the state sector, can be seen as a different, older, form of risk management. That is what Crook (1999: 182) calls 'neo-traditonalism', which can produce 'local solidarities, whether defined by taste, ethnicity, place or other markers that take their significance from a balance of inclusion (us) and exclusion (them)'. This takes us back to the issue of social closure (Chapter 4). The private school provides a definitive form of boundary maintenance, of closure. It avoids the possibilities of social pollution which can arise when order and boundaries are breached. Indiscriminate mixing can threaten 'ontological insecurities' (Giddens 1991). Private schooling limits the degree of social mixing to tolerable levels. Indeed for some, as we have seen, a managed degree of social mixing with some others is welcome. The private school provides an assurance of common enterprise – 'a convergence of interests, practices, preferences and priorities' (Sedden 2001: 137). It is a choice for exclusivity and also for advantage. It is, as Crook suggests, a basis of solidarity, in effect, of 'recognition' (see below). Here, in a paradoxical sense, is an enclave in which neo-liberal policies do not operate. The risks threatened by equality through choice can be avoided. And indeed, for some families the private sector has an obviousness to it. It is a non-choice.[3] It is 'an alternative to constant "choice", anxiety and isolation' (Crook: 181) and mobilizes 'versions of safety and certainty' (182). Choice of private school goes a good way towards avoiding the 'chronic problematization of the signifier' (Lash 1994: 157) that attends the question of what is a good state school. The private schools are 'instead rooted in shared meanings and routine background practices' (159).

These might also be thought of as 'taste communities'. They are able to trade upon a 'second order language of allusions and cultural complicities' (Bourdieu 1994: 8) which also involve an 'immediate investment of affect' (Lash 1994: 157). Perhaps in Lash's (1994) terms this produces kinds of 'reflexive communities'. However, as noted previously, while the private school may fit 'like a pair of comfy slippers' for some, they are jarring anachronisms for others.

It is those parents who for want of economic capital, or by principled choice, find themselves in the liminal space between the local school and private school who face the most fear, anxiety and uncertainty and who feel themselves to be most at risk (see Chapter 6). The risks of reproduction are inherent in the situation of those who depend for their class position on cultural capital. They are subject to the logic of scholastic competition.

Anxiety, emotion and class choosing

Obviously, various capitals are interwoven here. There is an emotional as well as social and material expenditure involved in choice-making. As Mrs Connelly's account indicates, economic capital (she does not need to work) facilitates the choice process – visits, information gathering – and secures emotional capital for deployment in this process. This is a small-scale example of what Bourdieu calls 'transubstantiation' whereby 'the most material types of capital (...) can present themselves in the immaterial form of cultural capital' (1986b: 242).

> I'm glad I wasn't working ... well yes, it takes up an awful lot of energy and an awful lot of your emotional energy as well ... in the space of a few weeks. I think it wasn't difficult for me because I'm not working and I've got somebody who can look after the other children if I went out in the evening ...

While I do not want to overplay the emotional and psychological aspects of the market behaviour of parents and students, there was in the interviews and transcripts a palpable sense of the emotional aspects of risk. Worries about getting things wrong, about failing the child, about mistaking priorities, about not finding the perfect school or right university. The other side of all this was various forms of guilt. Both a personal guilt about letting the child down or in some cases social guilt about choosing private school in preference to the state sector (see Chapter 6). As one parent put it simply, you make 'judgments about yourself' (Mrs Cornwell). All of this is set, as noted before, within a general sense of moral responsibility as a parent, based upon normative and classed models of good parenting (see also Gewirtz 2001); 'the extent of parents' ethical and social responsibility today ... is historically unprecedented ... The contemporary family is under a *pressure to educate*' (Beck-Gernsheim 1996: 143).

And there are always doubts about the future, whether things will stay the same, or decisions stand the test of time; risks are ever-present. The vicissitudes of state education policies give the state sector an additional dimension of risk.

> And I don't know how those are going to develop over the next years, it still makes me a bit nervous because I am not convinced that they will remain as they are ... either in funding or attention ... so if those deteriorate they'll be a nightmare.
>
> (Mrs Symons)

Concerns both about getting it right and doing the right thing are engendered and reinforced within social networks. Parents, in part, become middle-class moral subjects by learning and acquiring behaviours and attitudes from others in their class setting. In this anxiety can be contagious. Parents are 'manic'. There is a danger of feeling 'panicked'. Decisions are almost made and then not.

> I did it with my husband ... Allan [son] knew that we were looking at schools, because what happens is, in September and October and November, the school is abuzz with manic parents ... and that filters right down ... to even the third years ... they all know that all these people are going round looking at schools ... so he knew that we were going to have a look at them, and ... we just said we're going to have a look just to see so that when the time comes for you ... we don't feel panicked and rushed. The next year, when he was in the fifth year, I took Allan to see Overbury and Tideway, because we had almost made up our mind by then that we were going to go to the state sector.
>
> (Mrs Cornwell)

There are emotions both in and of choice. As suggested above certain sorts of information are valued more highly than others. Hot knowledge gleaned through social capital networks is one such. This provides a reassurance of community, of shared perceptions and values and is thus related to a second sort of information which was privileged in many of the parents' narratives; that is, their own emotional responses to schools, particularly the negative responses, such as aversion, or positive responses such as recognition. This is what I have called elsewhere class choosing; a part, if you like, of the lived reality of class, its emotional reality. What Reay (1998a: 267) calls 'the emotive intimacies of class'. Those 'gut feelings' that are a 'primitive' form of class awareness, an identification with 'people like us' – 'the taken-for-granted understandings they bring to their relationships with others' (Reay 1997: 226). A sense of belonging, of a shared 'style of life' or mode of being. The sense, as Bourdieu puts it, of being like 'a fish in water'. Such choosing is outside the rational, not irrational, but irreducible to a simple calculability. It is a cultural response, a class response, where class is a critical mediation of being (Charlesworth 2000).

Futurity

As I have tried to indicate at various points so far, choice has a history within families and also, crucially, it has a future. Choice is about getting from the present to a particular kind of class and social location in the future. It is about prediction, imagination and assurance. This is why control is so important and why also risk is ever-present. Planning and anxiety go hand-in-hand (Giddens 1991). The future is now 'more absorbing' but 'at the same time more opaque' (Giddens 1998: 28). Middle-class ontologies are founded upon incompleteness, they are about becoming, about the developmental self, about making something of yourself, realizing yourself, realizing your potential. These parents envisage certain sorts of futures for their children. They see themselves as having the responsibility to make these futures possible through their actions and planning in the here and now and in the making up of a child that is 'reasoning and reasonable' (see Vincent 2000: 36). It is not a matter of 'insisting' as Mr Symons makes clear below, it is about making certain things obvious and about 'backing up', creating the conditions for the realization of their children's interests. These are possibilities that cannot be taken for granted, but they are 'worth striving for' (Lewis and Maude 1950: 245). Individualism must be tempered by hard work and 'the productive use of time' (Allatt 1993: 153). The future has to be invested in and the future has to be actively joined up to the present. It is important to know what you want to be. Lewis and Maude (1950: 288) suggest that the English middle class 'are what they are ... because of what they wanted to be'. A good number of the parents were able to say what their child, aged 11, wanted to be.

> So I made him think about it, I said it was his choice and it was his future, as much as our guidance, there was no point in him going to a school he didn't want to go to.
>
> (Mrs Crais)

> She was crying, saying "well mummy I don't know what I want to do", but we have actually consciously talked to her about the idea that, if you want to be ... let's say ... purely for example, a doctor, you've got to spend a lot of years in college and training and it takes this long ... so we've actually talked to her about it ... just so she realizes what she's letting herself in for ... sometimes it worries her a bit because she's got friends who say "I want to be this".
>
> (Mr Pelecanos)

In particular, these parents were envisaging their choices at 11 as a precursor to, a step towards, their children's entry into higher education. As noted already, these parents work hard to naturalize higher education as an obvious future route for their offspring. They are very aware of the point made by Marshall and Swift (1997: 114) that currently in the relationships between education and the labour market 'it is degree type qualifications that are of greater relevance for obtaining advantaged conditions of employment' and at this level the differentials between classes are actually widening despite the increase in participation rates (Ball, Davies, Reay and David 2002b). These parents are in many cases envisaging their child's educational trajectory in order to position them advantageously in relation to higher education entry.

> ... ours both are above average, not geniuses but both above average. You therefore want to make sure you're going to be able to give them a good education that will allow them to go on and do higher education ... .
>
> (Mrs Mankell)

> Yes, now definitely ... we really really hope that they will stay on beyond 16 ... somewhere. We really really want them to do higher ed ... but we don't have restricted views about what that will be. I mean my husband and I went A level, university, first degree, post-graduate, I went straight through, he had to break for work between his first degree and his post grad, so we took if you like an intensely academic route. There is no way that we would insist that our children do that, we wouldn't insist. We'd back them all the way if they ... but it's already looking as if our daughter might well have real artistic talent, and she gets very excited about the possibility of design ... well she might need art college, and we'd back her all the way on that. So yes, I'd say utterly enthusiastic about higher education, but not saying ... it's got to be the route we took, or that it's got to be a particular route ... yes.
>
> (Mrs Symons)

Mrs Doyle is even going so far as to think about which universities her child might attend. And as she explains she can 'see' her children doing certain things, her 'imagined future' for them is clear. Nonetheless, it is a long haul, and a matter of 'sticking at it', and as Power, Edwards, Whitty and Wigfall (2002, Chapter 8) point out, it is still possible to 'fail against the odds'.

> We're hoping they'll go on to higher education ... hopefully ... I can't see them leaving school at sixteen ... I mean I see them going on to tertiary college ... at the moment ... but hopefully they're going on to higher education. I think they're both capable of doing so. But I don't know what they want to be in the end. I think Jeremy's an environmental scientist or something ... because he's always been in to bugs and bees and things ... and Anna wants to be an author ... she could do drama at Bristol or something, couldn't she. And he could go to Stirling or somewhere like that. I mean that's what we'd like them to do ... when you look in the long term. I think they've got the capabilities ... and if they can stick at it ... .
>
> (Mrs Doyle)

In the interviews many of the parents seemed careful not to appear as 'pushy', a fine line needed to be trod between attentive support and over-bearing pressure. The individuality of the child, their developmental self has to be recognized, at least to some extent – again this was a point of differentiation among the families. But the riskiness of the future also has to be made clear.

> ... well after secondary school ... we'd assume, and I'd be very disappointed if he didn't then go on to sixth form college, that is the sixth form college in Riverway, so that's what he'd do ... after secondary school I hope ... and then I hope after that, but you never know what might happen ... that he'd go to university.
>
> (Mr Parker)

> I felt really I wanted her to be in a school where she would have a good chance of getting good GCSE and A level results, and getting the university of her choice. I'm not fussed if she doesn't get ten As like they seem to do at JAGs ... I want a springboard really to go into whatever she wants to do in the future ... .
>
> (Mrs Cornwell)

In effect, these parents are seeking to achieve some narrative coherence, linking and making consistent the lives of their children with their own. They are also reproducing through their children their tastes, distinctions and world-view; although these are related to a set of 'flexible futures, a landscape of possibilities rather than discrete and rigid paths' (Beck-Gernsheim 1996: 153). Nonetheless, there are some very clear and fixed markers or way stations on those paths – like higher education. What is of central importance in all of this is the tendency towards 'planning and rationalisation in the conduct of life' (Beck-Gernsheim 1996: 139). Again we should not over-estimate the newness of this; after all, the middle class have always be denoted by an orientation to the future. It is the increased ubiquity and sophistication, and often its technicization, that is remarkable; '... the pressure of planning and expectation on parents is not only growing quantitatively, but also assuming qualitatively new forms' (Beck-Gernsheim 1996: 139). As we have glimpsed in previous chapters, planning is starting earlier and involves, for some families, the mobilization or buying in of a sophisticated set of preparatory experiences and guidance, as well as making the best possible use of state support and facilities. All of this takes place not within a void of social autonomy but inside, over and against 'a highly complex work of art of labyrinthine construction' (140) that is modern governmentality. Although Beck-Gernsheim (1996) argues that there is no class specificity to all this (143), she does identify what she calls 'social risk groups' (150) – 'the unemployed, single parents, the homeless, etc.' (150). However, as I have tried to suggest above, risk has a particular specificity for the middle class – best represented perhaps in what O'Malley (1996: 199) calls 'prudentialism'. It is deeply embedded in the middle-class habitus inflecting perceptions, appreciations and actions in a particular way. This sense of risk, or of social ordering, is productive, it makes certain things possible. And crucially risk, for the middle class, is thus offset by the deployment of capitals, in specific social fields, as a means of controlling the future. Again my point is that while the dispositions and advantages embedded in the relationship of the middle class to its own social reproduction have a long history, these dispositions and advantages have a particular significance within and harmony with current shifts in the predominant risk-regime. This prudentialist risk-regime is constantly reinforced by the state's emphasis of the responsibilities of parenthood, and particularly motherhood[4] (see Vincent 2000, Chapter 2); although older, punitive social technologies are also deployed here. Again in its role of providing information for parents on school performance, the state encourages them to act as rational and calculative choosers, to make the best choices in the interests of their family and their future. Within such a regime, the prudent subject will invest in their own family's future (O'Malley 1996: 201). The relationship between parent and professional is also reworked within this new regime. The parent is now partner or customer and their active participation or intervention in their child's education becomes entirely legitimate and increasingly a necessity (Vincent 2000: 130–31). The prevailing risk-regime is pre-eminently middle-class.

8 Class practices and inequality

Well ... especially with the first child, I think ... you feel that all the decisions you've ever made about your child's ... education ... way of life.. and all the rest of it, are on the line ... and that ... if the child then doesn't get into the sort of school ... you feel they could cope with, you would be asking yourself what you've done wrong ... so I felt it was a time when our whole parenting was under scrutiny and we would either be vindicated or not ... so that's what I mean and also ... there was definitely a feeling that ... this step, although not ... this step into secondary education, it wouldn't be irrevocable, but it would be ... that's really got to be it, and a very very big influence on what they do in the rest of their life ... and that it would be ... a big step to get wrong ... so you had to put a lot of your attention into the ... into each school and approach each school as if your child was definitely going to go there, and ... size it up, assess your own reactions to it and all the rest of it.

(Mrs Cornwell)

In this last brief chapter I have three main concerns. First, I will consider what the discussion and analyses in the foregoing chapters have to contribute to our understanding of class and inequality in relation to what Tomlinson (2001) calls 'education in a post welfare society'. Second, I will consider what the discussion and analyses in the foregoing chapters have to contribute to current debates about social class, class theory and in particular our understanding of the middle class in contemporary society. I think it is very evident from the material discussed in this monograph that class has not gone away. However, the task and the challenge are to understand the new forms that it takes.[1] Third, I offer some comments about the relationship between the public morality of the state and the private principles of parents. Generally, in the course of this closing discussion I will revisit the themes of ambivalence, boundary, fear and uncertainty, individualism and reflexivity. Mrs Cornwell (above) provides the touchstone for the closing discussion.

The main thrust of the argument running through the previous chapters is that choice policies, or post-welfare education policies, offer a social and political context, and produce social fields or social spaces, in which the middle class feel both at home and at risk, comfortable but uncertain. The

demands and use of market rules of exclusion and a neo-liberal risk management regime are challenges which the middle class are well placed to
meet. They are fearful, alert and strategic. They are adept at working on
and in public institutions to realize their interests and ends. In particular
they are well placed to take advantage of modes of engagement which rely
upon the practices of consumption and the skills of assertive talk (Graue
1993). I have noted this as a recurrent phenomenon in a diverse range of
countries (Chapter 3). In particular, within the social fields of education the
middle class have enough capitals in the right currency, to ensure a high
probability of success for their children. Their tactical deployment of these
capitals more often than not enables them to gain access to and monopolize
advantageous educational sites and trajectories. Nonetheless, the possibility
of failing works to maintain high levels of anxiety and assiduousness. The
exclusionary rules of the market are addressed and appropriate capitals
activated via certain sorts of individualism. Nonetheless, the science of distinctions upon which exclusion rests, and in particular the social capitals
which facilitate choice, through the language and relationships of us and
them, are realized within a form of collectivity located within a community
of aspirations; what Boltanski (1987: 279) calls 'the cohesion of a fluid
group'. Thus: 'while processes in the labour market tend[ed] to fragment
the middle classes according to the different types of career they pursued,
those based around family structures and neighbourhood tended to unify
them' (Savage, Barlow, Dickens and Fielding 1992: 151). The practical mastery of choice and its underpinning judgements of attribution erect social
barriers along the fault lines of alienation and recognition, attraction and
rejection, commonality and difference to achieve social closure. Social closure 'is a form of collective social action which, intentionally or otherwise,
gives rise to a social category of ineligibles or outsiders' (Parkin 1979: 45).
The degree of intentionality within choice and other social actions, as discussed in Chapter 6, varies from family to family – ranging from
comfortable exclusivity to principled discomfort. But, as I have tried to
demonstrate it is often the case that 'deliberately class-organized practices
... arise out of a field of inertia' (Connell 1983: 72); doing what people like
us do! Class identities are always here relational, made by distinctions and
classifications of self and others. The middle class seek out settings which
are both familiar and distinctive. They are 'one of a social group', a collectivity of individuals which offers 'the twofold blessing of being someone
and not having to be alone in doing so' (Berking, 1996: 199).

The perceptions and actions which recognize and realize these distinctions are important in the production of closures both between and within
educational institutions. With a degree of paradox, and subject to a variety
of interpretations, social mix may also be valued; but there are limits to
social mix and to the value of social realism as against scholastic success
and certification as part of a child's development or experience of higher
education. When success and social advantage are at stake universalisms

may have to be sacrificed or circumvented. The legitimate partiality of family interests weigh heavily against general social principles. The child must be stretched; talents and abilities made the most of. This is good parenting. Investment in the child begins early and financial capital enables the buying in of services and experiences which play their part in making up the child as an educational subject, constructing them as able or talented, reasonable and reasoning. The child is produced through particularly focused hopes aimed towards vividly imagined futures. They are a future to be realized in and through education, as Mrs Cornwell makes clear. Constant vigilance and the right kind of pressure, over and on the child, and their educational institutions, is vital. There are always new separations to be sought or taken advantage of, new boundaries to be forged, gateways to be found, trajectories assured and distractions to be avoided. Options must be kept open and the responsible parent considers all possibilities in their child's best interests, although those interests are defined differently within different families.

Writing in the 1970s Bernstein (1975: 126) made the point that for the new middle class, if it is 'to repeat its position in the class structure, then appropriate secondary socialisation into privileged education becomes crucial' – 'your child's education, way of life ... are on the line', as Mrs Cornwell puts it. As the middle-class child passes through the education system classifications and frames increase in strength over time but, Bernstein suggests, space remains for 'some ambivalent enthusiasm for the invisible pedagogy for the early socialisation of the child' (127). While some residues of those enthusiasms may be apparent in the foregoing chapters, the space in which they are exercised is increasingly small, closed down by educational reform; in Bernstein's terms the 'inter-positional' is in the ascendant against the 'inter-personal'. In relation to, or alongside this, in the 1990s and the twenty-first century 'the grim obduracy of the division of labour and of the narrow pathways to power and prestige' (126) are uppermost in the minds of the middle-class parent even when their children are still very young. Whatever ambivalence remains around invisible pedagogies is being forced lower and lower down the system, and perhaps out of education altogether in some private child care settings, as our glimpses of pre-school choice have suggested.[2] In the UK the inroads which had been made in primary, and to a lesser extent in secondary, school by invisible pedagogies during the 1970s and 1980s have been more or less thoroughly undone by post-1988 policy interventions. However, all of this was a possibility that Bernstein had anticipated. Writing of what he called the 'interrupter matrix, and the new middle class', that is, the 'interruption' of traditional relationships between educational forms and social reproduction, Bernstein goes on to speculate that 'it is possible that such a form of reproduction may at some point evoke its own interrupter, i.e. an increase in either classification or frame strength or both' (1975: 149). We can see this interruption both in policy changes and in the changing perspectives of the middle class themselves. Both elements in turn reflecting changes in class relationships, in and around the labour market. In this way in the UK the education policies of Thatcherism and in more sophisticated ways Blairism (New Labour) are thoroughly classed. In effect class and policy and class and educational practices are being realigned.

> After the Conservative interregnum, the aspirational middle class is now attracted to individualist forms of organization and signals of opportunity and excellence. New Labour's electoral success has been built on creating an association with such individualist responses to aspirational demand.
>
> (McCaig 2001: 201)

In so far as they do or did stand for variety against inflexibility, expression against repression, it is now clearer than ever that 'The new middle class, like the proponents of the invisible pedagogy, are caught in a contradiction; for their theories are at variance with their objective class relationship' (Bernstein 1975: 126). Here again we can see at least one basis of the ambivalence of values and principles that arises between claims made, by some parents, for some kind of liberal identity and over and against the necessities of 'putting the family first'. Some families as we have seen struggle with the dilemmas of principle that this ambivalence creates. New Labour education policies can bridge this gap by providing both a critique of universalism in education, which gives support to individualistic practices and perspectives, and a set of positive legitimations of and opportunities for distinctions and boundaries between and within educational institutions, which enable social closure to be more easily achieved – specialist and Faith schools, ability setting, talented and gifted programmes and so on. Bauman (1998: 61) offers a more cynical and immediate interpretation of this 'interruption' when he suggests that:

> The welfare state came nowhere near the fulfilment of its founding fathers' dreams of exterminating once and for all poverty, humiliation and despondency; yet it did produce a large enough generation of well educated, healthy, self-assured, self-reliant, self-confident people, jealous of their freshly acquired independence, willing to cut the ground from beneath the popular support for the idea that it is the duty of those who have succeeded to assist those who continue to fail.

However, the lines of distinction asserted inside the education marketplace are drawn in different places by different families within the diversity of educational provision. Family histories, family values and principles, social location and opportunity (including financial capital) produce different degrees of obviousness, urgency and risk in relation to distinction and choice. In some locations a balance between responsibility and principles, between the personal and impersonal standpoints is achievable. In others, especially those parts of cities where 'others' are numerous, such balance is impossible. Even so, the interests of the child, either as (a classed) individual or (unique) person (Bernstein 1975), and the concomitant responsibilities of parenthood, in either form, are taken very seriously by these families. Indeed it is not easy to convey the high levels of assiduousness and attentiveness and concomitant anxiety that are invested in processes of choice in education. In this and other respects these parents are models of good practice (Gewirtz 2001). The middle class, and middle-class mothers especially, are 'the purveyors of normality' (Walkerdine, Lucey and Melody 2001: 114). It is very clear to these parents that they 'must do everything to give their child the "best start in life"' (Beck and Beck-Gernsheim 1995: 143).[3] These high expectations are embedded in neighbourhoods and social networks, and in this way social capital, even in the form of weak ties, acts back through the medium of responsibility – 'our whole parenting was under scrutiny' (Mrs Cornwell). middle-class families are confident choosers beset with doubts and loaded with responsibility. Through social involvements and interactions in the local community of schooling the discourse and practices of good parenting are developed and 'come to have a directive force for organising parental behaviour' (Harkness, Super and Keefer 1992: 178). In their responses to such direction middle-class parents confirm themselves as one of us and as not something other. That is, 'A class is defined as much by its *being-perceived* as by its *being* by its consumption ...' (Bourdieu 1986a: 483). Responsibility must be acted out, and in and through this acting out, in relations with and participation in schools, the family itself is represented as the right sort of educational milieu for a successful child. The taking up of these responsibilities for participation also opens up possibilities of influence and fast-track access or support at moments of crisis.

These parents know a great deal about schools and schooling but never enough. Their social grapevines work well but are rarely conclusive. The pace of educational reform and the marketing tactics of schools in congested metropolitan education markets create areas of confusion and uncertainty. Trust is at a premium. 'In this world of difference, uncertainty, and hence suspicion (toward others) as well as refuge (for oneself, when scrutinized by others), "one never knows" and "nothing means anything"' (Boltanski 1987: 287). As Giddens (1994: 253) expresses it, somewhat dramatically, 'we are now in a runaway world where there are many others but also where there are no others'. Thus, for some, the private sector remains a haven of clarity providing 'class enclaves' (Teese 2000) and displaying familiar and reassuring 'symbolic codes and codings' (Bernstein 1975: 125), and relatively predictable and assured trajectories of educational advantage; 'achievement in this system appears natural, if not always effortless' (Brown and Scase 1994: 58). Here classifications and frames, on the whole, remain very strong. However, for some, ambivalences again come into play and these institutions can seem outmoded and inappropriate and, as we have seen, some families reject their studied traditionalism. Others seek out variations in codes and distinctions within the private sector, looking to balance exclusion with principles, and the personal and positional, in inventive ways. Perhaps though the effects of recent educational reforms are tending to blur the differences in forms of social control between the state and private sectors.

Generally, the sorts of fractional differences in socialization and solidarity which Bernstein postulates certainly exist within the data discussed, but are not related in any clear cut way to fractional occupational categories, nor 'conflicting forms of social control' (Bernstein 1975: 128) among the families, nor are they systematically related together with other differences in ideology or perspective. Clearly more research is needed here inside families.

One way of thinking about the patterns and interactions explored between families, educational institutions and state policies is that we are witnessing a managed (re)convergence between the ideologies, interests and resources of the middle class and the ideologies, interests and resource requirements that are embedded in educational policies. Furthermore, we might see this as giving rise to, or as part of, some sort of mutual conditioning. On the one hand, there is 'the role of politics and the actions of the state in shaping individual and family decision-making processes' (Devine 1997: 39). Class perspectives have to be understood as articulated from within changing discourse and policy regimes, in particular here within the discursive framework of 'the market society' and 'the aesthetic of consumption' (Bauman 1998). On the other hand I have also sketched out a way (Chapter 3) of thinking about how the strategies of the middle class 'have major implications for political conflicts' (Savage, Barlow, Dickens and Fielding 1992: 216). A dialectic is at work. All of this makes thinking otherwise about welfare politics very difficult.

Rather than heralding the disappearance of class, high modern, post-welfare societies are marked by new forms of class relations and new modalities of class struggle. Post-welfare class relations are relations of a generalized 'distributive struggle' (Parkin 1979: 112) – made up of collective, group and individual actions, in and around policy and in and around institutions; although Parkin believed that this was 'not necessarily impossible to "contain"' (112). The strategies of reproduction of the middle class, to maintain or improve their social position and the content and volume of their capitals within these struggles, 'constitute a system' (Bourdieu and Boltanski 2000: 896) – a set of structural relations between class structure and the education structure. As Bourdieu and Boltanski (2000: 917) put it: 'The education market has become one of the most important loci of class struggle'. Education itself is changed by all this. It becomes in Larabee's (1997) words 'an arena for zero-sum competition filled with self-interested actors seeking opportunities' (32).

Class, class identities and class theory

I have to begin here with a disclosure. I have the problem of having ended up somewhere that I had not anticipated. This has involved a process of re-writing the book alongside the process of writing it. What I am referring to is the significance, or rather the formulation and study, of class fractions[4] within the middle class. I had begun with an interest in differentiating the families within my samples in terms of professional/managerial, private/public, aesthetic/corporate, repairer/shaper type categories with the expectation of being able to at least shed some light on the relationship between these box categories and educational strategies, preferences and principles.[5] Such relationships have proved elusive. They are not totally unapparent but rather looser and vaguer than I had anticipated.[6] This is a problem that Murdock and McCron (1975: 75) noted some considerable time ago, that 'it soon becomes apparent that the same structural location can generate and sustain a variety of responses and modes of accommodation'. In the process of analysis and writing I have come to find myself much closer to the position outlined by Robson and Butler (2001: 71). That is:

> In analysing middle-class formation it is important to avoid simply read-ing different groups off from their 'objective' class/occupational positions. Processes of formation are, rather, better understood as emerging out of the dialectical interplay of varying forms of social and economic capital and habitus on the one hand, and the distinctive oppor-tunities – across a range of fields – offered by metropolitan marketplaces on the other.

A similar reconceptualization is advocated by Wynne (1998) in the conclu-sion to his study of a new middle-class housing estate in Cheshire and he notes that a 'failing of many analyses was to assume that one could simply "read" class structure from occupational position' (147). The general short-comings of a simple class to culture analysis of class formation was earlier outlined by Watson (1993). Watson's critique of the Birmingham tradition of cultural studies points up the need to re-examine and re-work a final binary, the one step decoding of culture into class (working or middle). His point is that what is in practice a multi-levelled social reality (as we have seen) is collapsed by this decoding (188). What is needed he suggests is 'a multi-staged process of abstraction' (188). Wacquant (1991: 52) argues, in a similar way, that '... the nature, composition and dispositions of the mid-dle classes cannot be directly "deduced" from an objectivist map of the class structure ... Rather, they must be discovered through analysis of the whole set of creative strategies of distinction, reproduction and subversion of all agents'. The point is that the relationships of families to class structure is complex and that the class structure, as I have outlined previously, is also changing. As Watson (1993: 189) argues research into class formation and reproduction 'requires a simultaneous engagement with the ethnography of the subject and the history of the structure'. We might note for instance the convergence of the public and private professions, and the professions and managerial middle class, in terms of working conditions and work ideologies (Hanlon 1998), and Savage (2000) notes that there may be an ongoing blurring of some of the distinctions in lifestyle, principles and family relations that seemed evident and clear-cut in the 1970s and 1980s. In other words, the search for clear-cut divisions, within the middle class, based on positional differences, may be structurally out of date.

Robson and Butler (2001) go on to point up especially one aspect of the processes of class formation and reproduction which is systematically neglected – the role of space: 'the spatial component of these processes is of central rather than marginal significance' (72). This has been pointed up in a variety of ways in the substantive chapters. Interestingly and importantly Robson and Butler attribute a particular significance in the 'processes of formation and reproduction of the resulting categories of class to education and the way in which local educational "circuits" (Ball, Bowe and Gewirtz 1995) are strategically manipulated and, in some instances constructed, by middle-class parents' (Robson and Butler 2001: 72). Thus, patterns of differentiation or fractioning within the middle class have to be sought in situated categories of consciousness. Families may be conceived of as unstable, situated, cultural ensembles whose relationships to structure and work practices are dynamic, in a number of senses, in space and time. I have tried to access this to a small extent in discussion of parents' educational experiences and the middle-class orientations to the developmental self and futurity (see also Bourdieu 1986a: 345–6).

Clearly then, this is by no means a fideistic account of class. Nonetheless, the obduracy of class and class struggles in and around educational fields remains clear and Pakulski and Waters' (1996: 24) argument that 'the continuation of the class paradigm merely obstructs the development of a robust sociological analysis' seems unrealistic and unhelpful to say the least. Rather, I believe the discussion here indicates that no robust sociological analysis of social advantage and social reproduction is possible without attending to class. However, such an analysis must seriously consider new ways of thinking about class as it happens.

Despite the arguments and efforts of those theorists who want to bring an 'end to class' and move on, debates around class theory continue to take up considerable space in sociological journals and stubbornly recur in discussions of empirical research, as here. In particular there has been a recent return to the difficult issues of class identity and awareness. Historically, class awareness has been given a key role in the theorization of class and class relations. Class identity within class theory is in effect one of the indicators of the existence of classes and an absence of such self-identification is taken by critics of the class paradigm as an indicator of the end of class, or a condition of classlessness. Thus: 'To be useful, class theory can't merely define specific divisions as consequential; it must show that these divisions correspond to the collective realities that people experience and perceive' (Kingston 2000: 3). Or as Pakulski and Waters (1996: 3) express it: 'Minimally, the members of a class have to be aware of their commonality and employ some recognised form of self-description. A sense of difference between "them" and "us"'. Such perceptions and awareness are very much in evidence within the field of educational choice and in the ways in which families think about themselves in this competitive and risky social environment. The labelling and judgement of others and the self-descriptions to which they give rise are a fundamental part of boundary maintenance and strategies of social closure.

However, class identity research is beset with problems of measurement, method and conceptualization. In the simplest sense, despite some recent shifts in the way class is conceptualized in this field, particularly through the work of Savage and Butler, class identities and awareness continue to be sought primarily within talk – responses to interviewers' questions, a very simple kind of empiricism. That is, if researchers want to establish the existence of the self-identification of class they ask people what class they belong to, how they perceive others and understand class structures. Unfortunately such research seems to be entrenched in forms of class relations and class action, especially in terms of politics, which are being realized differently, and the researchers are then surprised and disappointed when these cannot be found empirically (Savage 2000: 36). These studies seem set up to fail. I want to argue, drawing from the discussion and analyses in the substantive chapters of this text, that class identites are not to be found within talk about categories but in practices and accounts of practices – in practices of distinction, and closure and in the 'aesthetics of distance' (Savage 2000: 107). That is: '... groups and boundaries are made and unmade in history, not in theory' (Wacquant 1991: 51).

It is within these practices, in specific social fields, that individuals and families are aware of themselves and others as classed. Here behaviour is 'latent with meaning' (Charlesworth 2000: 22). Class, in this sense, is inductive and grounded – located in space and time. In order to identify and explore class identity, 'we need to forcefully jettison any notion of class as a category' and focus attention instead on 'practices and on collective social processes' (Watson 1993: 194). While a focus upon 'class practices' still begs questions about what class is, this should not be regarded as a 'retreat' (Savage 2000: 23) from a thoroughgoing class analysis. It rests upon a conception of class and its realization in terms of a playing out of class relations within social fields of competition, the reiterative 'clash of forces and drives' which recur 'in and through our everyday lives' (Rikowski 2001: 15); such that '... no ideology or identity is reality unless it is acted out in everyday life, experienced at the concrete micro-level of reality and formulated in the undisciplined structures of mundane speech' (Sulkunen 1992: 46). This is a view of class as relational, emergent, contextual, dynamic, localized, and eventualized. Class is not the membership of a category or the simple possession of certain capitals or assets. It is an activation of resources and social identities, or rather the interplay of such identities, in specific locations, for particular ends. Thus, '... class assets define the terrain on which class collectivities form, rather than specify the nature of social class *per se*. How actual classes form as distinct social groups will depend on context ...' (Savage, Barlow, Dickens and Fielding 1992: 211). Such assets underpin the capacity to act, they do not define or determine action. Class processes are relational in a strategic sense, in the recognition and realization of difference and markers of class identity. For the middle classes, class is 'encoded' (Savage 2000: 107) within the self, within identity and organized and imagined within a past and toward a future. It is about how they think about their present in relation to possible futures, fond or rejected pasts, and obstacles or dangers to be encountered along the way – 'past trajectory is conserved in the form of a striving towards the future which prolongs it' (Bourdieu 1986a: 333).

Within all this class identification 'in people's mind' (Savage 2000: 11) is not 'straightforward' – it is situated in social and physical space, and within time and events – but no less potent, meaningful and consequential for all that; 'it always refers to the particular situation in which it has to orient practices' (Bourdieu 1986a: 473). As Savage argues class is articulated primarily through differentiation, 'class becomes individualised' (2000: 69), but as I have tried to demonstrate in the social field of education differentiation is enacted as much through belonging, through a recognition of mutuality, fit and identification, as it is through distinctions. There is a straightforwardness to this. Class identification in this sense is both a reaffirmation of values, lifestyle and aspirations and a projection towards reproduction or social betterment. Class awareness then lies within and just beneath the obvious, in the practices of division. It is as much about who you are not, who you could not consider being, as who you are. Savage takes us to the brink of this but ultimately remains rooted in the mire of old class theory. Middle-classness, like other class identifications, has to be sought in the subtleties of the everyday, in the uncertainties of status, in fine distinctions as well as gross ones. As Bourdieu (1986a: 472) argues, this 'in no way implies the capacity to situate oneself in the classification (as so many surveys on social class ask people to do), still less to describe this class identification in any systematic way and state its principles'. Identities and awareness are worked at, threatened and reaffirmed; they may be simply or confidently asserted by some but not all or perhaps not even most (see (Savage, Bagnall and Longhurst 2001). Nonetheless, middle-classness has, almost by definition, a certain degree of reflexivity (cf. Charlesworth 2000), a knowingness which is based on both ambivalence and a certain sort of precariousness, but this reflexivity should not be mistaken for ironic distance which, in my data at least, seems in short supply.[7] Writing about the petit bourgeois, but very apt here, Bourdieu (1986a: 345) describes the class as 'constantly faced with ethical, aesthetic or political dilemmas forcing them to bring the most ordinary operations of existence to the level of consciousness and strategic choice'. Educational choice is a case in point.

Many class researchers seem to be looking in the wrong place, looking both too hard and not hard enough. The distinctions and identifications of class are embedded in non-cognitive dispositions as well as the minutiae of the everyday perceptions and fears. In one form, class struggles are realized within the everyday interweaving of diverse tapestries of behaviour. Class is made visceral and palpable in the practical closures and exclusions of choice, which are achieved and maintained within families and social networks and in the interactions between families and social networks and social institutions. This is by no means the be all and end all of class but it is part of the constitution and reproduction of class which cannot be ignored.

A great deal of the work of class, as outlined above, and of social reproduction within the family, is heavily gendered. It draws particularly and heavily upon the unpaid work and emotional labour of mothers (Smith 2000); 'parenting is an activity that is gendered and classed' (Graue 1993: 486). Smith (2000) also argues that the restructuring and privatization of education, what I have referred to as the neo-liberal risk management regime, what she calls a new regime of accumulation, in part through the demands it makes on middle-class women, who are better able than others to cope with its demands, is a new 'engine of inequality'. The activity of parenting as a dimension of social reproduction extends also into the development and maintenance of social networks, engagement with and involvement in schooling, the elicitation of information about and application of pressure on the school. Mothers much more than fathers are 'hooked into the life of the school' (Graue 1993: 474) and become active partners in the educational process.

Some might argue that the economic bases and aspects of class are muted in this account, but property assets and other economic capital are fundamental to the strategies which are involved in the reproductive constructions of class, and its meaning, the experience of class, in education. Economic capital is itself constitutive of the meaning and practices of class, in opening up certain possibilities of educational choice; private schooling, tutoring and cramming, early-start experiences and private child care, and house purchase. Most families on low incomes or living in poverty are by definition excluded from these possibilities. However, the capitals of class are not easily separable conceptually and certainly not within the practices of distinction. They are inter-facilitative and 'cannot be considered in isolation' (Allatt 1993: 142). 'The kinds of capital, like trumps in a game of cards, are powers which define the chances of profit in a given field' (Bourdieu 1992: 230). It is also important to recognize the extent of different distributions of capital within the middle class and the role for some of economic capital within reproduction as a form of denial, of 'negative magnitudes' (Bourdieu 1986a: 333) and sacrifice as expenditure; 'they must somewhere find the resources to make up for the absence of capital' (333).

Class is relational also in that the actions of one set of class agents have effects upon, and consequences for, the fate of others. Classes remain, to a great extent, 'communities of fate'; 'where you come from matters more today than it did in the past' (Blanden, Goodman and Gregg 2002 quoted in *The Guardian* 27 March 2002: 26). And these fates impinge on one another. In relation to schooling, class strategies contribute to the selection of policies and rules of exclusion. They enact physical divisions (e.g. between and within schools), contribute to social polarization and its achievement effects, and produce and entrench resource differences within institutions and within families. These are practical if sometimes unintended consequences of values and interests in action. And while Savage may be partly right that we need to 'abandon an approach to class which roots it as a collective enterprise' (2000: 101), as I have tried to demonstrate, it would be a mistake to throw out the collective aspects of class and class practices altogether. Indeed, individualism and collectivism may be one of those unhelpful binaries that prevent us from seeing the ambiguous nature of class reproduction that fails 'to capture the complex interweaving of class and individual identity' (Savage 2000: 101).

Based upon my discussion of closure, capital, values and risk I want to argue that when Beck (1992: 98) says that 'class loses its sub-cultural basis and is no longer experienced' he is simply wrong. The discussion here suggests that writers on social change in high modernity like Beck and Giddens may well be over-writing the disintegration of class, the loosening of bonds between individuals and institutions and the release of individuals from the socio-structural traditions of modernity. We should perhaps pay more attention to the ambivalence in Beck's work about the continuing role of the social arrangements of old modernity.

Education, the state and social justice

A final point on the 'social arrangements' of the education market. Nagel argues that political theories, and the 'social arrangements' to which they give rise, require of us a particular kind of relation between the personal and impersonal standpoints. That is a sense of our own best interests and those of our kith and kin over and against a general social good, and an awareness of the fate of others. He goes on to assert that 'I believe that any political theory that merits respect has to offer us an escape from the self-protective blocking out of the important of others ...' . (Nagel 1991: 19).[8] Neither choice theory specifically nor Thatcherite social theory more generally pass Nagel's test of being worthy of respect. As an unreconstructed enlightenment modernist Nagel appears not to have anticipated or taken account of the reinvention of political theories and social arrangements which operate in such a way as to 'externalize the demands of the personal standpoint' (5), rather than the impersonal. The current approach to the management of the public sector in the UK and increasingly almost everywhere else, takes up what Cohen (1992:

183) calls a Thatcherite theory, or rather the colonizing legacy of the 'discourse of Thatcherism' (Phillips 1996: 236), and it's 'assumption of a grotesquely simplistic notion of causality' with, in florid terms, a 'depiction of the individual whose self-direction has been beaten into dust by the reflex hammer of self-gratification' (Cohen 1992: 183).[9] As I argued in Chapter 2, the values and incentives of market policies being pursued and celebrated by the states of almost all Western societies (Ball 2001b) give legitimation and impetus to certain actions and commitments – enterprise, competition, excellence – and inhibit and delegitimize others – social justice, equity, tolerance. The need to give consideration to the fate of others has been lessened in all this and generally by the inroads of neo-liberalism, and the concomitant regime of prudentialism. Neither the individual morality of class members, with some exceptions, nor the operant political rules of exclusion,[10] contribute, in Nagel's terms to 'the creation of a context in which it will be possible for each of us to live a decent and integrated life' (Nagel 1991: 17).

As many writers have argued, the middle class is defined by a sense of precariousness and vulnerability, and confidence and social efficacy. Structure and consciousness intertwine within the ontology of the class. The absence of complacency and the constant activity of distinction and status maintenance is the best and the worst of the middle class. They are in a sense their own worst enemies. The commitment to individualism and 'putting the family first', the defence of borders and strategies of social closure undermine both security and moral vision and encourage fearfulness; 'by reflecting on these concerns and developing strategies to allay their fears, they may actually help to accentuate the [kinds of inequalities I have explored above] so that individualisation and social inequality are mutually constitutive' (Savage 2000 104). The middle-class dreams of order (Crook 1999: 186) and advantage are in Giddens' (1994: 9) words 'an unstable mix'. The values, culture and practices of the middle class are set within a set of contradictions; 'the wholesale expansion of a market society' (Giddens 1994: 9), as advocated by neo-liberalism, which offers the middle class certain strategic advantages, is also 'promoting those very disintegrative forces which neo-liberalism opposes' (9), and increasing social and other risks. 'Too much liberty and too little collective responsibility is the warning call of those who see social order threatened by the individualized lifestyles in which strategic interaction and pure self-interest dominate' (Berking 1996: 198).

In a different way we are back to the core of the middle-class ontology, back to that paradoxical mix of confidence and dread, of efficacy and uncertainty. That paradox which is embedded in the structural instabilities and contradictions of class positioning and the struggle for closure; which is played out in the relationships between the class and the state and liberal–democratic capitalism; which rests on the contradictory virtues of liberalism; which celebrates individualism and sociality. The future may be middle class but it is a future that is both open and 'beset with worries' (Lewis and Maude 1950: 288).

Appendix I
Who are these people?

Despite my disclaimers in the main text I do need to draw some clear limits around the groups of families represented and be clear about who they are. I need to specify what I mean by middle class in this study, if it is to speak to debates and developments in class theory and contribute to the burgeoning scholarship on the middle class and their social reproduction.

Very simply the families included in the study are members of what is sometimes called the 'saliariat' or more commonly the 'service class'. As Goldthorpe (1995: 314) makes very clear: 'the service class is a class of employees'. The main problem of demarcation is that of distinguishing them from other sorts of employees. There are two elements to this; first, benefits of employment over and above salary; that is, pension rights, increments, employment security and career opportunities – although as I have suggested these things are changing and are part of the threat to social reproduction (see Savage 2000, Chapter 8); second, some degree of professional autonomy and managerial or administrative authority – again professional autonomy is under threat for many public and private professionals, and there is a convergence of work practice between professional and managerial jobs. Nonetheless, these criteria do still provide a fairly robust basis for distinguishing service class employees from other middle-class groups, specifically the intermediate middle class; that is, those employed in routine, low-autonomy, white-collar jobs. I can add two further non-work criteria to this definition of the service class. One is education; the parents included in this study, with the exception of one couple and three other women, all experienced some form of higher education (the exceptions being a couple both of whom had attended private school and who were both employed in professional jobs, but who had not done formal higher education, but had done professional qualification courses, and three women, all with A levels). The other criterion is that they are house-owners.

On this basis, drawing on the four studies outlined below, I set about selecting the families with which I would engage and whose interviews I would analyse or re-analyse, by a process of exclusion. That is, I excluded all those families where one or both partners were working in routine, non-manual, white-collar jobs. Again one exception was made, a couple both of whom had higher education, the husband was a chartered accountant, but his wife worked on a college help desk. In most cases of divorced or separated couples I was able to collect data on the missing partners' education and work, and in the case of 'homeworkers' details of their education and previous jobs. (See below for more details.)

Still, it remains the case, as numerous commentators have pointed out that the service class is very diverse; it 'involves the aggregation of non-comparable jobs and occupations' (Crompton 1993: 115). In other words: 'There is no longer a "typical" middle-class family' (Savage, Barlow, Dickens and Fielding 1992: 156). In Bernstein's terms: regulators,[1] repairers,[2] diffusers,[3] shapers[4] and executors[5] are all included, and as Bernstein (1975: 128) points out: 'Further, each category has both its own hierarchy and its own internal ideological conflicts'.[6] There are problems involved in treating nurses and senior consultants, and infant teachers and professors in elite universities as having common commitments and perspectives. Both professional and managerial, and public and private sector employees are included, as are liberal/aesthetic and corporate lifestyles. That is a strength and a weakness; a weakness perhaps, making descriptive generalizations tricky, but a strength in so far as analytic generalizations become possible. As Butler and Robson (2002b) put it in a recent paper, my use of the concept of middle class is 'rather broadly conceived and internally undifferentiated' (6). These parents were drawn from four studies conducted over a ten-year period from 1991 to 2001, three ESRC funded studies and a pilot for an ongoing ESRC funded study. Each of the studies focused upon a particular point of choice and each one involved the collection of a variety of sorts of data on different aspects of the market in educational services operating at that point. Only the consumer data are considered here. Three of these studies were partly based in the south London district of Northwark. Three include Riverway. This provides a degree of continuity between the samples. The studies are as follows:

1 The school choice study

This research was conducted with Richard Bowe and Sharon Gewirtz. The study focused upon the dynamics of a set of specific education markets over a 39-month period. Three clusters of secondary schools in three adjacent Local Education Authorities (LEAs) were identified as sites of local competition – 15 schools in all, including LEA and grant-maintained, mixed and single-sex, a church school and a city technology college (CTC). The LEAs are very different in terms of social class and ethnic mix and each has as different majority party in control of the local council. Each LEA has a different orientation to and engagement with the education market. These adjacent sites were chosen not for any reasons of representativeness but because competition between schools was likely and they each provided different kinds of market conditions. Together they offered a social laboratory for research into choice and competition. Good transport links and the relative proximity of the schools ensure that competition for recruitment takes places within and between the three localities.

The research had three main elements. First of all, monitoring the market behaviour of the schools – attending meetings, collecting documents, visiting open evenings and interviewing a cross-section of staff and governors in each (121 interviews in all). Here we were interested in how the schools seek to attract parents, their responsiveness to market signals, as well as their changing relationships with one another and with their LEA. We also sought to explore the ways in which the LEAs were able to continue to influence or direct local provision when open choice, management and budgetary devolution to schools and grant-maintained status have been used in combination by central government to severely reduce their role in controlling and planning education. Second, in each of the three years of the study we conducted interviews with a sample of parents in each of the clusters (137 in all). The sample was designed to match roughly the social class and ethnic composition of the cluster localities. The interviews – 82 with mothers, 20 with fathers, 34 with both parents and one with another relative – were conducted in some depth. Parents were asked to talk about the processes of choice, reasons, constraints, sources of information, influences, the nature of their decision-making within the family and so on. The interviews were conducted during the period of choosing in order to capture the flux of choice-making rather than simply record *post factum* reconstructions and legitimations. We wanted to move away decisively from the emphasis on listing abstract criteria for choice which predominates in the school choice research literature. We were also able to interview 20 primary head teachers who feature in various ways in the choice-making process.

2 *The post-16 choice study*

This research was conducted with Meg Maguire and Sheila Macrae (see Ball, Maguire and Macrae 2000) for more detail. The research was focused on a single post-16 market in education, training and employment but the reach of the market extends over a wide inner-city/suburban setting based around the Northwark area of London and is defined in terms of the expressed interests and choices of a cohort of Year 11 students from one comprehensive school – Northwark Park – and one PRU (pupil referral unit). This local, lived market encompasses several different, small LEAs that organize their schools' provision in different ways. The main players in the market for our young people are two 11–18 secondary schools, five further education colleges, a tertiary college, a denominational sixth form college and two TECs. Three other further education colleges, another sixth form college, and an 11–18 denominational school impinge upon the margins of this market. We engaged with the main groups of actors in this market: providers, that is those offering education, training or employment;

intermediaries, that is those offering advice or support, including teachers, careers officers and parents; and consumers or choosers, that is the young people themselves and their families.

The study is small-scale, intensive, multidimensional and longitudinal. As indicated above, the data are based upon contacts initiated with a group of Year 11 students in 1995. The original sample comprised a total of 110 students: 81 from the 11–18, mixed comprehensive school and 29 from the local pupil referral unit (PRU). From this cohort of students a smaller group was selected for indepth study. This sub-sample was constituted to represent the range of Northwark Park school students in terms of sex, social class, academic attainment, ethnicity and destinations and routes from school to work and includes some young people who had already opted out of formal education. It consisted of 64 young people: 42 from the school and 17 from the PRU. They were interviewed once in each of the spring and summer terms of Year 11 and at some point in their first year post-16 and again at some point in the second and third years – when they were 19. Some were interviewed as many as six times. The sample is itself very diverse. All the young people whose narratives appear in this study were born between 1979 and 1980. Some were born in London to teenage single mothers or to new middle-class professional couples, the first from their families to go to university, struggling to manage a mortgage, having two jobs and coping with child care. Some were born in different nation states such as Somalia and Bangladesh and became refugees. Some were born into minority ethnic families and communities who had moved to the UK in the early 1970s from the Gujerat or from Hong Kong, for example. Others were third- and fourth-generation members of communities which had settled in London after the Second World War. All these children and their families eventually settled into the Northwark/Streetley area of south-west London. Some were housed in post-war council housing estates, some lived in newly gentrified Victorian terraced houses, some were looked after by the local authority. We also interviewed representatives of all major local providers, and collected and analysed some of their public documentation, and interviewed teachers, careers officers and a sample of parents. A total of 244 interviews were conducted with these young people, and a further 46 with various intermediaries – teachers, careers officers and parents – involved in supporting the transitions from school to further education or employment.

3 The higher education choice study

This research was conducted with Miriam David, Jackie Davies and Diane Reay. It is a qualitative study of English students' choice of higher education institutions. It is focused upon two cohorts of student choosers, their parents and various intermediaries (careers teachers, sixth form tutors, etc.) in six educational institutions: an 11–18 mixed comprehensive with a large minority ethnic, working class intake (Crieghton Community School – CCS), a comprehensive sixth form consortium which serves a socially diverse community (Maitland Union – MU), a tertiary college with a very large A level population (Riverway College – RC), a further education college which runs higher education access courses (Fennister further education College – FFEC), and two prestigious private schools, one single-sex boys' (Cosmopolitan Boys' – CB), one single-sex girls' (Hemsley Girls' – HG). All of the institutions are in or close to London. Our research is institutionally located in this way so that we are able to explore the effects of individual, familial and institutional influences and processes in choice-making. We administered a questionnaire to 502 Year 12 and 13 and further education students; ran focus groups and interviewed a sub-sample of students in each location (120 interviews in all); interviewed various intermediaries in these institutions (15), and interviewed a sub-sample of parents (40). A small number of careers advice interviews, higher education application preparation sessions, Oxbridge application advice sessions and meetings for parents on higher education choice were observed. Several features of the choice process have been examined in other projects and published papers (Ball 2001a; Ball 2001b; Reay, Davies, David and Ball 2001, and Reay 2000).

4 The child care choice study

The material used on the text comes from a small pilot study conducted with Carol Vincent; the main study, again funded by the ESRC, is now in progress, again with Carol Vincent and Sophie Kemp. This study addresses a set of issues embedded in the operation of lived, private, pre-school, child care markets – markets in love! We are, first of all, interested in: how parents and consumers make use of these markets; how market-use is related to gender roles within families; how the purchase of child care articulates with beliefs about child rearing, and finally how these markets work in particular localities. The vast majority of the consumers in these markets are middle-class. As a secondary issue we are interested in how different fractions of the middle class engage with, and solve the problems posed by, these markets in different ways. In the pilot we attempted to mark out some of the basic features of this market and identify issues for further research. The pilot work drew upon diverse forms of data: a small number of interviews with child care providers (seven), and interviews with parent-choosers (12); the close examination of a range of provider's brochures and websites, and inspection reports; the results of searches of newspapers and a key professional journal, *Nursery World*; and discussions with various interested parties. The research was based in two locations, one of which was, again, Northwark.

The samples

So who remains when those families interviewed in the studies above not fitting the service class criteria are excluded? The tables below describe very simply the parents (and the students in the case of the post-16 and higher education studies) directly or indirectly referred to in the text.

The school choice sample consists of 36 families, the same number as Jordan, Redley and James' (1994) study. Included are two women separated from their husbands and one widower.

The post-16 sample consists of six families. Given the small number the parents' occupations can be listed. They are: occupational therapist and civil engineer; primary teacher and locations officer; secondary teacher and carehome manager; secondary teacher and sales manager; nurse and customer services manager, and senior trade union official and solicitor. With the exception of the last family this group is somewhat different from those from the other studies. These parents are referred to least often.

The higher-education sample consists of both parents and students; 20 families were selected, although more than that number fitted the service class criteria, and some students from other service class families in the original sample are quoted on occasion. A relatively large number of these parents were divorced or separated.

Table A1.1 Parents' occupational sector (school choice sample)

	Mother	Father
Private	8	21
Public	25	12
Voluntary		2
Homeworker	2	
Total	35	35

Table A1.2 Parents' education (school choice sample)

	Mother	Father
Private	11	12
Grammar	14	17
Comprehensive and secondary	4	2
Private and grammar	2	1
State and grammar	1	
State	1	2
Total	33	34

Table A1.3 Parents' employment (school choice sample)

	Mother	Father
Professional	23	27
Managerial	3	7
Intermediate	6	1
Homeworker	3	
Total	35	35

Table A1.4 Parents' occupational sector (higher education sample)

	Mother	Father
Private	9	8
Public	7	6
Total	16	14

Table A1.5 Parents' employment (higher education sample)

	Mother	Father
Professional	13	14
Managerial	1	0
Intermediate	1	0
Entrepreneurial	1	0
Total	16	14

The child care choice sample consists of 11 families (one intermediate family was excluded). Twenty of the 22 parents had higher education qualifications, the exceptions being the wife of a City banker who had left grammar school and had taken a vocational cookery qualification and was a corporate chef and cookery writer, and the wife of a large corporation manager who left school after A levels and works as a secretary. Also included in this group are four other City bank or fund managers, two doctors, four solicitors, a barrister, an architect, an early years teacher, a clinical psychologist, three senior charity workers and a lobbyist. Nine of the parents had attended private schools, two others grammar schools. We also collected data on the parents of these couples.

Appendix II

This will be brief. I want to give a very simple account of my working methods with the data which are deployed in this text. The samples are outlined in Appendix I.

My engagement with the data is a mix of old and new research technologies. The first point to make is that none of this is new data. In the case of the school choice data these transcripts have been coded at least three times and as many as five times. The other material at least once previously. Thus, this is data with which I am familiar. Nonetheless in the way of these things the new round of coding produced ideas and material that had not been attended to before. In part new questions were being asked but also in my experience data always has something more to give.

The coding to which I am referring above is mainly hand coding using pens, highlighter and a code notebook. My approach draws on techniques recommended by Anselm Strauss. However, all of these data were also stored in NuDist and were subject to various searches. This was particularly useful in generating code-based reports which could then be intensively coded within. For example, searches were run on such topics as setting, streaming, comprehensive, private, Oxford/Cambridge, trust, anxious/panic/worry, etc. These searches also made it possible to do distribution counts of topics within the samples and some of these are reported in the text. Still, the issues and topics identified in the text are not treated exhaustively. There is still work to be done. I will certainly be returning to this material.

Notes

1 Introduction

1 Except that it is written against current attempts to make educational research into a search for simple certitudes.

2 This project might have benefited from a comparative research design, setting middle class strategies over and against those of working class families (Watson 1993). However, that would also have been a different kind of exercise, and a dissipation of focus. With Diane Reay I have already written two papers addressed to working class educational strategies – I shall refer to these at times in the text. Other work (Reay 1998a, Reay 1998b, Reay 2000) compares working class and middle class mothers and Skeggs (1997) and others (Mahony and Zmroczek 1997) focus on the social mobility of working class women. The comparisons which are undertaken here are those within and among the middle classes themselves. The text is also written from a partial and situated perspective. This situatedness is taken up substantively in the analysis (see Chapters 4 and 6). The middle class actors represented here are not representative in any technical sense (see Appendix I).

3 Although like many others I see Marx's and Weber's concepts of class, notwithstanding the basic differences, as overlapping rather than irrevocably opposed and antagonistic.

4 Bourdieu's (1990c) notion of symbolic violence is very apt here, as the right to impose legitimately arbitrary power, which it also conceals. Choice and competition are presented as in the general good but as argued here they actually work to strengthen 'the established balance of power in preventing the apprehension of power relations as power' (14–15).

2 Class and strategy

1 One valid question to ask here would be whether the sorts of choosing and sorts of strategies attributed here to the middle classes are exclusive to them. In an absolute sense clearly not; however, my previous work with Sharon Gewirtz and Richard Bowe indicated that other criteria for choice were employed by working class families and different constraints upon choice were confronted. The working class criteria were founded in cohesion and social reproduction but of a different sort. Parkin (1974: 5) argues that it is possible 'to visualize the fundamental cleavage in the stratification order as that point where one set of class strategies gives way to a radically different set'. Some critics and commentators appear to read our previous work as suggesting that working class choice is deficient. This is simply not the case. We began to outline a set of perspectives related to the cohesion and reproduction of community, as distinct from the positional competitivism

predominant among the middle-classes (see (Gewirtz, Ball and Bowe 1995: 45–52, and also Reay and Ball 1997 on working class rationality).

2 See Appendix I for an account of the projects and the data 'worked on' here and Appendix II for a brief discussion of my methods of analysis or 'working with' data.

3 Fielding (1998: 61–62) makes a similar point, drawing on the philosophy of John Macmurray. He argues that, 'whilst the functional, the personal, the political and the communal, are fundamentally different from each other, they are inextricably linked'.

4 The case of the Coopers' school in Essex provides a good example. This is a school which was using interviews with prospective parents to select students, a practice which had been proscribed by the Labour Government. The school was subject to criticism from, and required to stop its interviewing by, the Schools Ombudsman (*The Independent* 9 March 2002). The giving of false addresses by parents anxious to get their children into a particular school is an example of self-regarding behaviour on the demand side of education markets.

5 As I have tried to make very clear in this chapter and Chapter 1 my interest here is not in the 'limits and frontiers of class' (Bourdieu 1990a: 49–50) – it is not 'helpful to argue that there are a definite number of social classes, each with clear boundaries around them' (Savage, Barlow, Dickens and Fielding 1992: 211) – but rather in 'the dynamic process of class formation' (Savage, Barlow, Dickens and Fielding 1992: 100). We 'need to see how people draw upon different assets to actually form classes' (Savage, Barlow, Dickens and Fielding 1992: 59). I do not therefore operationalize a careful and precise definition or demarcation of class fractions. I do identify and categorize the families referred to and quoted in the text (see Appendix I) as middle class but throughout, with some few exceptions, refer rather loosely to 'the middle class'. I am ready to be criticised for this but my purpose here is to begin a general analysis of middle class formation and reproduction in the field of education, with an emphasis on the development of a framework of fairly well worked through concepts. I see the more precise deployment of these concepts in an analysis or examination of class fractions as a further step beyond the scope of the current exercise.

3 Class and policy

1 Alongside choice policies of deregulation, the devolution of budgets and managerial responsibilities to schools also work to ingrain and depoliticize class advantages. For example, the creation of a free market in educational labour, as in the UK, will mean that schools located in inner-city locations will find it financially and reputationally more difficult to recruit enough or the best qualified teachers or to retain teachers.

2 Leaving aside the not insignificant role of economic determination in the last instance there is an uncanny affinity between Poulantzas' 'condensate' and Parkin's view of the state as 'the locus and the crystallization of ... antagonisms arising in civil society that are channelled upwards for resolution' (140). If anything, Parkin gives less credence to state autonomy than Poulantzas does.

3 'Marx's 1847 formulae of "class-in-itself" and of "class-for-itself" are merely Hegelian reminiscences. Not only do they fail to explain anything, but they have for years misled Marxist theorists of social classes' (Poulantzas 1973: 76). The avoidance of a notion of class as 'first constituted' in the economic, and rather as inherent in practices, is fundamental to the conception of class underpinning this text.

4 (Poulantzas 1973: 113) argues that 'Power is located at the level of the various class practices, in so far as there are class interests concerning the economic, the

political and the ideological. In particular, in a capitalist formation character-ized by the specific autonomy of the levels of structures and practices and of the respective class interests, we can clearly see the distinction between economic power, political power, ideological power, etc., according to the capacity of a class to realize its relatively autonomous interests at each level. In other words, relations of power are not located at the political level alone any more than class interests are located at the economic level alone. The relations of these var-ious powers (their index of effectiveness, etc.) themselves relate to the articulation of the various class practices (class interests) which, in a dislocated manner, reflect the articulation of the various structures of a social formation or of one of its stages of phases'.

5 The allocation of children at age 11 to grammar, technical or secondary modern schools on the basis of intelligence test performance.

6 This raises difficult questions about how much we need to know. Or to put it another way, how long can advocates of choice maintain their position and ini-tiate new schemes without clear-cut evidence and in the face of counter evidence? Carnoy (2000) identifies what appear to be some major flaws in Goldhaber's review and his arguments.

7 Noden also suggests that his analysis and Gorard's 'are completely reconcilable' but that 'neither of them tell us much (if anything) about markets and segrega-tion' (personal communication).

8 The use by the middle class of illicit choice is cited by some advocates of choice as an argument for choice. They suggest that giving choice to everyone would be fairer.

4 Social class as social closure

1 This makes perfect sense in relation to UK Prime Minister Tony Blair's overt commitment to meritocracy in education.

2 Compared with the fatalism of working class parents (see Reay and Ball 1998) these middle class parents are environmentalist and developmentalist. They see the children's talents as subject to contingent advancement and decline and sus-ceptible to intervention. This led to a sense of fragility of talent and of children needing to be protected from untoward influences: '... if she's got the ability at 11, then I don't want it to be killed in secondary school ... for her not to achieve her potential' (Mrs Forsythe).

3 Cultural capital can exist in embodied form (dispositions), objectified form (cul-tural goods) or institutionalized form (e.g. qualifications).

4 There is perhaps a greater degree of reflexivity in all of this than Bourdieu (1986: 472) allows for, but it is certainly not a 'mastery' of classification. These families do display some aspects of the ability to reflect on the implications of social change and their own actions in response to change to which Beck (1992), in contrast to Bourdieu, gives particular emphasis.

5 Lash sees classes and the middle class in particular as interest groups rather than as communities but as Savage (2000: 102) asserts 'individual identities and rela-tional identities are more closely interrelated than theorists of individualisation suppose'.

6 However, there were two examples among the interviews treated here of the choice of a state school, as a matter of principle, against the cultural scripts of the extended family (see Chapter 6).

7 Similar systems, underpinning forms of working-class self-exclusion were very clear in our work on higher education choice (see Reay, Ball and David 2002).

8 Also here we see the instability of the liberal subject, an inconsistency of val-ues 'fulfilling diverse functions in direct accordance with both the needs of the

creative multiple self and the demands of the social situation' (Avnon and de-Shalit 1999: 9).

9 These differences in preferences for traditional or modern schooling could not be related to any categorical differences among the parents.

10 Pakulski and Waters (1996) over-estimate the extent to which class reproduction is attenuated or made less certain by a reliance on public sector institutions by under-estimating the strategic exertions of the middle class.

11 Again though it is important not to erase those differences between parents which give rise to more emphasis on social as opposed to academic development, and the here and now as opposed to the future in views about and choices of educations. But these are emphases rather than oppositions.

5 Social capital, social class and choice

1 By this I mean extensive, detailed and exemplified accounts.

2 Interview conducted by Diane Reay.

3 Bourdieu and Boltanski (2000: 906) primarily stress the role of strong ties and argue that: 'the volume of social capital possessed by an individual agent ... depends on the volume of capital held by each of the members [of the group of which they are a part] multiplied by the degree of integration of the group'.

4 This was typically matched by parents' confidence and sense of 'self-efficacy': 'she will get into Waldegrave even if I have to appeal' (Mrs West); 'if you are prepared to push you can get your own way' (Mrs Gosling).

5 Five of the parents were not asked a relevant question.

6 Allatt (1993: 143) defines emotional capital as 'emotionally valued assets and skills, love and affection, expenditure of time, attention, care and concern'.

6 Values and principles: social justice in the head

1 These themes also underpin arguments for the impossibility of middle class consciousness.

2 She goes on to assert that 'this places society in general – or its policy making representatives – in a considerable dilemma' (334).

3 Other parents saw Merrybush as 'very middle class'.

7 Risk, uncertainty and fear

1 Crook's analysis of choice is detailed and sophisticated and there is not the space to rehearse it here. He relates 'ordering' to risk management regimes and to the decline in organized risk management.

2 But there are some, from prep. to private to Oxbridge, and thence a prestigious well paid job is still a route of predictable privilege for some.

3 In some respects, as I have argued elsewhere (Gewirtz, Ball and Bowe 1995), working class choice of a local school, as a non-choice, can also be thought of as neo-tradition, based on the social reproduction of solidarity and community. It is the liminal space between the local and the private that fosters anxiety, fear and uncertainty.

4 Or as Walkerdine, Lucey and Melody (2001: 175) starkly put it, 'the bourgeois subject is feminine'.

8 Class practices and inequality

1 Qualitative research is frequently criticized for lacking cumulation and empirical and conceptual development. In a whole variety of respects, many of which I hope to have noted, the discussion in previous chapters links to and confirms

and develops findings offered by and analytical work done by Jordan Redley and James, Allatt, Devine, Lauder and colleagues, Butler and Robson, Reay, Vincent and others around the issues of class advantage and middle class use of and involvement in educational institutions.

2 There is now an Early Years Curriculum for 3–5-year-olds, and Nursery Schools are now Inspected by the Office for Standards in Education rather than Social Services. Nursery school is increasingly viewed as being as much about education as it is about general social development but invisible pedagogies are still in the ascendant.

3 From the point of view of the state, other parents need to have this impressed upon them, and various schemes of early intervention are now in place to achieve this.

4 Other sorts of fractioning, for example along lines of ethnicity, have not been touched upon here (see Ball, Reay and David 2002). The class experiences of different ethnic groups are likely to be different in terms of 'structures of feeling' and subjectivity and the possibilities of agency. Different kinds of historical relationships to British capitalism and Empire may well produce different textures in the lived experience of class.

5 While it may be that different occupational cultures foster different attitudinal sets, and attract people with different values orientations, it may also be that parenting is a conservative influence on social attitudes and values (Carol Vincent, personal communication).

6 It might be argued that my sample sizes are too small to trace such relationships systematically. However, other researchers have experienced similar problems and the up-close examination of the intestices of these relationships raises questions about the validity of reducing them to 'a basically two-tiered structure of class and culture' (Watson 1993: 188).

7 'Distance and parenthood are irreconcilable' (Carol Vincent, personal communication).

8 This also relates to the 'dilemmas' that Johnathan (1989) sees as confronting policymakers – see Chapter 6.

9 On the other hand, Crewe (1989), reflecting on an analysis of the British Social Attitudes Survey, concludes that the 'Thatcher crusade for values change' has failed.

10 Nagel (1991: 17) argues that 'The problem of integration has to be approached both through the morality of individual conduct and through the design of those institutions, conventions and rules in which it is embedded'.

Appendix I Who are these people?

1 Members of the legal system, police, prison service, church.
2 Members of the medical/psychiatric services and its derivatives; social services.
3 Teachers at all levels and in all areas. Mass and specialized media.
4 Creators of what counts as developments within or change of symbolic forms in the arts and sciences.
5 Civil servants and bureaucrats. (Bernstein 1975: 128)
6 The classification of the agencies/agents of symbolic control.

Bibliography

Adler, M. (1997) 'Looking backwards to the future: parental choice and educational policy.' *British Educational Research Journal,* 23(3): 297–313.

Adonis, A. and S. Pollard (1997) *A Class Act: The Myth of Britain's Classless Society.* London, Methuen.

Albrow, M. (1997) Travelling beyond local cultures: socioscapes in a global city. In J. Eade (ed.), *Living the Global City: Globalization as Local Process.* London, Routledge.

Allatt, P. (1993) Becoming privileged. In I. Bates and G. Riseborough (eds), *Youth and Inequality.* Buckingham, Open University Press.

Althusser, L. (1969) *For Marx.* Harmondsworth, Penguin.

Anthias, F. (2001) 'The material and the symbolic in theorising social stratification: issues of gender, ethnicity and class.' *British Journal of Sociology,* 52: 367–390.

Arnove, R. F., A. Torres, S. Franz and K. Morse (1997) A political sociology of education and development in Latin America. In Y. W. Bradshaw (ed.), *Education in Comparative Perspective.* New York, E. J. Brill.

Avnon, D. and A. de-Shalit (1999) Liberalism between promise and practice. In D. Avnon and A. de-Shalit (eds), *Liberalism and its Practice.* London, Routledge.

Bagley, C., P. A. Woods and R. Glatter (2000) *Rejecting Schools: Towards a Fuller Understanding of the Process of Parental Choice.* BEMAS, Robinson College, Cambridge.

Bagley, C., P. A. Woods and G. Woods (2001) 'Implementation of school choice policy: interpretation and response by parents of students with special educational needs.' *British Educational Research Journal,* 27(3): 287–307.

Ball, S. J. (1981) *Beachside Comprehensive: A Case Study of Secondary Schooling.* Cambridge, Cambridge University Press.

Ball, S. J. (1987) *The Micropolitics of the School: Towards a Theory of School Organisation.* London, Routledge.

Ball, S. J. (1990) *Politics and Policymaking in Education.* London, Routledge.

Ball, S. J. (1993) 'Education markets, choice and social class: the market as a class strategy in the UK and the USA.' *British Journal of Sociology of Education,* 14(1): 3–20.

Ball, S. J. (1994) *Education Reform: A Critical and Post-Structural approach.* Buckingham, Open University Press.

Ball, S. J. (1997a) 'On the cusp: parents choosing between state and private schools.' *International Journal of Inclusive Education*, 1(1): 1–17.

Ball, S. J. (1997b) 'Policy sociology and critical social research: a personal review of recent education policy and policy research.' *British Educational Research Journal* 23(3): 257–274.

Ball, S. J. (1997c) Markets, equity and values in education. In R. Pring and G. Walford (eds), *Affirming the Comprehensive Ideal*. London, Falmer.

Ball, S. J. (1998a) 'Big policies/small world: an introduction to international perspectives in education policy.' *Comparative Education*, 34(2): 119–129.

Ball, S. J. (1998b) Ethics, self interest and the market form in education. In A. Cribb (ed.) *Markets, Managers and Public Service? Occasional Paper No. 1*. London, Centre for Public Policy Research, King's College London.

Ball, S. J. (2000) 'Performativities and fabrications in the education economy: towards the performative society.' *Australian Educational Researcher*, 27(2): 1–24.

Ball, S. J. (2001a) 'Ethnic choosing: minority ethnic students and higher education choice.' *Race Ethnicity and Education*.

Ball, S. J. (2001b) Globaalit toiminta periaateet ja kansalliset politiikat eureooppalaisessa koulutuksessa. In A. Jaunhiainen, R. Rinne and J. Tahtinen (eds), *Koulutuspolitiikka Suomessa Ja Ylikansalliset Mallit*. Turku, Kasvatusalan Tutkimuksia.

Ball, S. J. (2001c) 'Urban choice and urban fears: the politics of parental choice'. *Urban Education*, Vienna, Padogogisches Institut der Stadt Wien, City of Vienna, Austria.

Ball, S. J. and C. Vincent (1998) 'I heard it on the grapevine: hot knowledge and school choice.' *British Journal of Sociology of Education*, 19(3): 377–400.

Ball, S. J. and C. Vincent (2001) New class relations in education. In J. Demaine (ed.), *Sociology of Education Today*. London, Palgrave.

Ball, S. J., R. Bowe and S. Gewirtz (1995) 'Circuits of schooling: a sociological exploration of parental choice of school in social class contexts.' *Sociological Review*, 43(1): 52–78.

Ball, S. J., R. Bowe and S. Gewirtz (1996) 'School choice, social class and distinction: the realisation of social advantage in education.' *Journal of Education Policy* 11(1): 89–112.

Ball, S. J., S. Macrae and M. Maguire (1998) 'Race, space and the further education marketplace.' *Race, Ethnicity and Education*, 1(2): 171–189.

Ball, S. J., M. Maguire and S. Macrae (1997) *The Post-16 Education Market: Ethics, Interests and Survival*. BERA Annual Conference, University of York.

Ball, S. J., M. Maguire and S. Macrae (2000) *Choice, Pathways and Transitions Post-16: New Youth, New Economies in the Global City*. London, Falmer Press.

Ball, S. J., D. Reay and M. David. (2002) "Ethnic choosing': minority ethnic students and higher education choice", *Race, Ethnicity and Education*, forthcoming.

Ball, S. J., J. Davies, D. Reay and M. David (2002) 'Classification and judgement: social class and the cognitive structures of choice of higher education.' *British Journal of Sociology of Education*, 23(1): 51–72.

Barbalet, J. M. (2001) *Emotion, Social Theory and Social Structure: A Macrosociological Approach*. Cambridge, Cambridge University Press.

Barber, B. (1994) *Strong Democracy*. Berkeley: CA, University of Cailifornia Press.

Bateson, M. C. (1994) *Peripheral Visions: Learning Along the Way*. New York, Harper Collins.

Bauman, Z. (1993) *Postmodern Ethics*. Oxford, Blackwell.

Bauman, Z. (1998) *Work Consumerism and the New Poor*. Buckingham, Open University Press.

Beales, J. R. and M. Wahl (1995) Private vouchers in Milwaukee: the PAVE program. In T. Moe (ed.) *Private Vouchers*. Stanford: CA, Hoover Institution Press.

Beck, U. (1992) *Risk Society: Towards a New Modernity*. Newbury Park, CA., Sage.

Beck, U. and E. Beck-Gernsheim (1995) *The Normal Chaos of Love*. Cambridge, Polity Press.

Beck-Gernsheim, E. (1996) Life as a planning project. In C. Lash, B. Szersynski and B. Wynne (eds) *Risk, Environment and Modernity*. London, Sage.

Berking, H. (1996) Solidary individualism: the moral impact of cultural modernisation in late modernity. In C. Lash, B. Szersynski and B. Wynne (eds) *Risk, Environment and Modernity: Towards a New Ecology*. London, Sage.

Berlak, A. and H. Berlak (1981) *Dilemmas of Schooling: Teaching and Social Change*. London, Methuen.

Bernstein, B. (1966) 'Sources of consensus and disaffection in education." *Journal of the Association of Assistant Mistresses*, 17(4–11).

Bernstein, B. (1975) *Class, Codes and Control*. Vol. 3. London, Routledge.

Bernstein, B. (1990) *The Structuring of Pedagogic Discourse*. London, Routledge.

Bernstein, B. (1996) *Pedagogy Symbolic Control and Identity*. London, Taylor and Francis.

Beynon, H. (1999) A classless society? In H. Beynon and P. Glavanis (eds), *Patterns of Social Inequality: Essay for Richard Brown*. London, Longman.

Birenbaum-Carmeli, D. (1999) 'Parents who get what they want: on the empowerment of the powerful.' *Sociological Review*, 47(1): 62–90.

Blair, T. (1995) Realising our true potential. *Press Release of Speech Given at the Institute of Education, University of London, 23rd June*. London, Labour Party.

Blair, T. (1996) *My Vision of a Young Country*. London, Fourth Estate.

Blank, R. (1990) Educational effects of magnet high schools. In W. Clune and J. Witte (eds) *Choice and Control in American Education* Vol 2: *The Practice of Choice, Decentralization and School Restructuring*. Basingstoke, Falmer.

Boltanski, L. (1987) *The Making of a Class: Cadres in French Society*. New York, Cambridge University Press.

Bottery, M. (1992) *The Ethics of Educational Management*. London, Cassell.

Bourdieu, P. (1986a) *Distinction: a Social Critique of the Judgement of Taste*. London, Routledge.

Bourdieu, P. (1986b) Forms of capital. In J. Richardson (ed.) *Handbook of Theory and Research for the Sociology of Education*. New York, Greenwood Press.

Bourdieu, P. (1988) *Homo Academicus*. Cambridge, Polity Press.

Bourdieu, P. (1990a) *In Other Words: Essays Towards a Reflexive Sociology.* Cambridge, Polity Press.

Bourdieu, P. (1990b) *The Logic of Practice.* Cambridge, Polity Press.

Bourdieu, P. (1990c) *Reproduction in Education, Society and Culture.* 2nd ed. London, Sage.

Bourdieu, P. (1992) *Language and Symbolic Power.* Cambridge, Polity Press.

Bourdieu, P. (1993) *Sociology in Question.* London, Sage.

Bourdieu, P. (1994) *State Nobility: Elite Schools in the Field of Power.* Oxford, Oxford University Press.

Bourdieu, P. and L. Boltanski (2000) Changes in the social structure and changes in the demand for education. In S. J. Ball (ed.) *Sociology of Education: Major Themes.* Vol. 2. London, RoutledgeFalmer.

Bourdieu, P. and J.-C. Passeron (1990) *Reproduction.* London, Sage.

Bourdieu, P. and L. J. D. Wacquant (1992) *An Invitation to Reflexive Sociology.* Chicago, University of Chicago Press.

Bourdieu, P. and M. de Saint Martin (1994) The meaning of property: class position and the ideology of home ownership. In M. Ryan and A. Gordon (eds) *Body Politics: Disease, Desire and the Family.* Boulder, Colorado, Westview Press.

Bourdieu, P., A. Accardo, G. Balazs, S. Beaud, F. Bonvin, S. Broccolichi, P. Campagne, R. Christin, F. Euvard, J.-P. Faguer, S. Garcia, D. Padalydes, M. Pailoux, L. Pinto, A. Sayad, C. Soulie and L. J. D. Wacquant (1999) *Weight of the World: Social Suffering in Contemporary Society.* Cambridge, Polity Press.

Bowe, R., S. J. Ball and S. Gewirtz (1994) 'Captured by the discourse? Issues and concerns in researching parental choice.' *British Journal of Sociology of Education,* 15(1): 63–78.

Bowe, R., S. J. Ball and S. Gewirtz (1995) Market forces, inequality and the city. In H. Jones and J. Lansley (eds) *Social Policy and the City.* Aldershot, Avebury Press.

Bowe, R., S. J. Ball and A. Gold (1992) *Reforming Education and Changing Schools: Case Studies in Policy Sociology.* London, Routledge.

Brantlinger, E., M. Majd-Jabbari and S.L. Guskin (1996) 'Self-interest and liberal educational discourse: how ideology works for middle-class mothers.' *American Educational Research Journal,* 33: 571–597.

Broccolichi, S. and A. van Zanten (2000) 'School competition and pupil flight in the urban periphery.' *Journal of Education Policy,* 15(1): 51–60.

Brown, P. (1990) 'The third wave: education and the ideology of parentocracy.' *British Journal of Sociology of Education,* 11(1): 65–86.

Brown, P. (1997) Cultural capital and social exclusion: some observations on recent trends in education, employment and the labour market. In A. H. Halsey, H. Lauder, P. Brown and A. Stuart Wells (eds) *Education: Culture, Economy and Society.* Oxford, Oxford University Press.

Brown, P. (2000) 'Globalisation of Positional Competition.' *Sociology* 34(4): 633–654.

Brown, P. and R. Scase (1994) *Higher Education and Corporate Realities: Class, Culture and the Decline of Graduate Careers.* London, UCL Press.

Butler, T. and G. Robson (2001) 'Social capital, gentrification and neighbourhood change in London: a comparison of three South London neighbourhoods.' *Urban Studies*, 38: 2145–2162.

Butler, T. and G. Robson (2002a) 'Middle class households and the remaking of urban neighbourhoods in London.' *Urban Studies* (forthcoming).

Butler, T. and G. Robson (2002b) 'Plotting the middle classes in London: gentrification and circuits of education in London.' *Housing Studies* (forthcoming).

Butler, T. and M. Savage (1995) *Social Change and the Middle Classes*. London, UCL Press.

Carnoy, M. (2000) 'School choice? Or is it privatization?' *Educational Researcher*, 29(7): 15–20.

Charlesworth, S. J. (2000) *A Phenomenology of Working Class Experience*. Cambridge, Cambridge University Press.

Chenoweth, T. (1987) 'Unanticipated consequences of schools of choice: some thoughts on the case of San Francisco.' *Equality and Choice*, 5(7).

Chubb, J. and T. Moe (1990) *Politics, Markets and America's Schools*. Washington, DC., The Brookings Institution.

Cohen, A. P. (1992) A personal right to identity: a polemic on the self in the enterprise culture. In P. Heelas and P. Morris (eds) *The Values of the Enterprise Culture*. London, Routledge.

Cohen, P. and V. Hey (2000) *Studies in Learning Regeneration: Consultation Document*. University of East London and Brunel University.

Colebrook, C. (2000) Introduction. In I. Buchanan and C. Colebrook (eds) *Deleuze and Feminist Theory*. Edinburgh, University of Edinburgh Press.

Coleman, J. S. (1988) 'Social capital and the creation of human capital.' *American Journal of Sociology*, 94(Supplement): S95-S120.

Collins, R. (1981) 'On the microfoundations of macrosociology.' *American Journal of Sociology*, 86(5): 984–1014.

Collins, R. (1986) *Weberian Sociological Theory*. Cambridge, Cambridge University Press.

Connell, R. W. (1983) *Which Way Is Up? Essays on Class, Sex and Culture*. Sydney, George Allen and Unwin.

Connell, R. W. (1989) 'Cool guys, swots and wimps: the interplay of masculinity and education.' *Oxford Review of Education*, 15(3): 291–303.

Cote, J. E. (1996) 'Sociological perspectives on identity formation: the culture identity link and identity capital.' *Journal of Adolescence*, 19: 417–428.

Craft, M. (1970) *Family, Class and Education*. London, Longman.

Crewe, I. (1989) Values: the crusade that failed. In D. Kavangh and A. Seldon (eds) *The Thatcher Effect*. Oxford, Oxford University Press.

Crompton, R. (1997) *Women and Work in Modern Britain*. Oxford, Oxford University Press.

Crompton, R. (1998) *Class and Stratification: An Introduction to Current Debates*. 2nd ed. Cambridge, Polity Press.

Crook, S. (1999) Ordering risks. In D. Lupton (ed.) *Risk and Sociocultural Theory: New Directions and Perspectives*. Cambridge, Cambridge University Press.

Crow, G. (1989) 'The use of the concept of strategy in recent sociological literature.' *Sociology*, 23(1): 1–24.

Crozier, G. (2000) *Parents and Schools: Partners or Protagonists?* Stoke-on-Trent, Trentham Books.

David, M. (1993) *Parents, Gender and Education Reform*. Cambridge, Polity Press.

David, M., A. West and J. Ribbens (1994) *Mothers' Intuition: Choosing Secondary Schools*. London, Falmer Press.

David, M., S.J. Ball, J. Davies and D. Reay (2002) 'Gender issues in parental involvement in student choices of higher education.' *Gender and Education*. (forthcoming).

Dean, M. (1999) Risk, calculable and incalculable. In D. Lupton (ed.) *Risk and Sociocultural Theory: New Directions and Perspectives*. Cambridge, Cambridge University Press.

Deem, R., K. Brehony and S. Heath (1995) *Active Citizenship and the Governing of Schools*. Buckingham, Open University Press.

Dehli, K. (2000) Travelling tales: education reform and parental choice in postmodern times. In S. J. Ball (ed.) *Sociology of Education: Major Themes*. Vol. 4. London, Routledge.

Deleuze, G. (1992) What is a dispositif? *Michel Foucault, Philosopher: Essays Translated from the French and German*. T. J. Armstrong. London, Harvester/Wheatsheaf.

Devine, F. (1997) *Privilege, Power and the Reproduction of Advantage*. British Sociological Association Annual Conference, University of York, 7–10 April.

Douglas, J. W. B. (1964) *The Home and the School*. London, McGibbon and Kee.

Douglas, M. (1994) *Risk and Blame: Essays in Cultural Theory*. London, Routledge.

Dreyfus, H. L. and P. Rabinow (1983) *Michael Foucault: Beyond Structuralism and Hermeneutics*. Chicago, University of Chicago Press.

Du Bois-Reymond, M. (1998) '"I don't want to commit myself yet": Young people's life concepts.' *Journal of Youth Studies*, 1(1): 63–79.

Duru-Bellat, M. (2000) 'Social inequalities in the French education system: the joint effect of individual and contextual factors.' *Journal of Education Policy*, 15(1): 33–40.

Echols, F. H. and Wilms, J. D. (1997) *Scottish Parents and Reasons for School Choice*. Vancouver, Department of Social and Educational Studies, University of British Columbia.

Eder, K. (1993) *The New Politics of Class: Social Movements and Cultural Dynamics in Advanced Societies*. London, Sage.

Edwards, T., J. Fitz and G. Whitty (1989) *The State and Private Education: An Evaluation of the Assisted Places Scheme*. Lewes, Falmer.

Ehrenreich, B. (1989) *Fear of Failing: The Inner life of the Middle Class*. New York, Pantheon.

Espinola, V. (1992) *Decentralization of the Education System and the Introduction of Market Rules in the Regulation of Schooling: The Case of Chile*. Santiago, Centro de Investigacion y Desarrollo de la Educacion.

Fevre, R. W. (2000) *The Demoralization of Western Culture: Social Theory and the Dilemmas of Modern Living*. London, Continuum.

Fielding, M. (1998) 'The point of politics: friendship and community in the work of John Macmurray.' *Renewal*, 6(1): 55–64.

Floud, J., A. H. Halsey and F. M. Marton (1956) *Social Class and Educational Opportunity*. London, Heinemann.

Foskett, N. and A. Hesketh (1997) 'Constructing choice in contiguous and parallel markets: institutional and school leavers' responses to the new post-16 market place.' *Oxford Review of Education*, 23(3).

Fossey, R. (1994) 'Open enrolment in Massachusetts: why families choose.' *Educational Evaluation and Policy Analysis* 16(3): 320–334.

Foucault, M. (1974) *The Archaeology of Knowledge*. London, Tavistock.

Foucault, M. (1980) *Two Lectures. Power/Knowledge*. C. Gordon. London, Longman.

Foucault, M. (1996) *Foucault Live: Collected Interviews, 1961–84 (edited by Lotringer, S.)*. New York, Semiotext(e).

Fowler-Finn, T. (1994) 'Why have they chosen another school system?' *Educational Leadership*, Dec 93/Jan 94: 60–62.

Fuller, B. and R. F. Elmore (1996) Empirical research on educational choice: what are the implications for policymakers? In B. Fuller, R. F. Elmore and G. Orfield. (eds) *Who Chooses? Who loses? Culture, Institutions and the Unequal Effects of School Choice*. New York, Teachers College Press.

Gamarnikow, E. and A. Green (2000) Citizenship, education and social capital. In D. Lawton, J. Cairns and R. Gardner (eds) *Education For Citizenship*. London, Continuum.

Gewirtz, S. (2001) 'Cloning the Blairs: New Labour's programme for the re-socialization of working class parents.' *Journal of Education Policy* 16(4): 365–378.

Gewirtz, S. (2002) *The Managerial School: Post-welfarism and Social Justice in Education*. London, Routledge.

Gewirtz, S., S. J. Ball and R. Bowe (1995) *Markets, Choice and Equity in Education*. Buckingham, Open University Press.

Gibson, A. and S. Asthana (2000) 'What's in a number? Commentary on Gorard and Fitz's 'Investigating the determinants of segregation between school.' *Research Papers in Education*, 15 (2): 133–153.

Giddens, A. (1971) *Capitalism and Modern Social Theory: An Analysis of the Writings of Marx, Durkheim and Weber*. Cambridge, Cambridge University Press.

Giddens, A. (1984) *The Constitution of Society*. Oxford, Polity Press.

Giddens, A. (1991) *Modernity and Self-Identity*. Cambridge, Polity.

Giddens, A. (1994) *Beyond Left and Right: The Future of Radical Politics*. Cambridge, Polity Press.

Giddens, A. (1998) Risk society: the context of British politics. In J. Franklin (ed.) *The Politics of Risk Society*. Cambridge, Polity Press.

Gillborn, D. and D. Youdell (2000) *Rationing Education: Policy, Practice, Reform and Equity*. Buckingham, Open University Press.

Glassman, R. M. (2000) *Caring Capitalism: A New Middle-Class base for the Welfare State*. Basingstoke, Macmillan.

Goldhaber, D. (2000) 'School choice: do we know enough.' *Educational Researcher*, 29(8): 21–22.

Goldring, E. B. and R. Shapira (1993) 'Choice, empowerment and involvement: what satisfies parents?' *Educational Evaluation and Policy Analysis*, 15(4): 396–409.

Goldthorpe, J. (1980) *Social Mobility and Class Structure in Modern Britain*. Oxford, Clarendon Press.

Goldthorpe, J. (1995) The service class revisited. In T. Butler and M. Savage (eds) *Social Change and the Middle Classes*. London, UCL Press.

Goldthorpe, J. (1996) 'Class analysis and the reorientation of class theory: the case of persisting differentials in educational attainment.' *British Journal of Sociology*, 47(3): 481–505.

Goldthorpe, J. H. (1983) 'Women and class analysis: in defence of the conventional view.' *Sociology*, 17(4): 467–478.

Gorard, S. (1997) *School Choice and the Established Market*. Aldershot, Ashgate.

Gorard, S. (1999) '"Well. That just about wraps it up for school choice research": a state of the art review.' *School Leadership and Management*, 19(25–47).

Gorard, S., J. Fitz and C. Taylor (2001) 'School choice impacts: what do we know?' *Educational Researcher*, 30(7): 18–23.

Grace, G. (1995) *School Leadership: Beyond Education Management: An Essay in Policy Scholarship*. London, Falmer.

Grace, G. (2002) *Catholic Schools: Mission, Market and Morality*. London, RoutledgeFalmer.

Granovetter, M. (1973) 'The strength of weak ties.' *American Journal of Sociology*, 78: 1360–1380.

Graue, M. E. (1993) 'Social networks and home–school relations.' *Educational Policy*, 7(4): 466–490.

Hallam, S. (2002) *Ability Grouping in Schools*. Institute of Education, University of London.

Halpin, D., S. Power and J. Fitz (1997) Opting into the past? Grant-maintained schools and the reinvention of tradition. In R. Glatter, P. A. Woods and C. Bagley (eds) *Choice and Diversity in Schooling: Perspectives and Prospects*. London, Routledge.

Halsey, A. H., A. Heath and J. Ridge (1980) *Origins and Destinations*. Oxford, Clarendon Press.

Halstead, M. J. (1994) *Parental Choice and Education: Principles, Policy and Practice*. London, Kogan Page.

Hanlon, G. (1998) 'Professionalism as Enterprise.' *Sociology*, 32(1): 43–63.

Harkness, S., C. Super and C. H. Keefer (1992) Learning to be an American parent: how cultural models gain directive force. In R. D'Andrade and C. Strauss (eds) *Human Motives and Cultural Models*. Cambridge, Cambridge University Press.

Hatcher, R. (1998) 'Class differentiation in education: rational choices?' *British Journal of Sociology of Education*, 19(1): 5–24.

Hatton, E. J. (1985) 'Equality, class and power: a case study.' *British Journal of Sociology of Education*, 6(3): 255–272.

Heise, J. R., K. D. Colburn Jr. and J. F. Lamberti (1995) Private vouchers in Indianapolis: the golden rule program. In T. Moe (ed.) *Private Vouchers*. Stanford: CA, Hoover Institution Press.

Hemsley-Brown, J. (1996) Decision-making among sixteen year olds in the further education market place. In N. Foskett. (ed.) *Markets in Education: Policy, Process and Practice*. Southampton, Centre for Research on Education Markets.

Henig, J. R. (1994) 'Race and choice in Montgomery County, Maryland, Magnet Schools.' *Teachers College Record*, 96(4): 729–734.

Hershkoff, H. and A. S. Cohen (1992) 'School choice and the lessons of Choctaw County.' *Yale Law and Policy Review* 10(1): 1–29.

Hirsch, D. (1994) 'School choice and the search for an education market.' London, paper presented to the parental choice and market forces seminar, King's College.

Hirsch, F. (1977) *Social Limits to Growth*. London, RKP.

Hirschmann, A. (1970) *Exit, Voice and Loyalty*. Cambridge, Mass., Cambridge University Press.

Jackson, B. and D. Marsden (1962) *Education and the Working Class*. Harmondsworth, Penguin.

Jimerson, L. (1998) *Hidden Consequences of School Choice: Impact on Programs, Finances and Accountability*. American Educational Research Association, San Diego.

Johnathan, R. (1989) 'Choice and control in education: parents' rights, individual liberties and social justice.' *British Journal of Educational Studies* 37 (4): 321–338.

Jones, K. (1999) 'In the shadow of the centre-left: post-conservative politics and rethinking educational change.' *Discourse* 20(3): 235–247.

Jordan, B., M. Redley and S. James (1994) *Putting the Family First: Identities, Decisions and Citizenship*. London, UCL Press.

Kenway, J. (1990) Class, gender and private schooling. In D. Dawkins (ed.) *Power and Politics in Education*. Lewes, Falmer Press.

Kenway, J. and E. Bullen (2001) *Consuming Children: Education-entertainment-advertising*. Buckingham, Open University Press.

Kingston, P. W. (2000) *The Classless Society*. Stanford: CA, Stanford University Press.

Kohn, A. (1998) 'Only for my kid: how privileged parents undermine school reform.' *Phi Delta Kappan*, 79(8): 569–577.

Labour Party, The (1997) 'New Labour: because Britain deserves better' (election manifesto). London, Labour Party.

Lacey, C. (1970) *Hightown Grammar*. Manchester, Manchester University Press.

Lacey, C. (1974) Destreaming in a pressured academic environment. In J. Eggleston (ed.) *Contemporary Research in the Sociology of Education*. London, Methuen.

Lane, R. (1991) *The Market Experience*. Cambridge, Cambridge University Press.

Larabee, D. (1997) *How to Succeed in School Without Really Learning: The Credentials Race in American Education.* New Haven, Yale University Press.

Lareau, A. and E. McNamara Horvat (1999) 'Moments of social inclusion and exclusion: race, class and cultural capital in family-school relationships.' *Sociology of Education,* 72(January): 37–53.

Lash, S. (1994) (eds) Reflexivity and its doubles. In U. Beck, T. Giddens and S. Lash. *Reflexive Modernization: Politics, Tradition and Aesthetics in the Modern Social Order.* Cambridge, Polity Press.

Lash, S. and J. Urry (1987) *The End of Organised Capitalism.* Cambridge, Polity.

Lauder, H., D. Hughes, S. Watson, S. Waslander, M. Thrupp, R. Strathdee, I. Simiyu, A. Dupuis, J. McGlinn and J. Hamlin. (1999) *Trading in Futures: Why Markets in Education Don't Work.* Buckingham, Open University Press.

Le Grand, J. (1982) *The Strategy of Equality: Redistribution and the Social Services.* London, George Allen and Unwin.

Lee, M. J. (1993) *Consumer Culture Reborn.* London, Routledge.

Levi, M. (1996) 'Social and unsocial capital: a review essay of Robert Putnam's *Making Democracy Work.*' *Politics and Society,* 24(1): 45–55.

Levin, B. (1998) 'An epidemic of education policy: what can we learn for each other?' *Comparative Education,* 34(2): 131–142.

Lewis, R. and A. Maude (1950) *The English Middle Classes.* London, Phoenix House.

Lipman, P. (1998) *Race, Class and Power in School Restructuring.* Albany, SUNY Press.

Lockwood, D. (1995) Marking out the middle class(es). In T. Butler and M. Savage (eds) *Social Change and the Middle Classes.* London, University College London Press.

Lucey, H. and D. Reay (2002) 'Carrying the beacon of excellence: social class differentiation and anxiety at a time of transition.' *Journal of Education Policy,* 17(3): 321–336.

Lukes, S. (1974) *Power: A Radical View.* London, MacMillan.

Lupton, D. (1999) 'Introduction'. In D. Lupton (ed.) *Risk and SocioCultural Theory: New Directions and Perspectives.* Cambridge, Cambridge University Press.

Maddaus, J. (1990) *Parental choice of school: what parents think and do.* In C. Cazden (ed.) *Review of Research in Education* 16. Washington: DC., AERA.

Maguire, M. (2001) 'The cultural formation of teachers' class consciousness: teachers in the inner city.' *Journal of Education Policy,* 16(4): 315–331.

Mahony, P. and C. Zmroczek (1997) *Class Matters: Working-Class Women's Perspectives on Social Class.* London, Taylor and Francis.

Marginson, S. (1997) *Markets in Education.* St Leonards: NSW, Allen and Unwin.

Marshall, G. and A. Swift (1997) Social class and social justice. In G. Marshall (ed.) *Repositioning Class.* London, Sage.

Marshall, G., (1997) *Repositioning Class.* London, Sage.

Martin, J. (2001) *Reconstructing Citizenship: The Structuration of Parental Voice.* British Educational Research Association Annual Conference, Leeds, September 2001.

Martin, J. and C. Vincent (1999) 'Parental voice: an exploration.' *International Studies in Sociology of Education*, 9(2): forthcoming.

McCaig, C. (2001) New Labour and education, education, education. In S. Ludlam and M. J. Smith (eds) *New Labour in Government*. Basingstoke, Macmillan.

McEwan, P. J. and M. Carnoy (2000) 'The effectiveness and efficiency of private schools in Chile's voucher system.' *Educational Evaluation and Policy Analysis*, 22(3): 213–239.

McGrath, D. J. and P. J. Kuriloff (1999) 'They're going to tear the doors off this place: upper-middle-class parents school involvement and the educational opportunities of other people's children.' *Educational Policy*, 13(5): 603–629.

McLaughlin, T. (1994) The scope of parents' educational rights. In M. J. Halstead (ed.) *Parental Choice and Education: Principles, Policy and Practice*, London, Kogan Page.

Merleau-Ponty, M. (1962) *Phenomenology of Perception*. London, Routledge.

Miles, M. and B. Gold (1981) *Whose School is it Anyway?* New York, Praegar Publishing.

Moe, T. (1995) *Private Vouchers*. Stanford: CA, Hoover Institution Press.

Moore, D. and S. Davenport (1990) Choice: the new improved sorting machine. In W. L. Boyd and H. J. Walberg (eds) *Choice in Education: Potential and Problems*. Berkeley, CA., McCutchan.

Morgan, D. (1989) 'Strategies and Sociologists: a Comment on Crow.' *Sociology* 23(1): 25–29.

Morrell, F. (1989) *Children of the Future*. London, Hogarth Press.

Morris, L. D. (1987) The household in the labour market. In C. C. Harris (ed.) *Redundancy and Recession*. Oxford, Basil Blackwell.

Morrow, V. (1999) 'Conceptualising social capital in relation to the well-being of children and young people: a critical review.' *The Sociological Review*, 47(4): 744–765.

Mouffe, C. (1993) *The Return of the Political*. London, Verso.

Munin, H. (1998) 'Freer forms of organisation and financing in Latin American education systems: two counties in comparison.' *Compare*, 28(3): 229–244.

Murdock, G. and R. McCron (1975) Consciousness of class and consciousness of generation. In S. Hall and T. Jefferson (eds) *Resistance Through Rituals – Youth Cultures in Post-War Britain*. London, Hutchinson.

Muth, R. (1993) *School Choice: A Comparative Analysis of Two Cases*. AERA, Atlanta, Georgia.

Nagel, T. (1991) *Equality and Partiality*. Oxford, Oxford University Press.

Narodowski, M. and M. Nores (2002) 'Socioeconomic segregation with (without) competitive education policies: a comparative analysis of Argentina and Chile.' *Compare* (forthcoming).

Nash, R. (1990) 'Bourdieu on education and social and cultural reproduction.' *British Journal of Sociology of Education*, 11(4): 431–447.

Noden, P. (2000) 'Rediscovering the impact of marketisation: dimensions of social segregation in England's secondary school 1994–99.' *British Journal of Sociology of Education*, 21(3): 371–390.

Oakes, J. and L. Lipton (2001) *Equity-focused Change in Diverse Educational Contexts: School Reform as Social Movement* Los-Angeles: CA, UCLA.

OECD (1995) *Governance in Transition: Public Management Reforms in OECD Countries.* Paris, Organisation for Economic Co-operation and Development.

O'Malley, P. (1996) Risk and responsibility. In A. Barry, T. Osborne and N. Rose. (eds) *Foucault and Political Reason: Liberalism, Neo-liberalism and Rationalities of Government.* London, UCL Press.

Owensby, B. P. (1999) *Intimate Ironies: Modernity and the Making of Middle Class Lives in Brazil.* Stanford, Stanford University Press.

Pahl, R. E. and C. D. Wallace (1985) Forms of work and privatisation on the Isle of Sheppey. In B. Roberts, R. Finnegan and D. Gallie. (eds) *New Approaches to Economic Life.* Manchester, Manchester University Press.

Pajackowska, C. and L. Young (1992) Race, representation and psychoanalysis. In J. Donald and A. Rattansi (eds) *Race, Culture, Difference.* London, Sage.

Pakulski, J. and M. Waters (1996) *The Death of Class.* London, Sage.

Parker, L. and A. Margonis (1996) 'School choice in the U.S. urban context: racism and policies of containment.' *Journal of Education Policy*, 11 (6): 717–728.

Parkin, F. (1974) Strategies of social closure in class formation. In F. Parkin (ed.) *The Social Analysis of Class Structure.* London, Tavistock.

Parkin, F. (1979) *Marxism and Class Theory: A Bourgeois Critique.* London, Tavistock.

Phillips, L. (1996) 'Rhetoric and the spread of the discourse of Thatcherism.' *Discourse and Society*, 7(2): 209–241.

Plant, R. (1992) Enterprise in its place: the moral limits of markets. In P. Heelas and P. Morris (eds) *The Values of the Enterprise Culture.* London, Routledge.

Pollard, S. (1995) 'School, selection and the market.' *Memorandum No. 16.* London, Social Market Foundation.

Poulantzas, N. (1973) *Political Power and Social Classes.* London, New Left Books.

Power, S. and G. Whitty (1999) 'New Labour's education policy: first, second or third way.' *Journal of Education Policy*, 14(5): 535–546.

Power, S., T. Edwards, G. Whitty and V. Wigfall (2002) *Education and the Middle Class.* Buckingham, Open University Press.

Power, S., G. Whitty, T. Edwards and V. Wigfall (1998a) 'Schools, families and academically able students: contrasting modes of involvement in secondary school.' *British Journal of Sociology of Education*, 19(2): 157–176.

Power, S., G. Whitty, T. Edwards and V. Wigfall (1998b) *Education and the Formation of Middle Class Identities.* European Conference on Educational Research, University of Ljubljana, Slovenia.

Powers, J. M. and J. Cookson (1999) 'The politics of school choice research: fact, fiction, and statistics.' *Educational Policy*, 13(1): 104–122.

Prout, A. (1999) 'Children – a suitable case for inclusion?' King's College London, CPPR Annual Lecture.

Pugsley, L. (1998) 'Throwing your brains at it: higher education, markets and choice.' *International Studies in Sociology of Education*, 8(8): 71–90.

Putnam, R. (1993) *Making Democracy Work: Civic Transitions in Modern Italy.* Princeton: NJ, University of Princeton Press.

Putnam, R. (2000) *Bowling Alone: The Collapse and Revival of American Community.* New York, Simon and Schuster.

Raftery, A. E. and M. Hout (1993) 'Maximally maintained inequality: expansion, reform, and opportunity in Irish education.' *Sociology of Education*, 66(1): 41–62.

Reay, D. (1997) The double-bind of the 'working class' feminist academic: the failure of success or the success of failure. In P. Mahony and C. Zmroczek (eds) *Class Matters: Working Class Women's Perspectives of Social Class.* London, Taylor and Francis.

Reay, D. (1998a) 'Rethinking social class: qualitative perspectives on class and gender.' *Sociology*, 32(2): 259–275.

Reay, D. (1998b) *Class Work: Mothers' Involvement in their Children's Primary Schooling.* London, UCL Press.

Reay, D. (1998c) 'Setting the agenda: the growing impact of market forces on pupil grouping in British secondary schooling.' *Journal of Curriculum Studies*, 30 (5): 545–558.

Reay, D. (2000) 'A useful extension of Bourdieu's conceptual framework?: emotional capital as a way of understanding mothers' involvement in their children's education.' *Sociological Review*, 48(4): 568–585.

Reay, D. and S. J. Ball (1997) 'Spoilt for choice: the working class and educational markets.' *Oxford Review of Education*, 23(1): 89–101.

Reay, D. and S. J. Ball (1998) 'Making their minds up: family dynamics of school choice.' *British Education Research Journal*, 24(4): 431–448.

Reay, D., S. J. Ball and M. David (2002) '"It's taking me a long time but I'll get there in the end": Mature students on access courses and higher education choice.' *British Educational Research Journal* 28(1): 5–19.

Reay, D., J. Davies, M. David and S. J. Ball (2001) 'Choices of degree and degrees of choice.' *Sociology*, 35(4): 855–874.

Rikowski, G. (2001a) *After the manuscript Broke Off: Thoughts on Marx, Social Class and Education.* BAS Sociology of Education Study Group, King's College London.

Rikowski, G. (2001b) *The Battle for Seattle: Its Significance for Education.* London, Tufnell Press.

Roberts, K. (2001) *Class in Modern Britain.* Basingstoke, Palgrave.

Robson, G. and T. Butler (2001) 'Plotting the middle classes in London.' *International Journal of Urban and Regional Research*, 25(1): 70–86.

Rose, N. (1992) Governing the enterprising self. In P. Heelas and P. Morris (eds) *The Values of the Enterprise Culture.* London, Routledge.

Rose, N. (1996) Governing advanced liberal democracies. In A. Barry, T. Osborne and N. Rose (eds) *Foucault and Political Reason: Liberalism, Neo-liberalism and Rationalities of Government.* London, UCL Press.

Sandel, M. (1982) *Liberalism and the Limits of Justice.* Cambridge, Cambridge University Press.

Saunders, P. (1981) *Social Theory and the Urban Question*. London, Hutchinson.

Savage, M. (2000) *Class Analysis and Social Transformation*. Buckingham, Open University Press.

Savage, M. and T. Butler (1995) Assets and the middle classes in contemporary Britain. In T. Butler and M. Savage (eds) *Social Change and the Middle Classes*. London, UCL Press.

Savage, M., G. Bagnall and B. Longhurst (2001) 'Ordinary, ambivalent and defensive: class identities in the northwest of England.' *Sociology*, 35(4): 875–892.

Savage, M., J. Barlow, P. Dickens and A.J. Fielding (1992) *Property, Bureaucracy and Culture: middle class formation in contemporary Britain*. London, Routledge.

Schneider, B. and D. L. Stevenson (1999) *The Ambitious Generation: America's Teenagers Motivated but Directionless*. New Haven, Yales University Press.

Scott, J. (2000) Class and stratification. In G. Payne (ed.) *Social Divisions*. Basingstoke, Macmillan.

Sedden, T. (2001) 'Revisiting inequality and education; a reminder of class; a retrieval of politics; a rethinking of governance.' *Melbourne Studies in Education*, 42(2): 131–144.

Sieber, R. T. (1982) 'The politics of middle class success in an inner-city public school.' *Journal of Education* 164: 30–47.

Skeggs, B. (1997) Classifying practices: representations, capitals and recognition. In P. Mahony and C. Zmroczek (eds). *Class Matters: Working Class Women's Perspectives on Social Class*. London, Taylor and Francis.

Slater, D. and F. Tonkiss (2001) *Market Society*. Cambridge, Polity Press.

Smith, D. (2000) The underside of schooling: restructuring, privatization and women's unpaid work. In S. J. Ball (ed.) *Sociology of Education: Major Themes*. Vol. 2. London, RoutledgeFalmer.

Stronach, I. and M. MacLure (1997) *Educational Research Undone: The Postmodern Embrace*. Buckingham, Open University Press.

Stuart Wells, A. and J. Oakes (1996) 'Potential pitfalls of systemic reform: early lessons from research on detracking.' *Sociology of Education*, 69.

Stuart Wells, A. and I. Serna (1997) The politics of culture: understanding local political resistance to detracking in racially mixed schools. In A. H. Halsey, H. Lauder, P. Brown and A. Stuart Wells (eds) *Education: Culture, Economy and Society*. Oxford, Oxford University Press.

Sulkunen, P. (1992) *The European New Middle Class: Individuality and Tribalism in mass society*. Aldershot, Avebury.

Szeter, S. (1998) 'A new political economy of New Labour: the importance of social capital.' *Policy Paper No. 15*. Political Economy Research Centre, University of Sheffield.

Taylor, I. (1996) 'Fear of crime, urban fortunes and suburban social movements: some reflections from Manchester.' *Sociology*, 30(2): 317–337.

Tedesco, J. C. (1994) 'Changes in managing education: the case of Latin-American countries.' *International Journal of Educational Research*, 21(8): 809–815.

Teese, R. (1981) 'The social function of private schools.' *Melbourne Working Papers*. University of Melbourne, Sociology Research Group.

Teese, R. (2000) *Academic Success and Social Power: Examinations and Inequality.* Melbourne, Melbourne University Press.

Thompson, E. P. (1980) *The Making of the English Working Class.* Harmondsworth, Penguin.

Thompson, J. B. (1990) *Ideology and Modern Culture: Critical Social Theory in an Era of Mass Communication.* Stanford, Stanford University Press.

Thrupp, M. (1999) *The School Mix Effect.* Buckingham, Open University Press.

Thrupp, M. and S.J. Ball (2000) 'Fighting for alternatives: the micropolitics of contesting British neo-Liberal reform.' Paper presented at the American Educational Research Association Annual Conference.

Tomlinson, S. (2001) *Education in a Post-Welfare Society.* Buckingham, Open University Press.

Townsend, P. (1979) *Poverty in the United Kingdom.* Harmondsworth, Penguin.

Troman, G. (2000) 'Teacher stress in the low-trust society.' *British Journal of Sociology of Education,* 21(3): 331–353.

Useem, E. L. (1992) 'Middle schools and math groups: parents' involvement in children's placement.' *Sociology of Education,* 65: 263–279.

van Zanten, A. (1997) 'Schooling immigrants in France in the 1990s: success or failure of the republican model of integration?' *Anthropology and Education Quarterly,* 28(3): 351–374.

van Zanten, A. (2001) *L'ecole de la Peripherie: Scolarite et Segregation en Banlieue.* Paris, Presses Universitaires de France.

van Zanten, A. and C. Veleda (2001) 'Contexts locaux et strategies scolaires: clivages et interactions entre classes et classes moyennes danes la peripherie urbaine.' *Revue du Centre de Recherche en Education,* 20: 57–87.

Vincent, C. (1997) 'Community and collectivism: the role of parents' organisations in the education system.' *British Journal of Sociology of Education,* 18(2): 271–284.

Vincent, C. (2000) *Including Parents? Education, Citizenship and Parental Agency.* Buckingham, Open University Press.

Vincent, C. (2001) 'Social class and parental agency.' *Journal of Education Policy,* 16(4): 347–364.

Vincent, C. and S. J. Ball (2001) 'A market in love? Choosing pre-school child care.' *British Educational Research Journal,* 27(5): 633–651.

Vincent, C. and J. Martin (2002) 'Class, Culture and Agency.' *Discourse* 23(1): 109–128.

Wacquant, L. J. D. (1991) Making class(es): the middle classes in social theory and social structure. In S. McNall, R. Levine and R. Fantasia (eds) *Bringing Class Back in: Contemporary and Historical Perspectives.* Boulder, West View Press.

Wade, R. (2001) 'Showdown at the world bank.' *New Left Review,* 7 second series: 124–137.

Walkerdine, V., H. Lucey and J. Melody (2001) *Growing up Girl.* London, Palgrave.

Wall, E., G. Ferrazzi and F. Schryer, (1998) 'Getting the goods on social capital.' *Rural Sociology,* 63(2): 300–322.

Walzer, M. (1984) *Spheres of Justice: A Defence of Pluralism and Equality.* Oxford, Martin Robertson.

Watson, I. (1993) 'Education, class and culture: the Birmingham ethnographic tradition and the problem of the new middle class.' *British Journal of Sociology of Education*, 14(2): 179–197.

Weber, M. (1915/48) Religious rejections of the world and their directions. In H. H. Gerth and C. Wright Mills (eds) *From Max Weber*. London, Routledge and Kegan Paul.

Weber, M. (1961) *General Economic History*. New York, Collier-Macmillan.

Webster, D. and K. Parsons (1999) 'British Labour Party policy on educational selection 1996–8: a sociological analysis.' *Journal of Education Policy*, 14(5): 547–559.

Weiss, M. (2000) Quasi-markets in Education: An Economic Analysis. *Futures of Education*, Zurich, Peter Lang.

Wells, A. S. and Associates (1998) *Beyond the Rhetoric of Charter School Reform: A Study of Ten California School Districts*. Los Angeles: CA, UCLA.

White, P. (1994) 'Parental choice and education for citizenship.' In M. J. Halstead (ed.) *Parental Choice and Education: Principles, Policy and Practice*, London, Kogan Page.

Wilkes, C. (1990) Bourdieu's class. In R. Harker, C. Mahar and C. Wilkes (eds) *An Introduction to the Work of Pierre Bourdieu*. London Macmillan.

Williams, R. (1959) *Keywords*. London, Fontana.

Williamson O. E. (1975) *Markets and Hierarchies: Analysis and Anti-Trust Implications*. New York, The Free Press.

Witte, J., C. A. Thorn, K. Pritchard and M. Claiborn (1994) Fourth Year Report: Milwaukee Parental Choice Program. Madison: WI, Department of Public Instruction.

Woods, P., C. Bagley and R. Glatter (1994) *Dynamics of Competition – The Effects of Local Competitive Arenas on Schools*. Changing Educational Structures: Policy and Practice Conference, University of Warwick, CEDAR.

Woods, P., C. Bagley and R. Glatter (1998) *School Choice and Competition*. London, Routledge.

Wynne, D. (1998) *Leisure, Lifestyle and the New Middle Class*. London, Routledge.

Yeandle, S. (1984) *Women's Working Lives*. London, Tavistock.

Index